# HOLIDAY

*Chocolate Drizzled Lace Cookies, see page 16; Chocolate Pinwheels, see page 18; Holiday Cutout Cookies, see page 28; Walnut Biscotti, see page 22; Hazelnut Rounds, see page 34; Holiday Meringues, see page 6; Pastel Mint Slices, see page 42; Raspberry Almond Shortbread Thumbprints, see page 44; Strawberry Lillies, see page 46*

## Land O'Lakes, Inc.

**Lydia Botham,** *Publisher*
**Mary Sue Peterson,** *Editor*
**Carolyn Patten,** *Senior Project Coordinator*

## Cy DeCosse Incorporated

**Becky Landes,** *Senior Art Director*
**Shawn Binkowski,** *Project Manager*
**Maren Frevert,** *Electronic Production*
**Gretchen Gundersen,** *Senior Production Manager*

### Cy DeCosse Photography
**Mike Parker,** *Director of Photography*
**Rex Irmen,** *Photographer*
**Beth Emmons,** *Food Stylist*
(Cover, pages 2, 4-5, 9, 17,19, 23, 29, 35, 37, 41, 43, 45,
47, 52-53, 57, 59, 61, 109, 127, 131, 133, 158-159, 163, 165,
226-227, 231, 234-235, 239, 240-241, 245)

Tony Kubat Photography

Recipes developed and tested by the Land O'Lakes Test Kitchens.

*Pictured on front cover:*

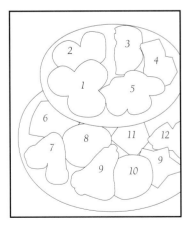

1 *Holiday Chocolate Butter Cookies, see page 30*

2 *Coconut Date Balls, see page 27*

3 *Raspberry Almond Shortbread Thumbprints, see page 44*

4 *Dark Chocolate Fudge, see page 84*

5 *Pastel Mint Slices, see page 42*

6 *Starlight Mint Sandwich Cookies, see page 48*

7 *Almond Logs Dipped In Chocolate, see page 7*

8 *Holiday Meringues, see page 6*

9 *Holiday Cutout Cookies, see page 28*

10 *Chocolate Pinwheels, see page 18*

11 *Black Forest Bars, see page 64*

12 *Melt-In-Your-Mouth Spritz, see page 32*

Holiday
p.  cm.  (Land O'Lakes collector series)
Includes index.
ISBN 0-86573-966-8 (hardcover)
1. Holiday cookery. 2. Desserts. 3. Menus. I. Land O'Lakes, Inc. II. Series.
TX739.H627 1995
641.5'68--dc20  95-18281

**PRINTED IN USA**

# Table of Contents

# Cookies

*The holidays*

*are a wonderful time*

*for families to enjoy*

*the pleasure of*

*cookie making.*

*Welcome the spirit*

*of the season*

*into your home*

*by baking one*

*of these delicious*

*cookie recipes.*

*Holiday Meringues, see page 6*

# Holiday Meringues

*Wreath shaped meringues are decorated with candied cherries.*

*Preparation time: 40 minutes • Baking time: 48 minutes*

4  egg whites, room temperature
1/2  teaspoon cream of tartar
2  teaspoons almond extract
1  cup sugar
4  drops green food coloring

Red and green candied cherries

Heat oven to 275°. In large mixer bowl combine egg whites, cream of tartar and almond extract. Beat at medium speed, scraping bowl often, until soft peaks form (about 1 minute). Increase speed to high. Continue beating, gradually adding sugar 2 tablespoons at a time and scraping bowl often, until stiff peaks form and sugar is almost dissolved (2 to 3 minutes). By hand, stir in food coloring. Place meringue in pastry bag fitted with large star tip (number 8). Pipe onto parchment-lined cookie sheets forming 2-inch wreaths; decorate with candied cherries. Bake for 25 minutes. <u>Reduce oven to 250°</u>. Continue baking for 23 to 27 minutes or until edges are lightly browned. Cool on parchment paper. **YIELD:** 3 1/2 dozen cookies.

TIP: Cookie sheets lined with aluminum foil which have been sprayed with no stick cooking spray can be substituted for parchment-lined cookie sheets.

*Nutrition Facts (1 cookie): Calories 20; Protein <1g; Carbohydrate 5g; Fat 0g; Cholesterol 0mg; Sodium 5mg*

# Brown Sugar Shortbread

*Brown sugar gives this classic shortbread a delightful caramel flavor.*

*Preparation time: 15 minutes • Baking time: 27 minutes • Cooling time: 30 minutes*

**Shortbread**
1  cup LAND O LAKES® Butter, softened
1/2  cup firmly packed brown sugar
1/2  cup powdered sugar
2 1/2  cups all-purpose flour
1  teaspoon vanilla

**Glaze**
1  cup powdered sugar
1  teaspoon grated orange peel
2  teaspoons light corn syrup
4 to 5  teaspoons orange juice

Heat oven to 300°. In large mixer bowl combine butter, brown sugar and 1/2 cup powdered sugar. Beat at medium speed, scraping bowl often, until creamy (1 to 2 minutes). Reduce speed to low; add flour and vanilla. Continue beating, scraping bowl often, until well mixed (1 to 2 minutes). Divide dough into thirds; form each piece into ball. Place each ball on cookie sheet. With floured rolling pin, roll out each ball into 7-inch circle. Crimp edge of each circle with fork; with floured knife score dough deeply into 12 wedges. Bake for 27 to 32 minutes or until set. Cool 5 minutes; cut into wedges. Cool completely on cookie sheets.

Meanwhile, in small bowl stir together all glaze ingredients <u>except</u> orange juice. Gradually stir in enough orange juice for desired glazing consistency. Drizzle over cooled shortbread. **YIELD:** 3 dozen cookies.

*Nutrition Information (1 cookie): Calories 110; Protein 1g; Carbohydrate 14g; Fat 5g; Cholesterol 15mg; Sodium 60mg*

# Holiday Thumbprint Cookies

*Make a beautiful cookie tray using one cookie dough with many variations.*

*Preparation time: 1 hour • Baking time: 14 minutes*

### Cookies
- 2 cups all-purpose flour
- $1/2$ cup firmly packed brown sugar
- 1 cup LAND O LAKES® Butter, softened
- 2 eggs, separated
- $1/8$ teaspoon salt
- 1 teaspoon vanilla or almond extract

### Suggested Coatings
- $1^1/2$ cups finely chopped peanuts, almonds, pecans or walnuts
- Colored sugars
- Cinnamon and sugar

### Suggested Toppings
- Chocolate stars
- Candied cherries
- Caramels, cut in half
- Maraschino cherries
- Fruit preserves

Heat oven to 350°. In large mixer bowl combine all cookie ingredients <u>except</u> egg whites. Beat at low speed, scraping bowl often, until well mixed (2 to 3 minutes). Shape rounded teaspoonfuls of dough into 1-inch balls.

In small bowl beat egg whites with fork until foamy. Dip each ball of dough into egg white; roll in choice of nuts. (If using colored sugars or cinnamon and sugar, do not dip balls of dough in egg white. Roll balls of dough in colored sugars or cinnamon and sugar.) Place 1 inch apart on greased cookie sheets. Make depression in center of each cookie with back of teaspoon. Bake for 8 minutes.

Remove cookies from oven; fill centers with choice of suggested toppings. Continue baking for 6 to 10 minutes or until lightly browned. **YIELD:** 3 dozen cookies.

*Nutrition Information (1 cookie): Calories 150; Protein 3g; Carbohydrate 12g; Fat 10g; Cholesterol 25mg; Sodium 70mg*

# Almond Logs Dipped in Chocolate

*These log shaped cookies are dipped in chocolate and nuts.*

*Preparation time: 45 minutes • Baking time: 13 minutes • Cooling time: 20 minutes*

### Cookies
- 1 cup LAND O LAKES® Butter, softened
- 1 (7-ounce) package almond paste
- 1 cup powdered sugar
- 2 egg yolks
- 1 teaspoon almond extract
- $1/2$ teaspoon vanilla
- 2 cups all-purpose flour

### Topping
- 1 (6-ounce) package (1 cup) semi-sweet real chocolate chips
- 1 tablespoon shortening
- 1 cup finely chopped almonds

Heat oven to 350°. In large mixer bowl combine butter and almond paste. Beat at low speed, scraping bowl often, until well mixed (1 to 2 minutes). Add powdered sugar, egg yolks, almond extract and vanilla. Beat at medium speed, scraping bowl often, until well mixed (1 to 2 minutes). Reduce speed to low. Continue beating, gradually adding flour and scraping bowl often, until well mixed (1 to 2 minutes).

Place dough in pastry bag with $1/2$-inch opening. Pipe onto parchment-lined cookie sheets forming $2^1/2$ to 3-inch logs. Bake for 13 to 17 minutes or until edges are very lightly browned. Cool completely on parchment paper.

In 1-quart saucepan melt chocolate chips and shortening over low heat, stirring often, until smooth (5 to 8 minutes). Remove cooled cookies from parchment paper and dip ends or top in chocolate and then in almonds. Place on waxed paper until set. **YIELD:** $4^1/2$ dozen cookies.

*Nutrition Facts (1 cookie): Calories 110; Protein 2g; Carbohydrate 10g; Fat 7g; Cholesterol 15mg; Sodium 35mg*

# Almond Spice Rugelach

*These buttery pastries are filled with almonds and rolled into delicious tiny crescents.*

*Preparation time: 1 hour • Chilling time: 4 hours • Standing time: 15 minutes • Baking time: 22 minutes*

## Pastry

- 2 cups all-purpose flour
- 3 tablespoons sugar
- 1/4 teaspoon salt
- 1 cup LAND O LAKES® Butter, cold
- 2 (3-ounce) packages cream cheese
- 1/3 cup LAND O LAKES® Sour Cream (Regular, Light or No·Fat)

## Filling

- 3/4 cup finely chopped blanched almonds
- 1/3 cup sugar
- 1 tablespoon LAND O LAKES® Butter, softened
- 1 teaspoon cinnamon
- 1/2 teaspoon ground nutmeg

## Glaze

- 1 egg white, beaten
  Ground nutmeg, if desired

In large bowl stir together flour, 3 tablespoons sugar and salt; cut in 1 cup butter until crumbly. Cut in cream cheese until well mixed. Stir in sour cream until mixture forms a soft dough. Form dough into ball. Cover; refrigerate until firm (at least 4 hours).

In small bowl stir together all filling ingredients; set aside. Remove dough from refrigerator; soften slightly at room temperature (about 15 minutes).

Heat oven to 350°. Divide dough into 4 pieces; form each piece into ball. Place 1 ball on lightly floured surface; flatten slightly. Roll dough into 9-inch circle about 1/8 inch thick. Sprinkle about 1/4 cup filling mixture over dough; gently press into dough. Using large sharp knife, cut circle into 12 wedges. Roll up each wedge tightly from wide end to point forming crescent. Place crescents, point side down, 1 inch apart on greased cookie sheets; curve slightly. Brush each crescent with beaten egg white; sprinkle lightly with nutmeg. Bake for 22 to 25 minutes or until light golden brown.

**YIELD:** 4 dozen cookies.

*Nutrition Facts (1 cookie): Calories 90; Protein 1g; Carbohydrate 7g;*
*Fat 7g; Cholesterol 15mg; Sodium 70mg*

*Almond Spice Rugelach*

# Brandied Buttery Wreaths

*This rich, buttery cookie is delicately flavored with brandy and nutmeg.*

*Preparation time: 45 minutes • Baking time: 8 minutes*

## Cookies

2¼  cups all-purpose flour
⅓  cup sugar
⅔  cup LAND O LAKES® Butter, softened
1  egg
1  teaspoon ground nutmeg
¼  teaspoon salt
2  tablespoons grated orange peel
2  tablespoons brandy*
⅓  cup chopped maraschino cherries, drained

## Glaze

1¼  cups powdered sugar
1 to 2  tablespoons milk
1  tablespoon brandy**
⅛  teaspoon ground nutmeg

Red and green maraschino cherries, halved, drained, if desired

Heat oven to 350°. In large mixer bowl combine all cookie ingredients <u>except</u> cherries. Beat at low speed, scraping bowl often, until well mixed (1 to 2 minutes). By hand, stir in cherries. Shape rounded teaspoonfuls of dough into 1-inch balls; form into 5-inch long strips. Shape strips into circles (wreaths), candy canes or leave as strips. Place 2 inches apart on greased cookie sheets. Bake for 8 to 12 minutes or until edges are lightly browned.

Meanwhile, in small bowl stir together all glaze ingredients. Dip or frost warm cookies with glaze. Decorate with maraschino cherries. **YIELD:** 2 dozen cookies.

*1 teaspoon brandy extract and 2 tablespoons water can be substituted for 2 tablespoons brandy.

**¼ teaspoon brandy extract and 1 tablespoon water can be substituted for 1 tablespoon brandy.

*Nutrition Facts (1 cookie): Calories 130; Protein 2g; Carbohydrate 18g; Fat 6g; Cholesterol 20mg; Sodium 80mg*

# Butter Pecan Tartlets

*These mini tarts taste like pecan pie.*

*Preparation time: 1 hour • Baking time: 12 minutes • Cooling time: 20 minutes*

## Tart Shells

½  cup LAND O LAKES® Butter, softened
½  cup sugar
1  egg
1  teaspoon almond extract
1¾  cups all-purpose flour

## Filling

1  cup powdered sugar
½  cup LAND O LAKES® Butter
⅓  cup dark corn syrup
1  cup chopped pecans

36  pecan halves

Heat oven to 400°. In large mixer bowl combine all tart shell ingredients. Beat at medium speed, scraping bowl often, until mixture is crumbly (2 to 3 minutes). Press <u>1 tablespoon</u> mixture into cups of mini muffin pans to form 36 (1¾ to 2-inch) shells. Bake for 7 to 10 minutes or until very lightly browned. Remove from oven. <u>Reduce oven to 350°.</u>

Meanwhile, in 2-quart saucepan combine all filling ingredients <u>except</u> chopped pecans and pecan halves. Cook over medium heat, stirring occasionally, until mixture comes to a full boil (4 to 5 minutes). Remove from heat; stir in chopped pecans. Spoon into baked shells. Top each with pecan half. Bake for 5 minutes. Cool 20 minutes; remove from pans. **YIELD:** 3 dozen cookies.

*Nutrition Facts (1 tartlet): Calories 130; Protein 1g; Carbohydrate 13g; Fat 8g; Cholesterol 20mg; Sodium 60mg*

*Brandied Buttery Wreaths*

# Buttery Butterscotch Cutouts

*This buttery cookie has melted butterscotch chips stirred in for a special cutout cookie flavor.*

*Preparation time: 1 hour • Chilling time: 1 hour • Baking time: 5 minutes • Cooling time: 15 minutes*

### Cookies

- 1 cup butterscotch-flavored chips
- 3 cups all-purpose flour
- 1/2 cup sugar
- 1/2 cup firmly packed brown sugar
- 1 cup LAND O LAKES® Butter, softened
- 1 egg
- 2 tablespoons milk
- 2 teaspoons vanilla

Decorator sugars, if desired
Powdered sugar, if desired
Frosting, if desired

In 1-quart saucepan melt butterscotch chips over low heat, stirring constantly, until smooth (3 to 5 minutes). Pour into large mixer bowl; add all remaining ingredients <u>except</u> decorator sugars, powdered sugar and frosting. Beat at low speed, scraping bowl often, until well mixed (1 to 2 minutes). Divide dough in half; wrap in plastic food wrap. Refrigerate until firm (at least 1 hour).

<u>Heat oven to 375°</u>. On lightly floured surface roll out dough, half at a time, to 1/8-inch thickness. Cut with 2 1/2-inch cookie cutters. Place 1 inch apart on cookie sheets. If desired sprinkle with decorator sugars. Bake for 5 to 8 minutes or until edges are lightly browned. Cool completely; decorate as desired. **YIELD:** 4 dozen cookies.

*Nutrition Facts (1 cookie): Calories 100g; Protein 1g; Carbohydrate 13g; Fat 5g; Cholesterol 15mg; Sodium 45mg*

# Chocolate Cinnamon Tea Cakes

*These cookies are a chocolate and cinnamon version of traditional Mexican wedding cakes.*

*Preparation time: 1 hour • Baking time: 8 minutes*

- 3/4 cup firmly packed brown sugar
- 3/4 cup LAND O LAKES® Butter, softened
- 2 (1-ounce) squares unsweetened baking chocolate, melted, cooled
- 1 teaspoon vanilla
- 2 cups all-purpose flour
- 1/2 teaspoon salt
- 1/2 teaspoon cinnamon

Powdered sugar, if desired

Heat oven to 350°. In large mixer bowl combine brown sugar and butter. Beat at medium speed, scraping bowl often, until creamy (1 to 2 minutes). Add cooled melted chocolate and vanilla. Continue beating until well mixed (1 to 2 minutes). Reduce speed to low; add all remaining ingredients <u>except</u> powdered sugar. Continue beating, scraping bowl often, until well mixed (2 to 3 minutes). Shape dough into 1-inch balls. Place 2 inches apart on cookie sheets. Bake for 8 to 10 minutes or until set. Cool 5 minutes; carefully remove from cookie sheets. Cool another 5 minutes. Roll in or sprinkle with powdered sugar while still warm and again when cool. **YIELD:** 4 dozen cookies.

*Nutrition Facts (1 cookie): Calories 60; Protein 1g; Carbohydrate 7g; Fat 4g; Cholesterol 10mg; Sodium 60mg*

*Buttery Butterscotch Cutouts*

*Holiday Meringues, see page 6*

# Chocolate Cherry Snowballs

*Dried cherries, pecans and coconut combine to make a delicious no-bake chocolate cookie.*

*Preparation time: 1 hour • Chilling time: 3 hours*

1 (9-ounce) package (about 2$^1$/$_4$ cups) chocolate cookie wafers, finely crushed
1$^1$/$_2$ cups (6 ounces) coarsely chopped dried cherries
1 cup flaked coconut
1 cup chopped pecans, toasted
1 (14-ounce) can sweetened condensed milk
1 teaspoon vanilla

Powdered sugar <u>or</u> unsweetened cocoa, if desired

In large bowl stir together all ingredients <u>except</u> powdered sugar. Cover; refrigerate until firm (at least 3 hours).

Form rounded tablespoonfuls into 1-inch balls. Sprinkle balls with powdered sugar. Place on waxed paper. Store refrigerated. **YIELD:** 5 dozen cookies.

*Nutrition Facts (1 cookie): Calories 80; Protein 1g; Carbohydrate 12g; Fat 3g; Cholesterol 3mg; Sodium 35mg*

# Cherry Jewels

*These delicate pink cookies are rich in buttery goodness and have the festive flavor of eggnog.*

*Preparation time: 45 minutes • Baking time: 10 minutes • Cooling time: 15 minutes*

2$^1$/$_4$ cups all-purpose flour
$^1$/$_2$ cup sugar
$^2$/$_3$ cup LAND O LAKES® Butter, softened
1 egg
$^1$/$_2$ teaspoon ground nutmeg
$^1$/$_4$ teaspoon salt
$^1$/$_2$ teaspoon brandy extract
$^1$/$_2$ cup chopped maraschino cherries, drained

Powdered sugar, if desired

Heat oven to 350°. In large mixer bowl combine all ingredients <u>except</u> powdered sugar. Beat at low speed, scraping bowl often, until well mixed (2 to 3 minutes). Shape rounded teaspoonfuls of dough into 1-inch balls. Place 2 inches apart on cookie sheets. Bake for 10 to 15 minutes or until edges are lightly browned. Cool completely; sprinkle with powdered sugar. **YIELD:** 3$^1$/$_2$ dozen cookies.

*Nutrition Facts (1 cookie): Calories 70; Protein 1g; Carbohydrate 9g; Fat 3g; Cholesterol 15mg; Sodium 45mg*

*Frosted Apricot Almond Cookies, see page 21; Chocolate Cherry Snowballs, see page 14; Buttery Butterscotch Cutouts, see page 12;*
*Starlight Mint Sandwich Cookies, see page 48*

# Chocolate Drizzled Lace Cookies

*Elegant lace cookies edged in chocolate.*

*Preparation time: 1 hour • Baking time: 13 minutes • Cooling time: 15 minutes*

<sup>1</sup>/2 cup light corn syrup
<sup>1</sup>/2 cup LAND O LAKES® Butter
1 cup all-purpose flour
<sup>1</sup>/2 cup firmly packed brown sugar
1 (2<sup>1</sup>/2-ounce) package (<sup>1</sup>/2 cup) slivered almonds, finely chopped

1 (6-ounce) package (1 cup) semi-sweet real chocolate chips, melted

Heat oven to 300°. In 2-quart saucepan over medium heat bring corn syrup to a full boil (2 to 3 minutes). Add butter; reduce heat to low. Continue cooking, stirring occasionally, until butter is melted (3 to 5 minutes). Remove from heat; stir in flour, brown sugar and almonds. Drop teaspoonfuls of dough 4 inches apart onto well-greased cookie sheets. Bake for 13 to 15 minutes or until cookies bubble and are golden brown. Let stand 1 minute. Working quickly, remove from cookie sheet; immediately wrap hot cookies around rolling pin or handle of wooden spoon. Hold in place a few seconds to set shape. Cool completely.

Dip edges or ends into melted chocolate or drizzle with melted chocolate. Place on waxed paper; let stand or refrigerate until chocolate has set (about 30 minutes).
**YIELD:** 5 dozen cookies.

*Nutrition Facts (1 cookie): Calories 50; Protein 1g; Carbohydrate 7g; Fat 3g; Cholesterol 5mg; Sodium 20mg*

# Double Mint Chocolate Cookies

*These puffy chocolate cookies are topped with a refreshing butter-mint frosting.*

*Preparation time: 1 hour • Baking time: 7 minutes • Cooling time: 15 minutes*

*Cookies*
2 cups sugar
1 cup unsweetened cocoa
1 cup LAND O LAKES® Butter, softened
1 cup buttermilk*
1 cup water
2 eggs
2 teaspoons baking soda
1 teaspoon baking powder
<sup>1</sup>/2 teaspoon salt
1 teaspoon vanilla
4 cups all-purpose flour

*Frosting*
4 cups powdered sugar
1 cup LAND O LAKES® Butter, softened
1 teaspoon salt
2 tablespoons milk
2 teaspoons vanilla
<sup>1</sup>/2 teaspoon mint extract
<sup>1</sup>/2 cup crushed starlight peppermint candies

Heat oven to 400°. In large mixer bowl combine all cookie ingredients except flour. Beat at low speed, scraping bowl often, until well mixed (1 to 2 minutes). By hand, stir in flour until well mixed (3 to 4 minutes). Drop dough by rounded teaspoonfuls 2 inches apart onto greased cookie sheets. Bake for 7 to 9 minutes or until top of cookie springs back when touched lightly in center. Cool completely.

In small mixer bowl combine all frosting ingredients except peppermint candy. Beat at medium speed, scraping bowl often, until light and fluffy (2 to 3 minutes). Spread <sup>1</sup>/2 tablespoon frosting on top of each cookie; sprinkle with peppermint candies.
**YIELD:** 8 dozen cookies.

*1 tablespoon vinegar plus enough milk to equal 1 cup can be substituted for 1 cup buttermilk.

*Nutrition Facts (1 cookie): Calories 90; Protein 1g; Carbohydrate 13g; Fat 4g; Cholesterol 15mg; Sodium 110mg*

*Chocolate Drizzled Lace Cookies*

# Chocolate Pinwheels

*Chocolate and white chocolate dough swirl together to form pinwheel cookies.*

*Preparation time: 40 minutes • Chilling time: 3 hours • Baking time: 7 minutes*

1 cup sugar
$1/2$ cup LAND O LAKES®
Butter, softened
1 egg
2 teaspoons vanilla
2 (1-ounce) squares white
baking bars, melted,
cooled
$1 2/3$ cups all-purpose flour
$1/2$ teaspoon baking powder
$1/4$ teaspoon salt
1 (1-ounce) square
unsweetened baking
chocolate, melted, cooled

In large mixer bowl combine sugar, butter, egg and vanilla. Beat at medium speed, scraping bowl often, until creamy (2 to 3 minutes). Reduce speed to low; add cooled melted white baking bars. Continue beating until well mixed (about 1 minute). Add flour, baking powder and salt. Continue beating, scraping bowl often, until well mixed (1 to 2 minutes). Remove <u>half</u> of dough; to remaining dough in bowl add cooled melted chocolate. Beat until well mixed (about 1 minute). Shape each half of dough into 6x3-inch rectangle. Wrap in plastic food wrap; refrigerate until firm (at least 1 hour).

On lightly floured waxed paper roll out white dough to 15x7-inch rectangle. Repeat with chocolate dough. Place chocolate dough on top of white dough. Roll up jelly roll style, starting with 15-inch side. (For easier handling, roll can be cut in half.) Wrap roll in plastic food wrap; refrigerate until firm (at least 2 hours).

<u>Heat oven to 375°.</u> Cut rolls into $1/4$-inch slices. Place 2 inches apart on cookie sheets. Bake for 7 to 9 minutes or until edges begin to brown. **YIELD:** 5 dozen cookies.

*Nutrition Facts (1 cookie): Calories 50; Protein 1g; Carbohydrate 7g;*
*Fat 3g; Cholesterol 5mg; Sodium 30mg*

# Chocolate-Dipped Shortbread

*Traditional shortbread dipped in semi-sweet chocolate and almonds.*

*Preparation time: 1 hour • Baking time: 18 minutes*

**Shortbread**
$1 1/4$ cups all-purpose flour
$1/2$ cup powdered sugar
$2/3$ cup LAND O LAKES®
Butter, softened
$1/2$ teaspoon almond extract

**Chocolate**
$1/2$ cup semi-sweet real
chocolate chips
2 teaspoons vegetable oil
$1/2$ cup finely chopped almonds

Heat oven to 325°. In large mixer bowl combine flour, sugar, butter and almond extract. Beat at medium speed, scraping bowl often, until mixture leaves side of bowl and forms a ball (3 to 4 minutes). With floured fingers press dough evenly on bottom of 9-inch square baking pan. Score dough in 16 squares; score each square into 2 triangles. Prick each triangle twice with fork. Bake for 18 to 22 minutes or until set and edges are very lightly browned. Let cool 5 minutes. Cut into triangles; cool completely in pan.

In 1-quart saucepan combine chocolate chips and vegetable oil. Cook over medium low heat, stirring constantly, until chocolate is melted (4 to 5 minutes). Remove from heat. Dip one cut edge of each triangle $1/4$ inch into melted chocolate; scrape against side of pan to remove excess chocolate. Dip chocolate-coated edge into chopped almonds; place on wire rack. Let stand until chocolate is firm. **YIELD:** 32 cookies.

*Nutrition Facts (1 cookie): Calories 90; Protein 1g; Carbohydrate 7g;*
*Fat 6g; Cholesterol 10mg; Sodium 40mg*

*Chocolate Pinwheels*

# Cinnamon Mocha Cookies

*Tender cinnamon mocha cookies are drizzled with a thin mocha cream glaze.*

*Preparation time: 45 minutes • Baking time: 7 minutes • Cooling time: 15 minutes*

## Cookies
- 2/3 cup firmly packed brown sugar
- 1 cup LAND O LAKES® Butter, softened
- 2 egg yolks
- 1 1/2 cups all-purpose flour
- 1/4 cup cornstarch
- 1 1/2 teaspoons cinnamon
- 1 teaspoon instant espresso or coffee powder*
- 1/4 teaspoon salt

## Glaze
- 1 cup powdered sugar
- 1/2 teaspoon instant espresso or coffee powder*
- 2 tablespoons milk

Heat oven to 375°. In large mixer bowl combine brown sugar and butter. Beat at medium speed, scraping bowl often, until well mixed (1 to 2 minutes). Add egg yolks; continue beating until well mixed (1 minute). Reduce speed to low. Add flour, cornstarch, cinnamon, espresso powder and salt. Continue beating, scraping bowl often, until well mixed (1 to 2 minutes). Divide dough in half. Place half of dough in large pastry bag fitted with large star tip. Pipe dough into 2 1/2-inch logs 1 inch apart on cookie sheets. Bake for 7 to 10 minutes or until very lightly browned. Do not overbake. Let cool on cookie sheets 1 minute; remove to cooling racks. Cool completely.

Meanwhile, in medium bowl stir together all glaze ingredients. Drizzle over cooled cookies. **YIELD:** 3 1/2 dozen cookies.

* Instant coffee granules can be substituted for espresso. Place coffee granules between sheets of waxed paper; crush with rolling pin. Measure amount called for in recipe after crushing.

TIP: To drizzle glaze over cookies place glaze in small plastic food bag; seal bag. Cut corner of bag just enough to allow thin stream of glaze. Drizzle glaze over cookies.

*Nutrition Facts (1 cookie): Calories 80; Protein 4g; Carbohydrate 10g; Fat 5g; Cholesterol 20mg; Sodium 60mg*

# Eggnog Snickerdoodles

*These eggnog snickerdoodles are a pleasant surprise.*

*Preparation time: 45 minutes • Baking time: 8 minutes*

## Cookies
- 2 3/4 cups all-purpose flour
- 1 1/2 cups sugar
- 1 cup LAND O LAKES® Butter, softened
- 2 eggs
- 2 teaspoons cream of tartar
- 1 teaspoon baking soda
- 1/4 teaspoon salt
- 1/2 teaspoon brandy extract
- 1/2 teaspoon rum extract

## Sugar Mixture
- 1/4 cup sugar or colored sugar
- 1 teaspoon ground nutmeg

Heat oven to 400°. In large mixer bowl combine all cookie ingredients. Beat at low speed, scraping bowl often, until well mixed (2 to 4 minutes).

In small bowl stir together sugar mixture ingredients. Shape rounded teaspoonfuls of dough into 1-inch balls; roll in sugar mixture. Place 2 inches apart on cookie sheets. Bake for 8 to 10 minutes or until edges are lightly browned. **YIELD:** 4 dozen cookies.

*Nutrition Facts (1 cookie): Calories 90; Protein 1g; Carbohydrate 13g; Fat 4g; Cholesterol 20mg; Sodium 80mg*

# Frosted Apricot Almond Cookies

*These tender, buttery almond apricot cookies are frosted and garnished with additional apricots.*

*Preparation time: 1 hour • Baking time: 11 minutes • Cooling time: 30 minutes*

## Cookies

- 1 1/2 cups powdered sugar
- 1 cup LAND O LAKES® Butter, softened
- 1 egg
- 1/2 teaspoon almond extract
- 2 cups all-purpose flour
- 1 teaspoon baking soda
- 1 teaspoon cream of tartar
- 1 cup coarsely chopped slivered almonds, toasted
- 1 (6-ounce) package chopped dried apricots, reserve 1/3 cup

## Frosting

- 2 1/4 cups powdered sugar
- 1/4 cup LAND O LAKES® Butter, softened
- 3 to 4 tablespoons milk
- 1/2 teaspoon almond extract

## Garnish

- Reserved chopped dried apricots

Heat oven to 350°. In large mixer bowl combine 1 1/2 cups powdered sugar and 1 cup butter. Beat at medium speed, scraping bowl often, until well mixed (1 to 2 minutes). Add egg and 1/2 teaspoon almond extract; continue beating until well mixed (1 minute). Reduce speed to low; add flour, baking soda and cream of tartar. Continue beating, scraping bowl often, until well mixed (1 to 2 minutes). By hand, stir in almonds and chopped apricots. Drop by rounded teaspoonfuls 2 inches apart onto cookie sheets. Bake for 11 to 15 minutes or until light golden brown. Cool completely.

Meanwhile, in small mixer bowl combine all frosting ingredients. Beat at medium speed, scraping bowl often, until well mixed (1 to 2 minutes). Spread about 1 teaspoon frosting on top of each cookie. Garnish with chopped apricots.
**YIELD:** 6 dozen cookies.

TIP: Cookies can be lightly sprinkled with powdered sugar instead of frosting.

*Nutrition Facts (1 cookie): Calories 100; Protein 1g; Carbohydrate 10g; Fat 4g; Cholesterol 10mg; Sodium 50mg*

# Cranberry Apricot Tartlets

*A tangy cranberry apricot mixture fills these orange-flavored tartlet shells.*

*Preparation time: 50 minutes • Baking time: 14 minutes • Cooling time: 1 hour • Cooking time: 20 minutes*

## Tartlet Shells

- 1/4 cup sugar
- 1/2 cup LAND O LAKES® Butter, cut into 4 pieces
- 1 1/3 cups all-purpose flour
- 1/4 teaspoon salt
- 1/2 teaspoon grated orange peel
- 1 to 3 tablespoons orange juice

## Filling

- 1 1/2 cups fresh or frozen cranberries
- 3/4 cup dried apricots, chopped
- 1 cup sugar
- 1/2 teaspoon grated orange peel
- 1/3 cup orange juice
- 1/4 cup water

  Sweetened whipped cream, if desired

Heat oven to 375°. In small mixer bowl combine 1/4 cup sugar, butter, flour and salt. Beat at low speed, scraping bowl often, until mixture is crumbly (1 to 2 minutes). Continue beating, adding orange peel and enough orange juice to form a dough. Divide dough into 30 equal pieces; set aside.

Grease and sugar mini muffin pans. Press dough evenly on bottom and up sides of prepared muffin cups. Bake for 14 to 18 minutes or until edges are lightly browned. Immediately loosen edges with knife; carefully remove shells using tip of sharp knife. Place on wire rack; cool completely.

Meanwhile, in 2-quart saucepan combine all filling ingredients except whipped cream. Cook over medium high heat until mixture comes to a full boil (5 to 7 minutes). Reduce heat to low. Continue cooking, stirring occasionally, until mixture thickens and liquid is absorbed (15 to 20 minutes). Cool completely. Just before serving, assemble tartlets. Spoon rounded teaspoonful filling into each shell; garnish with whipped cream.
**YIELD:** 30 tartlets.

*Nutrition Facts (1 tartlet): Calories 90; Protein 1g; Carbohydrate 16g; Fat 3g; Cholesterol 10mg; Sodium 50mg*

# Walnut Biscotti

*Toasted walnuts add flavor to this crisp biscotti.*

*Preparation time: 30 minutes • Baking time: 41 minutes • Cooling time: 15 minutes*

2 cups all-purpose flour
$3/4$ cup finely chopped
    walnuts, toasted
$1/2$ teaspoon baking powder
$1/2$ teaspoon baking soda
$1/4$ teaspoon salt
$3/4$ cup sugar
2 eggs
$1/4$ cup vegetable oil
1 tablespoon vanilla

2 to 3 teaspoons all-purpose
    flour

1 egg white
1 tablespoon water
    Sugar, if desired

Heat oven to 350°. In medium bowl combine 2 cups flour, walnuts, baking powder, baking soda and salt; set aside.

In large mixer bowl beat sugar and eggs at medium high speed until thick and lemon colored (2 to 3 minutes). Add oil and vanilla. Continue beating until well mixed (1 to 2 minutes). Reduce speed to low. Continue beating, gradually adding flour mixture and scraping bowl often, until well mixed (1 to 2 minutes).

Turn dough onto lightly floured surface (dough will be soft and sticky). Sprinkle dough lightly with 2 to 3 teaspoons flour; knead into dough. With floured hands shape into 2 (8x2-inch) logs. Place 3 to 4 inches apart on greased cookie sheet; flatten tops slightly. Combine egg white and water; brush over top of biscotti. Sprinkle with sugar. Bake for 25 to 30 minutes or until lightly browned and firm to the touch. Let cool on cookie sheet 15 minutes.

Reduce oven temperature to 300°. With serrated knife, cut logs diagonally into $1/2$-inch slices; arrange slices, cut side down, on cookie sheets. Bake for 8 to 10 minutes; turn slices. Continue baking for 8 to 10 minutes or until golden brown. Remove to wire rack; cool completely. **YIELD:** $2^1/2$ dozen cookies.

TIP: Drizzle cookies with or dip into melted chocolate.

*Nutrition Facts (1 cookie): Calories 150; Protein 3g; Carbohydrate 20g;*
*Fat 7g; Cholesterol 20mg; Sodium 80mg*

# Tangy Yule Balls

*An easy no-bake cookie flavored with orange juice concentrate.*

*Preparation time: 30 minutes • Chilling time: 2 hours*

4 cups vanilla wafer crumbs
    or graham cracker crumbs
2 cups powdered sugar
2 cups finely chopped walnuts
$1/2$ cup LAND O LAKES®
    Butter, melted
1 (6-ounce) can frozen orange
    juice concentrate, thawed

    Powdered sugar, if desired

In large bowl stir together all ingredients except powdered sugar for rolling. Shape into 1-inch balls. Roll in powdered sugar. Cover; refrigerate until firm (at least 2 hours). Store refrigerated. **YIELD:** 8 dozen cookies.

*Nutrition Facts (1 cookie): Calories 60; Protein 1g; Carbohydrate 7g;*
*Fat 3g; Cholesterol 5mg; Sodium 40mg*

*Walnut Biscotti*

# Favorite Teddy Bear Cookies

*Cookies become a special treat when shaped into cute little teddy bears.*

*Preparation time: 1 hour 30 minutes • Baking time: 7 minutes*

1 cup sugar
$^3/_4$ cup LAND O LAKES® Butter, softened
1 egg
2 teaspoons vanilla
$2^1/_4$ cups all-purpose flour
1 teaspoon baking powder
$^1/_4$ teaspoon salt
2 (1-ounce) squares unsweetened baking chocolate, melted

Heat oven to 375°. In large mixer bowl combine sugar, butter, egg and vanilla. Beat at medium speed, scraping bowl often, until well mixed (1 to 2 minutes). Add flour, baking powder and salt. Continue beating, scraping bowl often, until well mixed (1 to 2 minutes). Divide dough in half. Place half of dough in medium bowl; by hand, stir in chocolate.

For each teddy bear, form a portion of either color dough into a large ball (1-inch) for body, a medium ball ($^3/_4$-inch) for head, four small balls ($^1/_2$-inch) for arms and legs, two smaller balls for ears and one small ball for nose. If desired, add additional balls for eyes and mouth. Repeat with remaining dough, making either vanilla or chocolate teddy bears or mixing the doughs to make two-toned teddy bears.

To form each cookie, place large ball (body) on cookie sheet; flatten slightly. Attach head, arms, legs and ears by overlapping slightly onto body. Add nose, eyes and mouth. Bake for 7 to 8 minutes or until body is set. Cool 1 minute. Remove from cookie sheet; cool completely. **YIELD:** $1^1/_2$ dozen cookies.

TIP: If desired, decorate cookies with frosting.

*Nutrition Facts (1 cookie): Calories 190; Protein 2g; Carbohydrate 24g; Fat 10g; Cholesterol 30mg; Sodium 130mg*

# Favorite Chocolate Chip Cookies

*Ground oatmeal is the ingredient that makes these chocolate chip cookies a favorite.*

*Preparation time: 1 hour • Baking time: 10 minutes*

$2^1/_4$ cups uncooked quick-cooking <u>or</u> old-fashioned rolled oats
1 cup sugar
1 cup firmly packed brown sugar
1 cup LAND O LAKES® Butter, softened
2 eggs
2 teaspoons vanilla
2 cups all-purpose flour
1 teaspoon baking soda
$^1/_2$ teaspoon baking powder
$^1/_2$ teaspoon salt
1 (12-ounce) package semi-sweet chocolate chips

Heat oven to 375°. In 5-cup blender container or food processor bowl place oats. Cover; blend at high speed until oats are finely ground ($^1/_2$ to 1 minute). Set aside.

In large mixer bowl combine sugar, brown sugar and butter. Beat at medium speed, scraping bowl often, until creamy (1 to 2 minutes). Add eggs and vanilla; continue beating until well mixed (1 to 2 minutes). Reduce speed to low; add ground oats, flour, baking soda, baking powder and salt. Continue beating, scraping bowl often, until well mixed (1 to 2 minutes). By hand, stir in chocolate chips. Drop by rounded tablespoonfuls 2 inches apart onto cookie sheets. Bake for 10 to 13 minutes or until lightly browned. Let stand 1 minute; remove from cookie sheets. **YIELD:** 4 dozen cookies.

*Nutrition Facts (1 cookie): Calories 130; Protein 2g; Carbohydrate 18g; Fat 6g; Cholesterol 20mg; Sodium 90mg*

*Favorite Teddy Bear Cookies*

# Citrus Ribbons

*Layers of citrus flavors, in delicately tinted dough, make this cookie a must for special occasions.*

*Preparation time: 1 hour • Chilling time: 4 hours • Baking time: 9 minutes*

### Base Dough
- 1 cup sugar
- 1 cup LAND O LAKES® Butter, softened
- 1 egg
- 2¹/₂ cups all-purpose flour
- ¹/₄ teaspoon baking powder
- ¹/₄ teaspoon salt

### Orange Dough
- 1 teaspoon orange juice
- 1 teaspoon grated orange peel
- 2 drops yellow food coloring
- 1 drop red food coloring

### Lemon Dough
- 1 teaspoon lemon juice
- 1 teaspoon grated lemon peel
- 2 drops yellow food coloring

### Lime Dough
- 1 teaspoon lime juice
- 1 teaspoon grated lime peel
- 2 drops green food coloring

In large mixer bowl combine sugar, butter and egg. Beat at medium speed, scraping bowl often, until creamy (2 to 3 minutes). Reduce speed to low; add flour, baking powder and salt. Continue beating, scraping bowl often, until well mixed (1 to 2 minutes). Divide dough into 3 equal portions. To first portion add all orange dough ingredients; stir until well blended. To second portion add all lemon dough ingredients; stir until well blended. To third portion add all lime dough ingredients; stir until well blended. (Doughs will be soft.)

Line 8x4-inch loaf pan with waxed paper or aluminum foil. Press orange dough in even layer on bottom of lined pan. Top evenly with lemon dough, gently patting dough. Top evenly with lime dough, gently patting dough. Cover; refrigerate until firm (at least 4 hours).

Heat oven to 375°. Lift dough out of pan and peel off waxed paper or aluminum foil. Cut into ¹/₄-inch slices; cut each slice in half forming 2x1¹/₂-inch pieces. Place 1 inch apart on cookie sheets. Bake for 9 to 12 minutes or until edges are very lightly browned. **YIELD:** 5 dozen cookies.

*Nutrition Facts (1 cookie): Calories 60; Protein 1g; Carbohydrate 7g; Fat 3g; Cholesterol 10mg; Sodium 50mg*

# Grammie's Pfeffernusse

*These dime-size German cookies, flavored with anise, are eaten by the handful.*

*Preparation time: 1 hour • Standing time: 20 minutes • Chilling time: 2 hours • Baking time: 8 minutes*

- ¹/₄ cup boiling water
- 2 tablespoons anise seed
- 3¹/₂ cups all-purpose flour
- ²/₃ cup sugar
- ²/₃ cup LAND O LAKES® Butter, softened
- ²/₃ cup dark corn syrup
- ¹/₂ teaspoon baking soda

In large mixer bowl combine boiling water and anise seed; let stand 20 minutes. Add all remaining ingredients. Beat at low speed, scraping bowl often, until well mixed (3 to 4 minutes). Cover; refrigerate until firm (at least 1 hour).

On lightly floured surface roll portions of dough into ropes ¹/₂ inch in diameter. Place ropes on waxed paper-lined cookie sheet; cover. Refrigerate ropes until firm (at least 1 hour).

Heat oven to 350°. Cut ropes into ³/₈-inch slices. Place ¹/₂ inch apart on cookie sheets. Bake for 8 to 10 minutes or until very lightly browned around edges. Store in loosely covered container to keep cookies crisp. **YIELD:** 28 dozen dime-size cookies.

*Nutrition Facts (1 cookie): Calories 10; Protein 0g; Carbohydrate 2g; Fat 0g; Cholesterol 0mg; Sodium 5mg*

# Coconut Date Balls

*These moist cookies are filled with dates and rolled in coconut.*

*Preparation time: 45 minutes • Cooking time: 8 minutes • Chilling time: 1 hour*

½ cup LAND O LAKES® Butter
1 cup sugar
1 (8-ounce) package chopped dates
1 egg, slightly beaten
½ teaspoon salt
2 tablespoons milk
1 teaspoon vanilla
2 cups crushed cornflakes
½ cup chopped pecans
½ cup chopped maraschino cherries, drained
1½ cups flaked coconut

In 10-inch skillet melt butter over medium heat (3 to 4 minutes). Stir in sugar and dates. Remove from heat; stir in egg, salt, milk and vanilla. Cook over medium heat, stirring occasionally, until mixture comes to a full boil (4 to 7 minutes). Boil, stirring constantly, 1 minute. Remove from heat; stir in cornflakes, pecans and cherries. Shape into 1-inch balls; roll in coconut. Place on waxed paper. Refrigerate until set (at least 1 hour). **YIELD:** 4 dozen cookies.

Microwave Directions: In 2-quart casserole melt butter on HIGH (1 to 1½ minutes). Stir in sugar, dates, egg, salt, milk and vanilla. Microwave on HIGH, stirring every minute, until mixture comes to a full boil (2½ to 4 minutes). Microwave on HIGH 1 minute. Stir in cornflakes, pecans and cherries. Shape into 1-inch balls; roll in coconut. Place on waxed paper. Refrigerate until set (at least 1 hour).

*Nutrition Facts (1 cookie): Calories 90; Protein 1g; Carbohydrate 13g;*
*Fat 4g; Cholesterol 10mg; Sodium 80mg*

# Date Oatmeal Cookies

*Oatmeal and dates give this cookie old-fashioned goodness.*

*Preparation time: 30 minutes • Baking time: 7 minutes*

1 cup firmly packed brown sugar
½ cup LAND O LAKES® Butter, softened
½ cup shortening
2 eggs
2 teaspoons vanilla
2 cups all-purpose flour
½ teaspoon baking powder
1½ cups quick-cooking oats
1 (8-ounce) package chopped dates

Heat oven to 375°. In large mixer bowl combine brown sugar, butter and shortening. Beat at medium speed, scraping bowl often, until creamy (1 to 2 minutes). Add eggs and vanilla. Continue beating until well mixed (1 to 2 minutes). Reduce speed to low; add flour and baking powder. Continue beating, scraping bowl often, until well mixed (1 to 2 minutes). By hand, stir in oats and dates. Drop by heaping teaspoonfuls 2 inches apart onto cookie sheets. Bake for 7 to 10 minutes or until light golden brown.
**YIELD:** 4½ dozen cookies.

*Nutrition Facts (1 cookie): Calories 70; Protein 1g; Carbohydrate 11g;*
*Fat 4g; Cholesterol 10mg; Sodium 25mg*

# Holiday Cutout Cookies

*These crisp, tender cutout cookies can be decorated to capture the spirit of any time of the year.*

*Preparation time: 1 hour • Chilling time: 2 hours • Baking time: 6 minutes • Cooling time: 15 minutes*

2$^1$/2 cups all-purpose flour
1 cup sugar
1 cup LAND O LAKES® Butter, softened
1 egg
1 teaspoon baking powder
2 tablespoons milk
2 teaspoons almond extract
Food coloring, if desired

Colored sugars, if desired
Frosting, if desired
Decorator candies, if desired

In large mixer bowl combine all ingredients except colored sugars, frosting and candies. Beat at low speed, scraping bowl often, until well mixed (1 to 2 minutes). Divide dough into thirds; wrap in plastic food wrap. Refrigerate until firm (at least 2 hours).

Heat oven to 400°. On lightly floured surface roll out dough, one third at a time (keeping remaining dough refrigerated), to $^1$/4-inch thickness. Cut with 3-inch cookie cutters. Place 1 inch apart on cookie sheets. Sprinkle cookies with colored sugars or bake plain. Bake for 6 to 10 minutes or until edges are lightly browned. Cool completely. Decorate or frost cookies. **YIELD:** 3 dozen cookies.

TIP: For frosting recipe see Best Ever Butter Cookies page 32.

VARIATIONS
Pumpkins: Cut out dough with pumpkin shaped cookie cutter. Mix egg yolk and water with food coloring to make orange and green. Paint on pumpkin (orange), stems and leaves (green) before baking or after baked cookies are cooled, decorate as indicated above with white frosting that has been tinted to orange and green.

Candy Canes: Cut out dough with candy cane shaped cookie cutter. Sprinkle red decorator sugar to resemble candy cane stripes on cookie before baking or decorate cooled cookies with pastry bag filled with red tinted frosting to resemble candy cane stripes.

Christmas Trees: Cut out dough with tree shaped cookie cutter. Sprinkle with green colored sugar and decorate with cinnamon candies before baking or after baked cookies are cooled, frost cookies with frosting; immediately sprinkle with green colored coconut pressing lightly into frosting. Use decorator candies as ornaments.

*Nutrition Facts (1 cookie): Calories 100; Protein 1g; Carbohydrate 12g; Fat 5g; Cholesterol 20mg; Sodium 70mg*

# Lebkuchen Spice Spritz Cookies

*The popular flavors of Lebkuchen cookies come alive in this easy spritz cookie.*

*Preparation time: 1 hour • Baking time: 8 minutes*

*Cookies*
$^2$/3 cup sugar
1 cup LAND O LAKES® Butter, softened
1 egg
1 teaspoon cinnamon
1 teaspoon ground nutmeg
1$^1$/2 teaspoon ground allspice
$^1$/4 teaspoon ground cloves
2 teaspoons lemon juice
2 cups all-purpose flour

*Glaze*
1 cup powdered sugar
1 tablespoon milk
$^1$/2 teaspoon vanilla

Heat oven to 400°. In large mixer bowl combine all cookie ingredients except flour. Beat at medium speed, scraping bowl often, until well mixed (2 to 3 minutes). By hand, stir in flour until well mixed. If dough is too soft, cover; refrigerate until firm enough to form cookies (at least 1 hour).

Place dough in cookie press; form desired shapes 1 inch apart on cookie sheets. Bake for 8 to 12 minutes or until edges are lightly browned.

Meanwhile, in small bowl stir together all glaze ingredients. Drizzle over warm cookies. **YIELD:** 5 dozen cookies.

VARIATION
Traditional Spritz Cookies: Omit cinnamon, nutmeg, allspice, cloves and lemon juice. Add 1 teaspoon vanilla.

*Nutrition Facts (1 cookie): Calories 60; Protein 1g; Carbohydrate 8g; Fat 3g; Cholesterol 10mg; Sodium 30mg*

*Holiday Cutout Cookies*

# Holiday Chocolate Butter Cookies

*A rich, chocolate butter cookie with endless possibilities.*

*Preparation time: 1 hour • Baking time: 7 minutes*

## Cookies
- $1/2$ cup sugar
- $3/4$ cup LAND O LAKES® Butter, softened
- 1 egg yolk
- 1 teaspoon almond extract
- $1^1/2$ cups all-purpose flour
- $1/4$ cup unsweetened cocoa

## Suggested Coatings
- Semi-sweet real chocolate chips, melted
- Vanilla-flavored candy coating, melted

## Suggested Toppings
- Finely chopped almonds, pecans or walnuts
- Candy coated milk chocolate pieces
- Flaked coconut
- Fruit preserves
- Colored sugars
- Multicolored decorator candies
- Maraschino cherries

Heat oven to 375°. In large mixer bowl combine all cookie ingredients <u>except</u> flour and cocoa. Beat at medium speed, scraping bowl often, until mixture is creamy (2 to 3 minutes). Reduce speed to low. Continue beating, gradually adding flour and cocoa, until well mixed (2 to 3 minutes). Shape dough according to choice of variation directions. Bake for 7 to 9 minutes or until set. **YIELD:** 3 dozen cookies.

VARIATIONS

<u>Nut Rolls</u>: Shape dough into 2 to 3-inch logs. Place 1 inch apart on cookie sheets. Bake as directed above. Cool completely. Dip both ends of each cookie in melted chocolate chips, then in finely chopped nuts.

<u>Fruit Filled</u>: Shape dough into 1-inch balls. Place 1 inch apart on cookie sheets. Make a depression in center of each cookie with back of teaspoon. Bake as directed above. Cool completely. Fill centers with fruit preserves.

<u>Sugar Topped</u>: Shape dough into 1-inch balls. Place 1 inch apart on cookie sheets. Flatten cookies to $1/4$-inch thickness with bottom of buttered glass dipped in sugar.

<u>Spritz</u>: Place dough in cookie press; form desired shape 1 inch apart on cookie sheets.

<u>Decorated</u>: Shape rounded teaspoonfuls of dough into desired forms (logs, balls, flattened, etc.). Place 1 inch apart on cookie sheets. Bake as directed above. Cool completely. Drizzle cookies with melted chocolate chips or melted vanilla coating. Decorate with finely chopped nuts, coconut, colored sugars or multicolored decorator candies.

<u>Surprise Filled</u>: Shape dough into 1-inch balls. Place 1 inch apart on cookie sheets. Make a depression in center of each cookie with back of teaspoon. Bake as directed above. Cool completely. Place one of the following ingredients in center of each cookie: nut, candy coated milk chocolate piece, maraschino cherry half or $1/2$ teaspoon flaked coconut. Spoon melted chocolate chips over filled center. Let stand to harden chocolate.

<u>Snowballs</u>: Shape dough into 1-inch balls. Place 1 inch apart on cookie sheets. Bake as directed above. Roll in powdered sugar or unsweetened cocoa while still warm and again when cool.

<u>Bon Bons</u>: Shape dough into 1-inch balls. Place 1 inch apart on cookie sheets. Bake as directed above. Cool completely. Add food coloring and favorite flavor extract to melted vanilla coating. Dip top of each cookie in melted coating.

<u>Funny Faces</u>: Shape dough into 1-inch balls. Place 1 inch apart on cookie sheets. Flatten cookies to $1/4$-inch thickness with bottom of buttered glass dipped in sugar. Bake as directed above. Cool completely. Use melted chocolate chips or vanilla coating to attach chocolate chips, candy coated milk chocolate pieces, coconut, colored sugars, multicolored decorator candies, etc. making faces on cookies.

*Nutrition Facts (1 cookie): Calories 130; Protein 2g; Carbohydrate 10g;*
*Fat 10g; Cholesterol 15mg; Sodium 45mg*

*Holiday Chocolate Butter Cookies*

# Melt-In-Your-Mouth Spritz

*Perfect spritz cookies every time, plus variations to create variety.*

*Preparation time: 1 hour • Baking time: 6 minutes*

$2/3$ cup sugar
1 cup LAND O LAKES® Butter, softened
1 egg
$1/2$ teaspoon salt
2 teaspoons vanilla
$2^1/4$ cups all-purpose flour

Heat oven to 400°. In large mixer bowl combine all ingredients <u>except</u> flour. Beat at medium speed, scraping bowl often, until mixture is creamy (2 to 3 minutes). Reduce speed to low; add flour. Continue beating, scraping bowl often, until well mixed (2 to 3 minutes). If desired, add ingredients from one of the following variations. If dough is too soft, cover; refrigerate until firm enough to form cookies (30 to 45 minutes).

Place dough in cookie press; form desired shapes 1 inch apart on cookie sheets. Bake for 6 to 8 minutes or until edges are lightly browned. **YIELD:** 5 dozen cookies.

VARIATIONS

<u>Eggnog Spritz</u>: To dough add 1 teaspoon ground nutmeg. Glaze: In small bowl stir together 1 cup powdered sugar, $1/4$ cup softened LAND O LAKES® Butter, 2 tablespoons water and $1/4$ teaspoon rum extract until smooth; drizzle over warm cookies.

<u>Chocolate Mint Spritz</u>: To dough add $1/4$ teaspoon mint extract. Immediately after removing cookies from oven place 1 chocolate candy kiss on each cookie.

<u>Chocolate Flecked Spritz</u>: To dough add $1/4$ cup coarsely grated semi-sweet chocolate.

<u>Spiced Spritz</u>: To dough add 1 teaspoon cinnamon, 1 teaspoon ground nutmeg, $1/2$ teaspoon ground allspice and $1/4$ teaspoon ground cloves. Glaze: In small bowl stir together 1 cup powdered sugar, 2 tablespoons milk and $1/2$ teaspoon vanilla until smooth; drizzle over warm cookies.

*Nutrition Facts (1 cookie): Calories 50; Protein 1g; Carbohydrate 6g; Fat 3g; Cholesterol 10mg; Sodium 50mg*

# Best Ever Butter Cookies

*These crisp, tender cutout cookies can be decorated to capture the spirit of your occasion.*

*Preparation time: 1 hour • Chilling time: 2 hours • Baking time: 6 minutes • Cooling time: 15 minutes*

**Cookies**
$2^1/2$ cups all-purpose flour
1 cup sugar
1 cup LAND O LAKES® Butter, softened
1 egg
1 teaspoon baking powder
2 tablespoons orange juice
1 tablespoon vanilla

**Frosting**
4 cups powdered sugar
$1/2$ cup LAND O LAKES® Butter, softened
3 to 4 tablespoons milk
2 teaspoons vanilla

**Decorations**
Food coloring, colored sugars, flaked coconut, cinnamon candies

In large mixer bowl combine all cookie ingredients. Beat at low speed, scraping bowl often, until well mixed (1 to 2 minutes). Divide dough into thirds; wrap in plastic food wrap. Refrigerate until firm (at least 2 hours).

<u>Heat oven to 400°</u>. On lightly floured surface roll out dough, one-third at a time (keeping remaining dough refrigerated), to $1/4$-inch thickness. Cut with 3-inch cookie cutters. Place 1 inch apart on cookie sheets. Bake for 6 to 10 minutes or until edges are lightly browned. Cool completely.

In small mixer bowl combine all frosting ingredients. Beat at low speed, scraping bowl often, until fluffy (1 to 2 minutes). If desired, color frosting. Frost and decorate cookies. **YIELD:** 3 dozen cookies.

*Nutrition Facts (1 cookie): Calories 170; Protein 1g; Carbohydrate 23g; Fat 8g; Cholesterol 25mg; Sodium 90mg*

*Holiday Chocolate Butter Cookies, see page 30; Melt-In-Your-Mouth Spritz, see page 32; Orange Spiced Gingerbread Cookies, see page 38; Brandied Buttery Wreaths, see page 10*

# Hazelnut Rounds

*Finely chopped hazelnuts give this cookie its distinctive flavor.*

*Preparation time: 45 minutes • Chilling time: 1 hour • Baking time: 13 minutes*

1 cup sugar
1 cup LAND O LAKES®
    Butter, softened
1 egg
1 teaspoon vanilla
2 cups all-purpose flour
1/2 teaspoon baking soda
1/4 teaspoon salt
1 (2$^1$/2-ounce) package
    ($^1$/2 cup) hazelnuts <u>or</u>
    filberts, finely chopped

Heat oven to 350°. In large mixer bowl combine sugar and butter. Beat at medium speed, scraping bowl often, until creamy (1 to 2 minutes). Add egg and vanilla. Continue beating until well mixed (1 minute). Reduce speed to low; add flour, baking soda and salt. Continue beating, scraping bowl often, until well mixed (1 to 2 minutes). Cover; refrigerate until firm (at least 1 hour).

Shape dough into 1-inch balls; roll in hazelnuts. Place 2 inches apart on cookie sheets. Bake for 13 to 16 minutes or until edges are lightly browned. **YIELD:** 4 dozen cookies.

TIP: If desired, melt $^1$/2 cup semi-sweet real chocolate chips or raspberry-flavored chocolate chips with 1 teaspoon shortening over low heat. Drizzle over top of cookies.

*Nutrition Facts (1 cookie): Calories 80; Protein 1g; Carbohydrate 8g;*
*Fat 5g; Cholesterol 15mg; Sodium 60mg*

# Pineapple Macadamia Nut Cookies

*Pineapple, macadamia nuts and coconut are combined in this frosted drop cookie for a taste of the tropics.*

*Preparation time: 1 hour • Baking time: 10 minutes • Cooling time: 15 minutes*

**Cookies**
1/2 cup sugar
1/2 cup firmly packed brown
    sugar
1/2 cup LAND O LAKES®
    Butter, softened
1 (8-ounce) can ($^1$/2 cup)
    crushed pineapple in
    juice, well drained,
    <u>reserve juice</u>
1 egg
1 teaspoon vanilla
1$^3$/4 cups all-purpose flour
1 teaspoon baking powder
1 teaspoon baking soda
1/4 teaspoon salt
1 cup flaked coconut
1 (3$^1$/2-ounce) jar ($^3$/4 cup)
    macadamia nuts, coarsely
    chopped

**Frosting**
2 cups powdered sugar
1/4 cup LAND O LAKES®
    Butter, melted
1/2 teaspoon vanilla
2 to 3 tablespoons reserved
    pineapple juice

Toasted coconut, if desired

Heat oven to 375°. In large mixer bowl combine sugar, brown sugar and $^1$/2 cup butter. Beat at medium speed, scraping bowl often, until creamy (1 to 2 minutes). Add drained pineapple, egg and vanilla. Continue beating, scraping bowl often, until well mixed (1 to 2 minutes). Reduce speed to low; add flour, baking powder, baking soda and salt. Continue beating, scraping bowl often, until well mixed (1 to 2 minutes). By hand, stir in coconut and macadamia nuts. Drop by rounded teaspoonfuls 2 inches apart onto greased cookie sheets. Bake for 10 to 12 minutes or until lightly browned. Let stand 1 minute; remove from cookie sheets. Cool completely.

In small mixer bowl combine powdered sugar, $^1$/4 cup melted butter and vanilla. Beat at low speed, scraping bowl often and gradually adding enough pineapple juice for desired spreading consistency. Frost cooled cookies; sprinkle with toasted coconut. **YIELD:** 3$^1$/2 dozen cookies.

*Nutrition Facts (1 cookie): Calories 120; Protein 1g; Carbohydrate 18g;*
*Fat 6g; Cholesterol 15mg; Sodium 90mg*

*Hazelnut Rounds*

# Lemon Krumkake

*To make these Scandinavian favorites, a special krumkake iron is needed.*

*Preparation time: 1 hour • Baking time: 35 seconds*

3 eggs
³/₄ cup sugar
¹/₂ cup LAND O LAKES® Butter, melted, cooled
¹/₂ cup whipping cream
1¹/₄ cups all-purpose flour
1 teaspoon grated lemon peel

In small mixer bowl beat eggs at medium high speed until thick and lemon colored (1 to 2 minutes). Continue beating, gradually adding sugar, until well mixed (1 to 2 minutes). Reduce speed to low. Continue beating, gradually adding cooled melted butter and whipping cream, until well mixed (1 to 2 minutes). Continue beating, gradually adding flour, until smooth (1 to 2 minutes). By hand, stir in lemon peel.

Heat krumkake iron over medium high heat on range top. (Iron is hot when a drop of water sizzles when dropped on open iron.) Drop 1 heaping teaspoonful batter onto hot iron. Bring top of iron down gently, pressing firmly but not squeezing out batter; scrape any excess batter from edges. Bake 20 seconds; turn iron over. Continue baking for 15 to 20 seconds or until light golden brown. Open iron; lift krumkake off with thin spatula. Immediately wrap hot cookies around cone or handle of wooden spoon. Hold in place a few seconds to set shape. **YIELD:** 4 dozen cookies.

TIP: Krumkake irons are available in specialty food stores or in Scandinavian gift stores.

*Nutrition Facts (1 cookie): Calories 50; Protein 1g; Carbohydrate 6g; Fat 3g; Cholesterol 20mg; Sodium 25mg*

# Lemon Gingerbread Rounds

*Old-fashioned gingerbread cookies flavored with lemon.*

*Preparation time: 45 minutes • Chilling time: 2 hours • Baking time: 7 minutes*

¹/₃ cup firmly packed brown sugar
¹/₃ cup LAND O LAKES® Butter, softened
²/₃ cup light molasses
1 egg
2 teaspoons grated lemon peel
2³/₄ cups all-purpose flour
1 teaspoon ground ginger
¹/₂ teaspoon baking soda
¹/₂ teaspoon salt

Sugar

In large mixer bowl combine brown sugar, butter, molasses, egg and lemon peel. Beat at medium speed, scraping bowl often, until well mixed (1 to 2 minutes). Reduce speed to low; add all remaining ingredients except sugar. Continue beating, scraping bowl often, until well mixed (1 to 2 minutes). Divide dough in half; wrap each half in plastic food wrap. Refrigerate until firm (at least 2 hours).

Heat oven to 375°. On well floured surface roll out dough, half at a time (keeping remaining dough refrigerated), to ¹/₈-inch thickness. Cut with 3-inch round cookie cutter. Place 1 inch apart on greased cookie sheets. Sprinkle with sugar; press lightly into cookies. Bake for 7 to 10 minutes or until set. **YIELD:** 3 dozen cookies.

*Nutrition Facts (1 cookie); Calories 70; Protein 1g; Carbohydrate 13g; Fat 2g; Cholesterol 10mg; Sodium 60mg*

*Lemon Krumkake*

# Orange Spiced Gingerbread Cookies

*Traditional cutout gingerbread cookies are spiced with grated orange peel for a subtle new taste sensation.*

*Preparation time: 1 hour • Chilling time: 2 hours • Baking time: 6 minutes • Cooling time: 15 minutes*

### Cookies
- $1/3$ cup firmly packed brown sugar
- $1/3$ cup LAND O LAKES® Butter, softened
- $2/3$ cup light molasses
- 1 egg
- 2 teaspoons grated orange peel
- $2^3/4$ cups all-purpose flour
- 1 teaspoon ground ginger
- $1/2$ teaspoon baking soda
- $1/2$ teaspoon salt

### Frosting
- 4 cups powdered sugar
- $1/2$ cup LAND O LAKES® Butter, softened
- 2 teaspoons vanilla
- 3 to 4 tablespoons milk
- Food coloring, if desired

In large mixer bowl combine brown sugar, $1/3$ cup butter, molasses, egg and orange peel. Beat at medium speed, scraping bowl often, until smooth and creamy (1 to 2 minutes). Add all remaining cookie ingredients. Beat at low speed, scraping bowl often, until well mixed (1 to 2 minutes). Cover; refrigerate until firm (at least 2 hours).

Heat oven to 375°. On well floured surface roll out dough, half at a time, to $1/4$-inch thickness. Cut with 3 to 4-inch cookie cutters. Place 1 inch apart on greased cookie sheets. Bake for 6 to 8 minutes or until no indentation remains when touched. Cool completely.

In small mixer bowl combine all frosting ingredients <u>except</u> milk and food coloring. Beat at low speed, scraping bowl often and gradually adding enough milk for desired spreading consistency. Color frosting with food coloring. Decorate cooled cookies with frosting. **YIELD:** 4 dozen cookies.

*Nutrition Facts (1 cookie): Calories 100; Protein 1g; Carbohydrate 18g; Fat 3g; Cholesterol 15mg; Sodium 70mg*

# Old-Fashioned Chewy Molasses Cookies

*These chewy, spiced molasses cookies are sure to stir up fond memories.*

*Preparation time: 30 minutes • Chilling time: 2 hours • Baking time: 14 minutes*

- $4^1/2$ cups all-purpose flour
- 2 cups sugar
- 1 cup LAND O LAKES® Butter, softened
- 1 cup light molasses
- $1/2$ cup milk
- 2 eggs
- 1 teaspoon baking soda
- 1 teaspoon ground ginger
- $1/2$ teaspoon cinnamon
- $1/4$ teaspoon salt

  Sugar

In large mixer bowl combine all ingredients <u>except</u> additional sugar. Beat at low speed, scraping bowl often, until well mixed (2 to 3 minutes). Cover; refrigerate until firm (at least 2 hours).

Heat oven to 350°. Shape rounded tablespoonfuls of dough into balls; roll in sugar. Place 2 inches apart on cookie sheets. Bake for 14 to 16 minutes or until slightly firm to the touch. **YIELD:** $4^1/2$ dozen cookies.

*Nutrition Facts (1 cookie): Calories 120; Protein 1g; Carbohydrate 20g; Fat 4g; Cholesterol 20mg; Sodium 70mg*

*Orange Spiced Gingerbread Cookies*

# Mocha Toffee Crescents

*Crescent shaped cookies, flavored with espresso and toffee chips.*

*Preparation time: 45 minutes • Baking time: 13 minutes*

1 teaspoon instant espresso granules
1 tablespoon water
2/3 cup powdered sugar
1 cup LAND O LAKES® Butter, softened
2 cups all-purpose flour
1/4 teaspoon salt
1/2 cup toffee chips

Heat oven to 325°. In small bowl dissolve instant espresso granules in water. In large mixer bowl combine coffee mixture, powdered sugar and butter. Beat at medium speed, scraping bowl often, until creamy (1 to 2 minutes). Reduce speed to low; add flour and salt. Continue beating, scraping bowl often, until well mixed (1 to 2 minutes). By hand, stir in toffee chips. Shape heaping teaspoonfuls of dough into crescents. Place 1 inch apart on cookie sheets. Bake for 13 to 17 minutes or until set but not brown. Let stand 1 minute; remove from cookie sheets. **YIELD:** 3 1/2 dozen cookies.

TIP: Cookies can be rolled in powdered sugar when warm or cool, or dip ends in a mixture of 1/2 cup semi-sweet real chocolate chips and 2 teaspoons shortening, melted.

TIP: Cookies can also be shaped into 2 1/2-inch logs or 1-inch balls. Bake as directed above.

*Nutrition Facts (1 cookie): Calories 80; Protein 1g; Carbohydrate 8g;
Fat 5g; Cholesterol 15mg; Sodium 60mg*

# Slice & Bake Ginger Cookies

*The delightful aroma these cookies have while baking will appeal to all ages.*

*Preparation time: 50 minutes • Chilling time: 4 hours • Baking time: 7 minutes*

2 1/3 cups all-purpose flour
1 1/2 teaspoons baking soda
1 teaspoon baking powder
1 teaspoon cinnamon
1 teaspoon ground ginger
1/2 teaspoon salt
1/2 teaspoon ground cloves
1 cup sugar
3/4 cup LAND O LAKES® Butter
1 egg
1/4 cup dark molasses

In medium bowl combine flour, baking soda, baking powder, cinnamon, ginger, salt and cloves; set aside.

In large mixer bowl combine sugar and butter. Beat at medium speed, scraping bowl often, until creamy (1 to 2 minutes). Add egg and molasses. Continue beating until well mixed (1 to 2 minutes). Reduce speed to low. Continue beating, gradually adding flour mixture and scraping bowl often, until well mixed (1 to 2 minutes). Divide dough in half. On waxed paper shape each half into 9x1 1/2-inch roll. Wrap in plastic food wrap; refrigerate until firm (at least 4 hours).

Heat oven to 375°. Cut rolls into 1/4-inch slices. Place 2 inches apart on cookie sheets. Bake for 7 to 10 minutes or until set. **YIELD:** 5 dozen cookies.

TIP: If desired, cut rolls into 1/8-inch slices. **YIELD:** 9 dozen cookies.

*Nutrition Facts (1 cookie): Calories 60; Protein 1g; Carbohydrate 8g;
Fat 3g; Cholesterol 10mg; Sodium 70mg*

*Mocha Toffee Crescents*

# Pastel Mint Slices

*This three-color mint-flavored cookie is perfect for the holidays and other special occasions.*

*Preparation time: 20 minutes • Chilling time: 3 hours • Baking time: 9 minutes*

1 cup sugar
1 cup LAND O LAKES® Butter, softened
1 egg
1 teaspoon peppermint extract
2$\frac{1}{3}$ cups all-purpose flour
$\frac{1}{4}$ teaspoon baking powder
3 drops red food coloring
3 drops green food coloring

In large mixer bowl combine sugar and butter. Beat at medium speed, scraping bowl often, until creamy (1 to 2 minutes). Add egg and peppermint extract. Continue beating until well mixed (1 to 2 minutes). Reduce speed to low; add flour and baking powder. Continue beating, scraping bowl often, until well mixed (1 to 2 minutes). Divide dough into thirds. Add red food coloring to one third. Add green food coloring to another third. Stir each until well mixed. Leave remaining dough white. Wrap dough in plastic food wrap; refrigerate until firm (at least 1 hour).

Divide each color of dough into thirds; on waxed paper shape each into 12 x $\frac{1}{2}$-inch rope. Gently press together 1 pink and 1 green rope. Add 1 white rope; gently press to form 1 cloverleaf shaped multicolored roll. Wrap each multicolored roll in plastic food wrap; refrigerate until firm (at least 2 hours or overnight).

Heat oven to 350°. Cut rolls into $\frac{1}{4}$-inch slices. Place 1 inch apart on cookie sheets. Bake for 9 to 12 minutes or until edges are very lightly browned.
**YIELD:** 11 dozen cookies.

*Nutrition Facts (1 cookie): Calories 25; Protein 0g; Carbohydrate 3g; Fat 2g; Cholesterol 5mg; Sodium 15mg*

# Pink Lemonade Wafers

*A delicately flavored lemon wafer, tinted pink and drizzled with a pink lemonade glaze.*

*Preparation time: 40 minutes • Chilling time: 1 hour • Baking time: 5 minutes • Cooling time: 15 minutes*

### Wafers
$\frac{1}{4}$ cup LAND O LAKES® Butter, softened
$\frac{1}{2}$ cup sugar
1 egg
2 teaspoons grated lemon peel
1 teaspoon lemon juice
1 to 2 drops red food coloring
1 cup all-purpose flour
$\frac{1}{2}$ teaspoon baking powder
$\frac{1}{4}$ teaspoon salt

Sugar

### Glaze
1$\frac{1}{2}$ cups powdered sugar
$\frac{1}{2}$ teaspoon grated lemon peel
1 drop red food coloring
2 to 4 teaspoons lemon juice

Heat oven to 400°. In large mixer bowl combine butter, $\frac{1}{2}$ cup sugar, egg, 2 teaspoons lemon peel, 1 teaspoon lemon juice and 1 to 2 drops red food coloring. Beat at medium speed, scraping bowl often, until creamy (2 to 3 minutes). Reduce speed to low; add all remaining wafer ingredients except sugar for rolling. Continue beating, scraping bowl often, until well mixed (1 to 2 minutes). Cover; refrigerate until firm (at least 1 hour).

Shape dough into $\frac{1}{2}$-inch balls; roll in sugar. Place 2 inches apart on greased cookie sheets. Flatten balls to $\frac{1}{4}$-inch thickness with bottom of buttered glass dipped in sugar. Bake for 5 to 7 minutes or until edges are lightly browned. Remove to waxed paper sprinkled with sugar; cool completely.

In small bowl stir together all glaze ingredients except lemon juice. Gradually stir in enough lemon juice for desired glazing consistency. Drizzle over cooled cookies.
**YIELD:** 4$\frac{1}{2}$ dozen cookies.

TIP: If desired, omit glaze and dust with powdered sugar.

*Nutrition Facts (1 cookie): Calories 35; Protein <1g; Carbohydrate 7g; Fat 1g; Cholesterol 5mg; Sodium 25mg*

*Pastel Mint Slices*

# Raspberry Almond Shortbread Thumbprints

*A thumbprint cookie filled with raspberry jam and drizzled with an almond glaze.*

*Preparation time: 50 minutes • Baking time: 14 minutes*

### Cookies
$2/3$ cup sugar
1 cup LAND O LAKES® Butter, softened
$1/2$ teaspoon almond extract
2 cups all-purpose flour

$1/2$ cup raspberry jam*

### Glaze
1 cup powdered sugar
$1^1/2$ teaspoons almond extract
2 to 3 teaspoons water

Heat oven to 350°. In large mixer bowl combine sugar, butter and almond extract. Beat at medium speed, scraping bowl often, until creamy (1 to 2 minutes). Reduce speed to low; add flour. Continue beating until well mixed (1 to 2 minutes). Shape dough into 1-inch balls. Place 2 inches apart on cookie sheets. With thumb, make indentation in center of each cookie. (Edges may crack slightly.) Fill each indentation with about $1/4$ teaspoon jam. Bake for 14 to 18 minutes or until edges are lightly browned. Let stand 1 minute; remove from cookie sheets.

In small bowl stir together powdered sugar and $1^1/2$ teaspoons almond extract. Gradually stir in enough water to make a thin glaze. Drizzle over warm cookies. **YIELD:** $3^1/2$ dozen cookies.

* $1/2$ cup your favorite flavor jam can be substituted for $1/2$ cup raspberry jam.

*Nutrition Facts (1 cookie): Calories 90; Protein 1g; Carbohydrate 13g;*
*Fat 4g; Cholesterol 10mg; Sodium 45mg*

# Sandbakkels
## (Sugar Cookie Tarts)

*Small sandbakkel molds are used to make these delicate Scandinavian cookie tarts.*

*Preparation time: 1 hour • Chilling time: 2 hours • Baking time: 8 minutes*

$1/2$ cup sugar
$1/2$ cup firmly packed brown sugar
1 cup LAND O LAKES® Butter, softened
1 egg
1 teaspoon almond <u>or</u> brandy extract
$2^1/2$ cups all-purpose flour

Heat oven to 350°. In large mixer bowl combine all ingredients <u>except</u> flour. Beat at medium speed, scraping bowl often, until well mixed (1 to 2 minutes). Reduce speed to low; add flour. Continue beating, scraping bowl often, until well mixed (2 to 3 minutes). If dough is too soft, cover and refrigerate until firm (at least 2 hours).

Press 2 to 3 teaspoonfuls dough evenly into each 3-inch sandbakkel mold. Place molds on cookie sheets. Bake for 8 to 11 minutes or until lightly browned. Cool 3 minutes; remove from molds by tapping on table or loosening with knife. Cookies can be served plain or filled with fresh fruit, fruit filling, pudding or whipped cream. **YIELD:** 3 dozen cookies.

TIP: If using $2^1/2$-inch sandbakkel molds, press $1^1/2$ to 2 teaspoonfuls dough evenly into each mold. Bake for 7 to 10 minutes. **YIELD:** 5 dozen cookies.

*Nutrition Facts (1 cookie): Calories 60; Protein 1g; Carbohydrate 7g;*
*Fat 3g; Cholesterol 10mg; Sodium 35mg*

*Raspberry Almond Shortbread Thumbprints*

# Strawberry Lilies

*Tender cream cheese pastry circles are folded over jam to form a lily.*

*Preparation time: 1 hour 30 minutes • Chilling time: 2 hours • Baking time: 7 minutes*

$1/4$ cup sugar
1 cup LAND O LAKES® Butter, softened
1 (3-ounce) package cream cheese, softened
1 teaspoon vanilla
2 cups all-purpose flour
$1/4$ teaspoon salt

$1/2$ cup strawberry jam*

Powdered sugar, if desired

In large mixer bowl combine sugar, butter, cream cheese and vanilla. Beat at medium speed, scraping bowl often, until well mixed (about 1 minute). Reduce speed to low; add flour and salt. Continue beating, scraping bowl often, until well mixed (1 to 2 minutes). Divide dough into fourths. Wrap in plastic food wrap. Refrigerate until firm (at least 2 hours).

Heat oven to 375°. On lightly floured surface, roll out dough, one-fourth at a time (keeping remaining dough refrigerated), to $1/8$-inch thickness. Cut with 2-inch round cookie cutter. Place 1 inch apart on cookie sheets. Spoon $1/4$ teaspoon jam onto center of each unbaked circle; spread to within $1/4$ inch of edge of cookie. With thin spatula, fold dough over jam to form a lily shape; gently press narrow end to seal. (Jam will show at top and cookies will be cone-shaped.) Repeat with remaining dough and jam. Bake for 7 to 11 minutes or until edges are very lightly browned. Cool completely. Sprinkle cooled cookies lightly with powdered sugar. **YIELD:** 8 dozen cookies.

* $1/2$ cup your favorite fruit preserves or jam can be substituted for $1/2$ cup strawberry jam.

*Nutrition Facts (1 cookie): Calories 35; Protein 1g; Carbohydrate 4g; Fat 2g; Cholesterol 5mg; Sodium 30mg*

# Swedish Coconut Cookies

*A Scandinavian heritage is the foundation for this buttery, tender cookie.*

*Preparation time: 20 minutes • Chilling time: 2 hours • Baking time: 9 minutes*

$3^1/2$ cups all-purpose flour
2 cups sugar
2 cups LAND O LAKES® Butter, softened
1 tablespoon baking powder
1 teaspoon baking soda
1 teaspoon vanilla
1 cup flaked coconut

In large mixer bowl combine all ingredients except coconut. Beat at low speed, scraping bowl often, until well mixed (3 to 4 minutes). By hand, stir in coconut. Divide dough in half; shape each half into 12x2-inch roll. Wrap each roll in plastic food wrap; refrigerate until firm (at least 2 hours).

Heat oven to 350°. Cut rolls into $1/4$-inch slices; place 2 inches apart on cookie sheets. Bake for 9 to 14 minutes or until edges are lightly browned. Let stand 1 minute; remove from cookie sheets. **YIELD:** 8 dozen cookies.

*Nutrition Facts (1 cookie): Calories 70; Protein 1g; Carbohydrate 8g; Fat 4g; Cholesterol 10mg; Sodium 70mg*

*Strawberry Lilies*

# Starlight Mint Sandwich Cookies

*Use geometric shaped cookie cutters such as stars, diamonds, etc., to add sparkle to your cookie tray.*

*Preparation time: 1 hour 30 minutes • Chilling time: 1 hour • Baking time: 6 minutes • Cooling time: 15 minutes • Standing time: 1 hour*

### Cookies
- 1 cup sugar
- 1 cup LAND O LAKES® Butter, softened
- 2 egg yolks
- 1 1/2 teaspoons vanilla
- 1/2 teaspoon peppermint extract
- 2 1/4 cups all-purpose flour
- 1/2 cup finely crushed starlight mint candies
- 1/4 teaspoon salt

### Filling
- 6 (1-ounce) squares semi-sweet baking chocolate, melted
- Crushed starlight mint candies

In large mixer bowl combine sugar and butter. Beat at medium speed, scraping bowl often, until well mixed (1 to 2 minutes). Add egg yolks, vanilla and peppermint extract. Continue beating, scraping bowl often, until well mixed (1 minute). Reduce speed to low. Add flour, 1/2 cup crushed candies and salt. Continue beating, scraping bowl often, until well mixed (1 to 2 minutes). Divide dough in half. Wrap in plastic food wrap; refrigerate at least 1 hour.

Heat oven to 350°. On lightly floured surface roll out dough, half at a time, to 1/8-inch thickness. Cut into shapes with 1 1/2-inch cookie cutters. Place 1 inch apart on greased cookie sheets. Bake for 6 to 10 minutes or until edges are lightly browned. Let stand 1 minute; remove from cookie sheets. Cool completely.

To assemble cookies spread about 1 teaspoon melted chocolate on bottom of one cookie; top with bottom of another cookie. Repeat to assemble all cookies. Decorate as desired by rolling edges in melted chocolate, then crushed candies; dipping half of sandwich cookie in melted chocolate; drizzling top with melted chocolate, then sprinkling with crushed candies. Place on waxed paper; let stand 1 hour to set. **YIELD:** 2 1/2 dozen cookies.

TIP: If desired, cut out cookies using 2 1/2-inch cookie cutters. To assemble cookies spread about 2 teaspoons melted chocolate on bottom of one cookie; top with bottom of another cookie. **YIELD:** 1 1/2 dozen cookies.

*Nutrition Facts (1 cookie): Calories 160; Protein 1g; Carbohydrate 20g; Fat 9g; Cholesterol 30mg; Sodium 90mg*

# Snowball Cookies

*A favorite at Christmastime, pecan-filled Snowball Cookies are scrumptious all year 'round.*

*Preparation time: 1 hour • Baking time: 18 minutes*

- 2 cups all-purpose flour
- 2 cups finely chopped pecans
- 1/4 cup sugar
- 1 cup LAND O LAKES® Butter, softened
- 1 teaspoon vanilla

- Powdered sugar

Heat oven to 325°. In large mixer bowl combine all ingredients except powdered sugar. Beat at low speed, scraping bowl often, until well mixed (3 to 4 minutes). Shape rounded teaspoonfuls of dough into 1-inch balls. Place 1 inch apart on cookie sheets. Bake for 18 to 25 minutes or until very lightly browned. Cool 5 minutes. Roll in or sprinkle with powdered sugar while still warm and again when cool. **YIELD:** 3 dozen cookies.

*Nutrition Facts (1 cookie): Calories 130; Protein 1g; Carbohydrate 11g; Fat 9g; Cholesterol 15mg; Sodium 50mg*

*Starlight Mint Sandwich Cookies*

# Cookie Making Questions & Answers

### What kind of cookie sheet should I use for best results?

A shiny cookie sheet at least 2 inches narrower and shorter than the oven is best for evenly browned cookies. The sheet can be open on 1, 2 or 3 sides. Do not grease unless recipe states to do so. If a coated or dark cookie sheet is used, watch carefully for browning. Always place cookie dough on cool cookie sheets.

### Where should I place cookie sheets in the oven during baking?

For evenly browned cookies, place 1 cookie sheet at a time on the center rack.

### What can I do if my cookies stick to the cookie sheet?

Warm the cookies in the oven for 30 to 60 seconds; remove immediately. Use no stick cooking spray or solid shortening (not butter or margarine) to grease cookie sheets.

### Why are my cookies spreading too much?

Cookies can be spreading too much for a variety of reasons. Your dough may be too soft. Try refrigerating dough until well chilled. Be sure the butter or margarine you use is not too soft. Use only butter or margarine, not low fat or light spreads, when baking. Let cookie sheets cool completely before putting more cookie dough on them. You can also bake test cookies to give you an idea of the condition of the dough. Bake 1 to 3 cookies; if they spread more than desired, add 1 to 2 tablespoons flour to the dough. If they are too dry, add 1 to 2 tablespoons of cream or milk.

### What is the best way to cool cookies if I do not have a wire rack?

If you do not use a wire rack to cool your cookies, they can become soft or soggy. To prevent this from happening, place a sheet of waxed paper on the counter and sprinkle with granulated sugar. Place the cooling cookies on the sugared waxed paper.

# Cookie Making Questions & Answers

### Can I refrigerate or freeze my cookie dough?

Most cookie dough can be packaged in an airtight container and stored in the refrigerator up to two days or frozen up to three months. Thaw dough in the refrigerator.

### How can I make soft cookies? Mine are always too crisp.

- Do not overbeat the dough once the dry ingredients have been mixed in. Overworking the dough will toughen the cookies.

- Do not overbake the cookies. They continue to set as they cool.

- Soft cookie doughs usually have more moisture than doughs for crisp cookies. If your dough looks dry, add 1 to 2 tablespoons of milk, cream, buttermilk or sour cream.

- Cake flour will give a tender crumb to your baked cookies.

- Excess sugar often results in crisp, not soft, cookies.

### How should I store my cookies?

- Store soft cookies in a container with a tight-fitting lid.

- Store crisp cookies in a container with a loose-fitting lid.

- Do not mix soft and crisp varieties in the same container or the crisp cookies will become soft.

- Cookies can be frozen for up to six months.

### How can I mail cookies?

- Use a heavy cardboard box or empty coffee can as a mailing container.

- Bar, drop or fruit cookies can best withstand mailing.

- Wrap 4 to 6 cookies of the same size together in aluminum foil, plastic wrap or plastic food bags and seal securely.

- Layer wrapped cookies with crumpled paper toweling around them.

- Seal container with freezer, plastic or adhesive tape.

- Mark package with "Fragile" to ensure careful handling.

# Bars

*Easy-to-make*

*bar cookies are*

*always popular during*

*the holidays. Fill your*

*cookie platter with*

*scrumptious bars*

*like Apple Cranberry*

*Bars and Fudgy Orange*

*Pecan Brownies.*

*They're sure to satisfy*

*any sweet tooth.*

*Minted Cheesecake Bars, see page 54*

# Minted Cheesecake Bars

*These mint-flavored cheesecake bars have a chocolate graham cracker crust.*

*Preparation time: 20 minutes • Baking time: 35 minutes • Cooling time: 1 hour 30 minutes*

**Crust**
- $1/3$ cup LAND O LAKES® Butter
- 1 cup [6 (5x2$1/2$-inch)] finely crushed chocolate graham crackers

**Filling**
- $1/2$ cup sugar
- 2 (8-ounce) packages cream cheese, softened
- 2 eggs
- $3/4$ teaspoon peppermint extract
- 1 to 2 drops green food coloring, if desired

**Glaze**
- $1/4$ cup semi-sweet real chocolate chips
- $1/2$ teaspoon shortening

Heat oven to 350°. In 9-inch square baking pan melt butter in oven (4 to 6 minutes). Stir in crushed graham crackers. Press evenly on bottom of pan; set aside.

In small mixer bowl combine all filling ingredients. Beat at medium speed, scraping bowl often, until smooth (3 to 4 minutes). Spread filling over crust. Bake for 35 to 40 minutes or until filling is set. Cool completely.

In 1-quart saucepan melt chocolate chips and shortening over low heat, stirring often, until smooth (2 to 3 minutes). Drizzle glaze over cooled bars; refrigerate until firm. Cut into bars. Store refrigerated. **YIELD:** 25 bars.

TIP: To get a fine line when drizzling chocolate, pour melted chocolate mixture into a recloseable plastic food bag. Cut a <u>very small</u> opening in one corner; gently press out chocolate.

*Nutrition Facts (1 bar): Calories 140; Protein 2g; Carbohydrate 9g; Fat 10g; Cholesterol 40mg; Sodium 110mg*

# Lemon-Butter Bars

*Tangy lemon and creamy butter combine to make these classic bars.*

*Preparation time: 30 minutes • Baking time: 33 minutes*

**Crust**
- 1$1/3$ cups all-purpose flour
- $1/4$ cup sugar
- $1/2$ cup LAND O LAKES® Butter, softened

**Filling**
- $3/4$ cup sugar
- 2 eggs
- 2 tablespoons all-purpose flour
- $1/4$ teaspoon baking powder
- 3 tablespoons lemon juice

Powdered sugar

Heat oven to 350°. In small mixer bowl combine all crust ingredients. Beat at low speed, scraping bowl often, until mixture is crumbly (2 to 3 minutes). Press on bottom of 8-inch square baking pan. Bake for 15 to 20 minutes or until edges are lightly browned.

Meanwhile, in small mixer bowl combine all filling ingredients <u>except</u> powdered sugar. Beat at low speed, scraping bowl often, until well mixed. Pour filling over hot partially baked crust. Continue baking for 18 to 20 minutes or until filling is set. Sprinkle with powdered sugar while still warm and again when cool. Cut into bars. **YIELD:** 16 bars.

<u>Microwave Directions</u>: Prepare crust as directed above. Press on bottom of 8-inch square baking dish. Microwave on HIGH until top looks dry (4 to 5 minutes). Meanwhile, in small microwave-safe mixer bowl combine all filling ingredients <u>except</u> powdered sugar. Beat at low speed, scraping bowl often, until well mixed. Microwave filling on HIGH, stirring every minute, until warm and slightly thickened (2 to 4 minutes). Pour over hot crust. Microwave on HIGH, turning dish $1/4$ turn after half the time, until filling is just set in center (2 to 5 minutes). Sprinkle with powdered sugar while still warm and again when cool. Cut into bars.

*Nutrition Facts (1 bar): Calories 150; Protein 2g; Carbohydrate 22g; Fat 6g; Cholesterol 40mg; Sodium 70mg*

# Cheesecake Squares

*The flavor of cheesecake in an easy-to-make bar.*

*Preparation time: 30 minutes • Baking time: 31 minutes*

## Crust
- 1 cup all-purpose flour
- $1/2$ cup firmly packed brown sugar
- $1/3$ cup LAND O LAKES® Butter, softened
- $1/2$ cup chopped walnuts <u>or</u> pecans

## Filling
- 1 (8-ounce) package cream cheese, softened
- $1/4$ cup sugar
- 1 egg
- 2 tablespoons lemon juice
- 2 tablespoons milk
- $1/2$ teaspoon vanilla

Heat oven to 350°. In large mixer bowl combine flour, brown sugar and butter. Beat at low speed, scraping bowl often, until mixture is crumbly (2 to 3 minutes). By hand, stir in walnuts. <u>Reserve 1 cup mixture for topping</u>; press remaining mixture on bottom of 8-inch square baking pan. Bake for 8 to 10 minutes or until lightly browned.

Meanwhile, in small mixer bowl combine all filling ingredients. Beat at medium speed, scraping bowl often, until smooth (4 to 5 minutes). Spread over hot partially baked crust. Sprinkle with reserved crumb mixture. Continue baking for 23 to 30 minutes or until golden brown. Cool completely; cut into bars. Store refrigerated. **YIELD:** 25 bars.

<u>Microwave Directions</u>: Prepare crust as directed above. <u>Reserve 1 cup mixture for topping</u>; press remaining mixture on bottom of 8-inch square baking dish. Microwave on HIGH until edges look dry (2 to 4 minutes). Meanwhile, in small microwave-safe mixer bowl combine all filling ingredients. Beat at medium speed, scraping bowl often, until smooth (4 to 5 minutes). Microwave filling on HIGH, stirring every minute, until warm and slightly thickened (2 to $2^1/2$ minutes). Spread over hot crust. Sprinkle with reserved crumb mixture. Microwave on HIGH, turning dish $1/4$ turn after half the time, until filling is just set in center (2 to $3^1/2$ minutes). Cool completely; cut into bars. Store refrigerated.

VARIATION

<u>Holiday Squares</u>: Stir $1/4$ cup chopped red candied cherries and $1/4$ cup chopped green candied cherries into filling mixture.

*Nutrition Facts (1 bar): Calories 120; Protein 2g; Carbohydrate 11g;*
*Fat 7g; Cholesterol 25mg; Sodium 60mg*

# Raspberry Pecan Bars

*Raspberry preserves and pecans are combined in this rich bar with an old-world flavor.*

*Preparation time: 15 minutes • Baking time: 35 minutes*

2 cups all-purpose flour
$^1/_2$ cup sugar
$^3/_4$ cup LAND O LAKES® Butter, cut into pieces
$^1/_4$ teaspoon salt
$^1/_2$ teaspoon vanilla
$^1/_2$ cup chopped pecans

1 (10-ounce) jar raspberry preserves
$^1/_2$ cup chopped pecans

Heat oven to 350°. In large mixer bowl combine flour, sugar, butter, salt and vanilla. Beat at low speed, scraping bowl often, until mixture resembles coarse crumbs (1 to 2 minutes). By hand, stir in $^1/_2$ cup pecans; reserve $^3/_4$ cup crumb mixture. Press remaining crumb mixture on bottom of 9-inch square baking pan. Spread preserves over crumb mixture; sprinkle with $^1/_2$ cup pecans and reserved crumb mixture. Bake for 35 to 40 minutes or until crumb mixture is lightly browned and preserves are bubbly. Cool completely; cut into bars. **YIELD:** 25 bars.

*Nutrition Facts (1 bar): Calories 160; Protein 1g; Carbohydrate 21g; Fat 9g; Cholesterol 15mg; Sodium 80mg*

# Holiday Fruit & Nut Bars

*Candied red and green cherries give these bars a holiday look. Sprinkle lightly with powdered sugar for a finishing touch.*

*Preparation time: 20 minutes • Baking time: 30 minutes*

$^1/_2$ cup sugar
$^1/_2$ cup firmly packed brown sugar
$^1/_2$ cup LAND O LAKES® Butter, softened
1 egg
$^1/_4$ cup orange juice
$1^1/_2$ teaspoons brandy extract
$1^1/_3$ cups all-purpose flour
$^1/_2$ teaspoon baking powder
$^1/_4$ teaspoon salt
1 cup red candied cherries, quartered
1 cup green candied cherries, quartered
1 cup coarsely chopped pecans

Powdered sugar, if desired

Heat oven to 350°. In large bowl combine sugar, brown sugar and butter. Beat at medium speed, scraping bowl often, until creamy (1 to 2 minutes). Add egg, orange juice and brandy extract. Continue beating until well mixed (1 to 2 minutes). Reduce speed to low; add 1 cup flour, baking powder and salt. Continue beating, scraping bowl often, until well mixed (1 to 2 minutes). In medium bowl combine remaining $^1/_3$ cup flour with red and green candied cherries. By hand, stir cherry mixture and pecans into batter. Spread in greased 13x9-inch baking pan. Bake for 30 to 35 minutes or until light golden brown. Cool completely; sprinkle with powdered sugar. Cut into bars. **YIELD:** 48 bars.

*Nutrition Facts (1 bar): Calories 70; Protein 1g; Carbohydrate 8g; Fat 4g; Cholesterol 10mg; Sodium 35mg*

*Raspberry Pecan Bars*

# Cranberry Vanilla Chip Bars

*The tang of cranberries and the sweetness of vanilla chips are combined for a great taste.*

*Preparation time: 25 minutes • Baking time: 25 minutes • Cooling time: 1 hour*

## Bars
- $1/2$ cup sugar
- $1/4$ cup firmly packed brown sugar
- $1/3$ cup LAND O LAKES® Butter, softened
- 1 egg
- 1 teaspoon vanilla
- 1 cup all-purpose flour
- $1/2$ teaspoon baking powder
- $1/4$ teaspoon salt
- $1/2$ cup vanilla milk chips
- $1/2$ cup coarsely chopped fresh or frozen cranberries
- $1/2$ cup chopped pecans, if desired

## Glaze
- $1/4$ cup vanilla milk chips
- $1/2$ teaspoon shortening

Heat oven to 350°. In large mixer bowl combine sugar, brown sugar, butter, egg and vanilla. Beat at medium speed, scraping bowl often, until well mixed (2 to 3 minutes). Reduce speed to low; add flour, baking powder and salt. Continue beating, scraping bowl often, until well mixed (1 to 2 minutes). By hand, stir in $1/2$ cup vanilla milk chips, cranberries and pecans. Spread in greased and floured 8-inch square baking pan. Bake for 25 to 30 minutes or until toothpick inserted in center comes out clean. Cool completely.

In 1-quart saucepan melt $1/4$ cup vanilla milk chips and shortening over low heat, stirring constantly, until smooth (1 minute). Drizzle over cooled bars; cut into bars. **YIELD:** 16 bars.

*Nutrition Facts (1 bar): Calories 140; Protein 2g; Carbohydrate 20g; Fat 7g; Cholesterol 25mg; Sodium 100mg*

# Apple Cranberry Bars

*Apples and cranberries are paired in this bar and frosted with an orange buttercream.*

*Preparation time: 40 minutes • Baking time: 30 minutes • Cooling time: 1 hour*

## Bars
- $1 1/2$ cups sugar
- 1 cup LAND O LAKES® Butter, softened
- 2 eggs
- 2 teaspoons grated orange peel
- 2 teaspoons vanilla
- $2 1/4$ cups all-purpose flour
- 1 teaspoon baking soda
- $1/4$ teaspoon salt
- 2 (2 cups) medium cooking apples, peeled, chopped
- 1 cup coarsely chopped fresh or frozen cranberries
- 1 cup chopped nuts

## Orange Buttercream
- $1/3$ cup LAND O LAKES® Butter, softened
- 1 (3-ounce) package cream cheese, softened
- 1 teaspoon vanilla
- 2 cups powdered sugar
- 1 teaspoon grated orange peel
- 2 to 4 teaspoons milk

Heat oven to 350°. In large mixer bowl combine sugar, 1 cup butter, eggs, 2 teaspoons orange peel and 2 teaspoons vanilla. Beat at medium speed, scraping bowl often, until well mixed (2 to 3 minutes). Reduce speed to low; add flour, baking soda and salt. Continue beating, scraping bowl often, until well mixed (1 to 2 minutes). By hand, stir in apples, cranberries and nuts. Spread in greased 15x10x1-inch jelly roll pan. Bake for 30 to 35 minutes or until toothpick inserted in center comes out clean. Cool completely.

In small mixer bowl combine $1/3$ cup butter, cream cheese and 1 teaspoon vanilla. Beat at medium speed, scraping bowl often, until well mixed (1 to 2 minutes). Reduce speed to low. Continue beating, gradually adding powdered sugar, 1 teaspoon orange peel and enough milk for desired spreading consistency. Thinly frost cooled bars; cut into bars. **YIELD:** 48 bars.

*Nutrition Facts (1 bar): Calories 140; Protein 1g; Carbohydrate 17g; Fat 8g; Cholesterol 25mg; Sodium 90mg*

*Cranberry Vanilla Chip Bars*

# Glistening Fruitcake Jewels

*A buttery shortbread crust is topped with colorful fruit for an easy version of a holiday favorite.*

*Preparation time: 15 minutes • Baking time: 32 minutes • Cooling time: 1 hour*

## Crumb Mixture
2 cups all-purpose flour
$1/2$ cup sugar
$3/4$ cup LAND O LAKES® Butter, softened

## Filling
$1/2$ cup sugar
$1/2$ cup raisins
$1/4$ cup orange juice or lemon juice
1 (8-ounce) package chopped dates
1 ($2^1/2$-ounce) package sliced almonds
1 egg
$1/4$ cup chopped candied cherries

## Glaze
$3/4$ cup powdered sugar
1 tablespoon milk
$1/2$ teaspoon vanilla

Heat oven to 350°. In small mixer bowl combine all crumb mixture ingredients. Beat at low speed, scraping bowl often, until well mixed and particles are fine (1 to 2 minutes). Press crumb mixture on bottom of greased 13x9-inch baking pan. Bake for 15 to 20 minutes or until edges are lightly browned.

Meanwhile, in same bowl stir together all filling ingredients except candied cherries. Spread filling evenly over hot partially baked crust. Sprinkle with candied cherries. Continue baking for 17 to 20 minutes or until edges are lightly browned. Cool completely.

In small bowl stir together all glaze ingredients; drizzle over cooled bars. Cut into bars. **YIELD:** 36 bars.

*Nutrition Facts (1 bar): Calories 130; Protein 2g; Carbohydrate 21g; Fat 5g; Cholesterol 15mg; Sodium 40mg*

*Glistening Fruitcake Jewels*

# Create-Your-Own Bars

*Four variations can top one buttery crust in these holiday bars.*

*Preparation time: 15 minutes • Baking time: 33 minutes*

**Crust**
1$^{1}$/$_{3}$  cups all-purpose flour
$^{1}$/$_{4}$  cup sugar
$^{1}$/$_{2}$  cup LAND O LAKES®
     Butter, softened

**Filling**
    Choice of variations

Heat oven to 350°. In small mixer bowl combine all crust ingredients. Beat at low speed, scraping bowl often, until mixture is crumbly (2 to 3 minutes). Press on bottom of 9-inch square baking pan. Bake for 15 to 20 minutes or until edges are lightly browned. Follow directions for variation of choice for filling. **YIELD:** 16 bars.

VARIATIONS

<u>Lemon</u>: In small mixer bowl combine $^{3}$/$_{4}$ cup sugar, 2 eggs, 2 tablespoons all-purpose flour, $^{1}$/$_{4}$ teaspoon baking powder and 3 tablespoons lemon juice. Beat at low speed, scraping bowl often, until well mixed. Pour filling over hot crust. Continue baking for 18 to 20 minutes or until filling is set. Sprinkle with powdered sugar. Cool; cut into bars.

<u>Cheesecake</u>: In small mixer bowl combine $^{1}$/$_{4}$ cup sugar, 1 (8-ounce) package softened cream cheese, 1 egg and 1 tablespoon lemon juice. Beat at medium speed, scraping bowl often, until well mixed. By hand, stir in $^{1}$/$_{2}$ cup miniature semi-sweet chocolate chips. Spread filling over hot crust. Continue baking for 18 to 20 minutes or until set. Cool; cut into bars. Cover; store refrigerated.

<u>Pecan</u>: In small mixer bowl combine $^{1}$/$_{2}$ cup sugar, $^{3}$/$_{4}$ cup dark corn syrup, 2 eggs, 2 tablespoons all-purpose flour and $^{1}$/$_{2}$ teaspoon vanilla. Beat at medium speed, scraping bowl often, until well mixed. By hand, stir in 1 cup chopped pecans. Pour filling over hot crust. Continue baking for 30 to 35 minutes or until set. Cool; cut into bars.

<u>Cherry Coconut</u>: In small mixer bowl combine $^{3}$/$_{4}$ cup flaked coconut, $^{1}$/$_{2}$ cup firmly packed brown sugar, 2 eggs, $^{1}$/$_{4}$ teaspoon salt and $^{1}$/$_{2}$ teaspoon almond extract. Beat at medium speed, scraping bowl often, until well mixed. By hand, stir in $^{1}$/$_{2}$ cup sliced almonds and $^{1}$/$_{2}$ cup chopped maraschino cherries, well drained. Spread over hot crust. Continue baking for 25 to 30 minutes or until set. In medium bowl stir together 1 cup powdered sugar, 2 tablespoons water and $^{1}$/$_{2}$ teaspoon almond extract. Drizzle over hot bars. Cool; cut into bars.

*Nutrition Facts (1 bar of lemon variation): Calories 150; Protein 2g; Carbohydrate 22g;*
*Fat 6g; Cholesterol 40mg; Sodium 70mg*

*Create-Your-Own Bars*

# Black Forest Bars

*Chocolate chips and cherries combine in this easy bar.*

*Preparation time: 20 minutes • Baking time: 40 minutes*

### Crumb Mixture
2¼ cups all-purpose flour
1 cup sugar
1 cup sliced almonds
1 cup LAND O LAKES® Butter, softened
1 egg
½ teaspoon almond extract

### Filling
1 (12-ounce) jar (1 cup) cherry preserves
½ teaspoon almond extract

½ cup miniature semi-sweet real chocolate chips

Heat oven to 350°. In large mixer bowl combine all crumb mixture ingredients. Beat at low speed, scraping bowl often, until crumbly (1 to 2 minutes). Reserve 1 cup crumb mixture. Press remaining crumb mixture on bottom of 11x7-inch or 9-inch square baking pan; set aside.

In small bowl combine cherry preserves and almond extract; spread over crumb mixture to within ½ inch of edge. Sprinkle chocolate chips over cherry mixture. Crumble reserved crumb mixture over chocolate chips. Bake for 40 to 45 minutes or until edges are light golden brown. Cool completely; cut into bars. **YIELD:** 32 bars.

*Nutrition Facts (1 bar): Calories 170; Protein 2g; Carbohydrate 23g; Fat 8g; Cholesterol 20mg; Sodium 60mg*

# Fudgy Orange Pecan Brownies

*Dress up these orange-flavored brownies with an orange frosting and garnish with shaved chocolate or orange curls.*

*Preparation time: 20 minutes • Baking time: 20 minutes • Cooling time: 30 minutes*

### Brownie
½ cup LAND O LAKES® Butter
2 (1-ounce) squares unsweetened baking chocolate
1 cup sugar
2 eggs, slightly beaten
1 teaspoon vanilla
½ cup all-purpose flour
½ cup chopped pecans
¼ teaspoon salt
1 tablespoon grated orange peel

### Frosting
1½ cups powdered sugar
2 tablespoons LAND O LAKES® Butter, softened
1 teaspoon grated orange peel
½ teaspoon vanilla
1 to 2 tablespoons orange juice

### Garnish
Shaved chocolate or orange peel curls, if desired

Heat oven to 350°. In 2-quart saucepan combine butter and chocolate. Cook over low heat until melted (3 to 6 minutes). Remove from heat; stir in sugar. Stir in eggs and vanilla just until mixed. Stir in all remaining brownie ingredients until well mixed. Spread in greased 11x7-inch or 9-inch square baking pan. Bake for 20 to 23 minutes or until brownies just begin to pull away from sides of pan. DO NOT OVERBAKE. Cool completely.

In small mixer bowl combine all frosting ingredients except orange juice. Beat at low speed, scraping bowl often and gradually adding enough orange juice for desired spreading consistency. Spread over cooled brownies; cut into bars. Garnish with shaved chocolate or orange peel curls. **YIELD:** 32 brownies.

*Nutrition Facts (1 brownie): Calories 110; Protein 1g; Carbohydrate 15g; Fat 6g; Cholesterol 25mg; Sodium 60mg*

# German Chocolate Brownies With Coconut Pecan Topping

*The flavors of German chocolate cake are combined in this brownie.*

*Preparation time: 25 minutes • Baking time: 23 minutes • Cooling time: 30 minutes*

### Brownie
- $3/4$ cup sugar
- $1/2$ cup LAND O LAKES® Butter, softened
- 2 eggs
- $1/2$ teaspoon vanilla
- 1 (4-ounce) bar sweet cooking chocolate, melted, cooled
- $1^1/4$ cups all-purpose flour
- $1/2$ teaspoon baking soda
- $1/4$ teaspoon salt
- $1/2$ cup buttermilk*

### Topping
- $1/2$ cup firmly packed brown sugar
- 3 tablespoons LAND O LAKES® Butter
- $1/2$ cup evaporated milk
- 1 egg
- $1/2$ teaspoon vanilla
- 1 cup flaked coconut
- 1 cup chopped pecans

Heat oven to 350°. In large mixer bowl combine sugar and $1/2$ cup butter. Beat at medium speed, scraping bowl often, until creamy (1 to 2 minutes). Add eggs and vanilla. Continue beating until well mixed (1 to 2 minutes). Add cooled melted chocolate. Continue beating until well mixed (about 1 minute). Reduce speed to low; add all remaining brownie ingredients. Continue beating, scraping bowl often, until well mixed (1 to 2 minutes). Spread in greased and floured 13x9-inch baking pan. Bake for 23 to 28 minutes or until toothpick inserted in center comes out clean. Cool completely.

Meanwhile, in 2-quart saucepan combine brown sugar, 3 tablespoons butter, evaporated milk and 1 egg. Cook over medium heat, stirring constantly, until mixture comes to a full boil (5 to 7 minutes). Continue cooking until mixture thickens (1 to 2 minutes). Remove from heat; stir in all remaining topping ingredients. Cool until thick enough for spreading consistency (10 minutes). Spread over cooled brownies; cut into bars. **YIELD:** 36 brownies.

*$1^1/2$ teaspoons vinegar plus enough milk to equal $1/2$ cup can be substituted for $1/2$ cup buttermilk.

*Nutrition Facts (1 brownie): Calories 130; Protein 2g; Carbohydrate 13g; Fat 8g; Cholesterol 25mg; Sodium 80mg*

# Big Batch Fudgy Brownies

*When you need brownies for a crowd, this fudge brownie with chocolate frosting will be a hit.*

*Preparation time: 15 minutes • Baking time: 20 minutes • Cooling time: 30 minutes*

### Brownie
- 1 cup LAND O LAKES® Butter
- 4 (1-ounce) squares unsweetened baking chocolate
- 2 cups sugar
- 4 eggs, slightly beaten
- $1/2$ cup LAND O LAKES® Sour Cream (Regular, Light or No·Fat)
- 2 teaspoons vanilla
- $1^3/4$ cups all-purpose flour
- $1/2$ teaspoon salt

### Frosting
- 1 cup semi-sweet real chocolate chips
- 2 tablespoons shortening
- $1^1/2$ cups powdered sugar
- $1/2$ teaspoon vanilla
- 3 to 5 tablespoons milk

Heat oven to 350°. In 3-quart saucepan melt butter and chocolate over low heat, stirring often (5 to 8 minutes). Remove from heat; stir in sugar. Stir in eggs, sour cream and vanilla just until mixed. Stir in flour and salt just until moistened. Spread in greased 15x10x1-inch jelly roll pan. Bake for 20 to 25 minutes or until brownies just begin to pull away from sides of pan. DO NOT OVERBAKE. Cool completely.

In 1-quart saucepan melt chocolate chips and shortening over low heat, stirring often (3 to 5 minutes). Stir in powdered sugar, vanilla and enough milk for desired spreading consistency. Spread over cooled brownies; cut into bars. **YIELD:** 48 brownies.

*Nutrition Facts (1 brownie): Calories 140; Protein 1g; Carbohydrate 19g; Fat 8g; Cholesterol 25mg; Sodium 70mg*

# Caramel N' Chocolate Pecan Bars

*Popular candy flavors combined in an easy bar.*

*Preparation time: 30 minutes • Baking time: 18 minutes*

### Crust
- 2 cups all-purpose flour
- 1 cup firmly packed brown sugar
- $1/2$ cup LAND O LAKES® Butter, softened

- 1 cup pecan halves

### Caramel Layer
- $2/3$ cup LAND O LAKES® Butter
- $1/2$ cup firmly packed brown sugar

- 1 (6-ounce) package (1 cup) semi-sweet real chocolate chips

Heat oven to 350°. In large mixer bowl combine all crust ingredients <u>except</u> pecans. Beat at medium speed, scraping bowl often, until well mixed and particles are fine (2 to 3 minutes). Press on bottom of 13x9-inch baking pan. Sprinkle pecans evenly over unbaked crust.

In 1-quart saucepan combine $2/3$ cup butter and $1/2$ cup brown sugar. Cook over medium heat, stirring constantly, until mixture comes to a full boil. Boil, stirring constantly, until candy thermometer reaches 242°F or small amount of mixture dropped into ice water forms a firm ball (about 1 minute). Pour evenly over pecans and crust. Bake for 18 to 22 minutes or until entire caramel layer is bubbly. Remove from oven. Sprinkle with chocolate chips; let stand 2 to 3 minutes. With knife, swirl chips leaving some whole for marbled effect. Cool completely; cut into bars. **YIELD:** 36 bars.

*Nutrition Facts (1 bar): Calories 160; Protein 1g; Carbohydrate 18g; Fat 10g; Cholesterol 15mg; Sodium 70mg*


# Chocolate Graham Cookie Bars

*A crunchy bar with a chocolate graham cracker crust.*

*Preparation time: 15 minutes • Baking time: 25 minutes*

- $1^1/2$ cups [9 (5x2$^1/2$-inch)] crushed chocolate graham crackers
- $1/2$ cup LAND O LAKES® Butter, melted
- 1 (14-ounce) can sweetened condensed milk
- 1 cup butterscotch-flavored chips
- 1 cup vanilla milk chips
- $1^1/3$ cups flaked coconut
- 1 cup chopped nuts

Heat oven to 350°. In medium bowl stir together crushed crackers and butter; press on bottom of 13x9-inch baking pan. Evenly pour sweetened condensed milk over crust. Sprinkle with butterscotch chips and vanilla chips. Sprinkle with coconut and nuts, pressing gently into sweetened condensed milk. Bake for 25 to 30 minutes or until lightly browned. Cool completely; cut into bars. **YIELD:** 36 bars.

*Nutrition Facts (1 bar): Calories 180; Protein 3g; Carbohydrate 20g; Fat 10g; Cholesterol 15mg; Sodium 90mg*

*Caramel N' Chocolate Pecan Bars*

# Pecan Pie Bars

*Try this version of pecan pie baked as a bar.*

*Preparation time: 15 minutes • Baking time: 40 minutes*

2 cups all-purpose flour
1/2 cup powdered sugar
1 cup LAND O LAKES® Butter, cold
1 (14-ounce) can sweetened condensed milk
1 egg
1 teaspoon vanilla
1 cup chopped pecans
1 (7.5-ounce) package almond brickle bits

Heat oven to 350°. In large bowl combine flour and powdered sugar; cut in butter until crumbly. Press firmly on bottom of 13x9-inch baking pan. Bake 15 minutes.

Meanwhile, in large bowl stir together sweetened condensed milk, egg and vanilla. Stir in pecans and brickle bits. Spread evenly over hot partially baked crust. Continue baking for 25 to 28 minutes or until golden brown. Cool completely. Cover; refrigerate until firm. Cut into bars. Store refrigerated. **YIELD:** 36 bars.

*Nutrition Facts (1 bar): Calories 160; Protein 2g; Carbohydrate 16g; Fat 10g; Cholesterol 25mg; Sodium 70mg*

# Apricot Bars With Brown Butter Frosting

*This chewy apricot-pecan filling on a crust is topped with brown butter frosting.*

*Preparation time: 40 minutes • Baking time: 23 minutes • Cooling time: 1 hour*

**Apricots**
2/3 cup dried apricots
1/2 cup water

**Crust**
1/2 cup all-purpose flour
1/4 cup LAND O LAKES® Butter, softened
3 tablespoons firmly packed brown sugar

**Filling**
2/3 cup firmly packed brown sugar
1 egg
1/2 teaspoon vanilla
1/3 cup all-purpose flour
1/2 teaspoon baking powder
1/4 teaspoon salt
1/2 cup chopped pecans

**Frosting**
1 1/2 cups powdered sugar
3 tablespoons LAND O LAKES® Butter, browned*
1/2 teaspoon vanilla
2 to 3 tablespoons milk

Heat oven to 350°. In 1-quart saucepan combine apricots and water. Cook over high heat until water comes to a full boil (3 to 5 minutes). Reduce heat to low. Continue cooking, stirring occasionally, until all water is absorbed (7 to 9 minutes). Cool 10 minutes; chop. Set aside.

Meanwhile, in small mixer bowl combine all crust ingredients. Beat at low speed until mixture is crumbly (1 to 2 minutes). Press on bottom of greased 9-inch square baking pan. Bake for 10 to 13 minutes or until lightly browned.

In same bowl combine brown sugar, egg and vanilla. Beat at medium speed until well mixed (1 to 2 minutes). Reduce speed to low; add all remaining filling ingredients <u>except</u> pecans. Continue beating, scraping bowl often, until well mixed (1 to 2 minutes). By hand, stir in cooled apricot mixture and pecans. Spread mixture over hot partially baked crust. Bake for 23 to 28 minutes or until golden brown. Cool completely.

In small mixer bowl combine powdered sugar, browned butter and vanilla. Beat at low speed, gradually adding enough milk for desired spreading consistency. Spread over cooled bars; cut into bars. **YIELD:** 25 bars.

*To brown butter, place in 1-quart saucepan. Cook over medium heat until browned (3 to 5 minutes). DO NOT BURN. Let cool to room temperature (10 minutes).

*Nutrition Facts (1 bar): Calories 120; Protein 1g; Carbohydrate 18g; Fat 5g; Cholesterol 15mg; Sodium 70mg*

# Bar Cookie Making Questions & Answers

### How can I prevent my bar cookies from crumbling when cut?

Bar cookies are less crumbly and easier to cut if cooled in the pan before cutting.

### What causes my bar cookies to be hard and crusty after baking?

Overbaking causes hard and crusty bar cookies. The correct size pan is important, too. If the pan is larger than recommended, the dough will be thin and bars will become hard from overbaking.

### What causes my bar cookies to be soft and doughy in the center?

Underbaking causes doughy bar cookies. If the pan is smaller than recommended, dough will be thick and will not bake completely in the time indicated in the recipe. Test bars for doneness before removing them from the oven.

### How can I tell when my brownies are done?

Brownies are done when they just begin to pull away from the sides of the pan. They should be firm to the touch in the center and the top will appear dry but shiny.

### Why do my bar cookies and brownies crack and get a ridge around the outside edge?

Overbeating can make the product rise too quickly when baking. As they cook, they fall. Beat ingredients just enough to mix well.

### How should I store my bar cookies?

Store bar cookies in the pan in which they were baked. Cover pan tightly with aluminum foil or plastic food wrap.

# Candy

Treat family and friends

to the delicious taste

of homemade candy

this holiday season.

Keep some at home,

then fill decorative tins

with extra batches

and give to

those you love.

*Melt-In-Your-Mouth Truffles, see page 72*

# Chocolate Swirl Divinity

*Swirls of chocolate make this divinity extra special.*

*Preparation time: 45 minutes • Cooking time: 30 minutes*

3 cups sugar
3/4 cup light corn syrup
3/4 cup water
1/8 teaspoon salt
3 egg whites
1 (12-ounce) package (2 cups) semi-sweet real chocolate chips
2 teaspoons vanilla

In 2-quart saucepan combine sugar, corn syrup, water and salt. Cook over low heat, stirring constantly, until sugar is dissolved (5 to 8 minutes). Without stirring, continue cooking until candy thermometer reaches 260°F or small amount of mixture dropped into ice water forms a hard ball (30 to 60 minutes).

Meanwhile, in large mixer bowl beat egg whites at high speed until stiff peaks form (2 to 3 minutes). Reduce to medium speed; continue beating while slowly pouring hot syrup into egg whites in a thin stream. Beat at high speed, scraping bowl often, until mixture loses gloss and starts to hold shape (4 to 6 minutes). By hand, stir in chocolate chips and vanilla just until chocolate melts and forms swirls. Quickly drop by tablespoonfuls onto buttered cookie sheets. Cool completely. **YIELD:** 3 dozen.

TIP: Divinity should be made with a standing mixer; a hand held mixer does not have the power to beat the syrup to a stiff consistency.

*Nutrition Facts (1 candy): Calories 130; Protein 1g; Carbohydrate 27g; Fat 3g; Cholesterol 0mg; Sodium 15mg*

# Melt-In-Your-Mouth Truffles

*These rich chocolate truffles are pure indulgence.*

*Preparation time: 30 minutes • Cooking time: 2 minutes • Cooling time: 30 minutes • Chilling time: 10 hours*

1/2 cup whipping cream
8 ounces dark sweet chocolate, coarsely chopped*
1/4 cup LAND O LAKES® Butter, softened
2 teaspoons vanilla**

Finely chopped nuts, if desired
Unsweetened cocoa, if desired
Powdered sugar, if desired

In 2-quart saucepan combine whipping cream and chocolate. Cook over low heat, stirring constantly, until chocolate is melted and mixture is smooth (2 to 4 minutes). Stir in butter until melted. Cool to room temperature (about 30 minutes). Stir in vanilla. Cover; refrigerate until firm enough to shape (at least 8 hours). Mixture can be kept in refrigerator for up to 3 days.

To make truffles, shape about 1 teaspoonful chocolate mixture into 1-inch balls. (Mixture will be soft.) Roll in finely chopped nuts, cocoa or powdered sugar. Refrigerate until firm (at least 2 hours). Store refrigerated or frozen. **YIELD:** 3 dozen.

*8 (1-ounce) squares semi-sweet chocolate, coarsely chopped, can be substituted for 8 ounces dark sweet chocolate, coarsely chopped.

**1/2 teaspoon mint extract or 4 teaspoons your favorite liqueur can be substituted for 2 teaspoons vanilla.

Microwave Directions: In 2-cup measure place whipping cream and chocolate. Microwave on HIGH, stirring after half the time, until chocolate is melted (1 to 2 minutes). Stir until smooth; stir in butter until melted. Cool to room temperature (about 30 minutes). Stir in vanilla. Cover; refrigerate until firm enough to shape (at least 8 hours). Mixture can be kept in refrigerator for up to 3 days. To make truffles, shape about 1 teaspoonful chocolate mixture into 1-inch balls. (Mixture will be soft.) Roll in finely chopped nuts, cocoa or powdered sugar. Refrigerate until firm (at least 2 hours). Store refrigerated or frozen.

*Nutrition Facts (1 candy): Calories 60; Protein 0g; Carbohydrate 4g; Fat 5g; Cholesterol 8mg; Sodium 15mg*

Chocolate Swirl Divinity

# Peanut Butter Cups

*A great gift idea or a fun addition to your holiday dessert plate.*

*Preparation time: 1 hour • Cooking time: 7 minutes • Freezing time: 2 hours*

### Cups
1 (11$^1$/$_2$-ounce) package (2 cups) real milk chocolate chips
2 tablespoons shortening

### Filling
$^1$/$_2$ cup LAND O LAKES® Butter
$^1$/$_2$ cup chunky peanut butter
1 cup powdered sugar
$^2$/$_3$ cup graham cracker crumbs

30 (1$^3$/$_4$x1$^1$/$_4$-inch) mini paper cups

In 1-quart saucepan combine chocolate chips and shortening. Cook over low heat, stirring occasionally, until melted and smooth (3 to 5 minutes). Loosen top paper cup from stack, but leave in stack for greater stability while being coated. With small paintbrush coat inside of top cup evenly with about 1 teaspoon melted chocolate to about $^1$/$_8$-inch thickness, bringing coating almost to top of cup but not over edge. Repeat until 30 cups are coated; refrigerate cups.

In 2-quart saucepan combine butter and peanut butter. Cook over medium heat, stirring occasionally, until melted (4 to 6 minutes). Stir in powdered sugar and graham cracker crumbs. Press about $^1$/$_2$ tablespoon filling into each chocolate cup. Spoon about $^1$/$_2$ teaspoon melted chocolate on top of filling; spread to cover. Freeze until firm (about 2 hours); carefully peel off paper cups. Store refrigerated. **YIELD:** 2$^1$/$_2$ dozen.

*Nutrition Facts (1 candy): Calories 140; Protein 2g; Carbohydrate 12g; Fat 10g; Cholesterol 10mg; Sodium 80mg*

# Creamy Nut Dipped Candies

*Nuts are hidden inside these dipped coconut buttercreams.*

*Preparation time: 1 hour 30 minutes • Chilling time: 2 hours*

4 cups powdered sugar
$^3$/$_4$ cup flaked coconut
$^1$/$_3$ cup LAND O LAKES® Butter, softened
$^1$/$_4$ teaspoon salt
3 tablespoons milk
2 teaspoons vanilla
1 cup powdered sugar

1 cup mixed nuts

1 (10-ounce) package almond bark, vanilla or chocolate candy coating or dipping chocolate

In large mixer bowl combine 4 cups powdered sugar, coconut, butter, salt, milk and vanilla. Beat at medium speed, scraping bowl often, until light and fluffy (4 to 5 minutes). By hand, knead in 1 cup powdered sugar. (Dough may be soft.) Form 1 teaspoonful of dough around each nut; roll into ball. Refrigerate until firm (at least 2 hours).

In 2-quart saucepan over low heat, melt almond bark, vanilla or chocolate candy coating, or dipping chocolate. Dip chilled balls into melted coating; place on waxed paper. If desired, drizzle with remaining almond bark, vanilla or chocolate candy coating, or dipping chocolate to decorate. Store refrigerated. **YIELD:** 5$^1$/$_2$ dozen.

*Nutrition Facts (1 candy): Calories 80; Protein 1g; Carbohydrate 11g; Fat 4g; Cholesterol 5mg; Sodium 20mg*

*Peanut Butter Cups*

# Chocolate Covered Cherries

*A candy store favorite you can make at home.*

*Preparation time: 2 hours • Chilling time: 2 hours*

$^1/_3$  cup LAND O LAKES® Butter
$^1/_3$  cup light corn syrup
$^1/_4$  teaspoon salt
$^1/_2$  teaspoon almond extract
 4  cups powdered sugar

 2  (10-ounce) jars maraschino
    cherries without stems,
    drained
    Chocolate for dipping

In large mixer bowl combine butter, corn syrup, salt and almond extract. Beat at medium speed, scraping bowl often, until well mixed (1 to 2 minutes). By hand, gradually stir in 3 cups powdered sugar. Turn mixture onto lightly powdered sugar dusted surface. Knead in remaining 1 cup powdered sugar. Continue kneading until mixture is smooth (1 to 2 minutes). Using about 1 teaspoonful mixture, completely enclose each cherry. Place on waxed paper-lined cookie sheets. Loosely cover; refrigerate until firm (at least 2 hours).

Coat cherries with dipping chocolate. Store at room temperature until centers soften (3 to 5 days). For longer storage freeze or refrigerate. **YIELD:** 6 dozen.

TIP: Maraschino cherries with stems can be used. Carefully seal sugar mixture around stems.

*Nutrition Facts (1 candy): Calories 70; Protein 0g; Carbohydrate 16g; Fat 1g; Cholesterol 2mg; Sodium 29mg*

# Chocolate For Dipping

*An easy way to dip homemade candies.*

*Preparation time: 1 hour*

1¹/₂ **cups semi-sweet miniature
real chocolate chips**
2 **tablespoons shortening***

Remove candy centers to be dipped from refrigerator about 10 minutes before coating; dipping cold centers can result in cracked coating or bloom (white crystals) on the coating. Chop 1¹/₂ teaspoons chocolate chips; set aside.

In 2-cup measure place remaining chocolate chips and shortening. Place measure in large bowl which contains very warm (100 to 110°F) water that reaches halfway up 2-cup measure. <u>Don't let even one drop of water mix with chocolate</u>. Stir mixture constantly with rubber spatula until chocolate is melted and mixture is smooth (18 to 22 minutes). (Do not rush melting process.) If necessary, replace water with more very warm water. Remove 2-cup measure from water; continue stirring until chocolate is cooled slightly (2 to 3 minutes). Stir reserved chopped chocolate chips into melted chocolate until smooth (1 to 2 minutes).

Set one center on tines of fondue fork or 2 pronged fork. Completely dip center into melted chocolate. Gently tap fork against side of 2-cup measure to remove excess melted chocolate. Invert candy onto waxed paper-lined cookie sheet. Repeat with remaining centers. If melted chocolate becomes too thick for dipping, place 2-cup measure containing chocolate into bowl of very warm water until desired consistency.
**YIELD:** Coats about 2¹/₂ dozen 1-inch centers.

* Do not use butter, margarine or oil.

TIPS ON HOW TO WORK WITH DIPPING CHOCOLATE:
- ◆ Do not dip chocolate on humid days.
- ◆ Avoid all types of moisture when melting chocolate. Steam or drops of moisture can cause mixture to "seize" or become very firm, crumbly and grainy. If this occurs, it can be corrected by stirring in 1 teaspoon shortening for each 2 ounces of melted chocolate.
- ◆ If not following recipe above, melt chocolate over low heat, in a double boiler or on MEDIUM (50% power) in microwave. If chocolate is melted at too high a temperature it will become crumbly and grainy. This can be corrected as directed above.
- ◆ Chop chocolate into small pieces for smooth and even melting.
- ◆ Store chocolate tightly wrapped, in a cool dry place. Do not refrigerate.

*Nutrition Facts (chocolate to dip one center): Calories 50; Protein 0g; Carbohydrate 5g;
Fat 4g; Cholesterol 0mg; Sodium 0mg*

# Cashew Butter Crunch

*No one will have to dig to the bottom of the bowl to find the cashews in this toffee-like candy.*

*Preparation time: 10 minutes • Cooking time: 25 minutes*

1 cup sugar
1 cup LAND O LAKES® Butter
1 tablespoon light corn syrup
$1^1/2$ cups salted cashew pieces

In 2-quart saucepan combine sugar, butter and corn syrup. Cook over low heat, stirring occasionally, until candy thermometer reaches 290°F or small amount of mixture dropped into ice water forms brittle strands (25 to 30 minutes). Remove from heat; stir in cashews. Spread to $1/4$-inch thickness on waxed paper-lined 15x10x1-inch jelly roll pan. Cool completely; break into pieces. **YIELD:** $1^1/4$ pounds (2 dozen pieces).

TIP: $1^1/2$ cups your favorite salted nuts can be substituted for $1^1/2$ cups salted cashew pieces.

*Nutrition Facts (1 piece): Calories 180; Protein 2g; Carbohydrate 14g;*
*Fat 14g; Cholesterol 25mg; Sodium 160mg*

# Buttery Chocolate Nut Toffee

*One taste of this old-time favorite and you'll be back for more!*

*Preparation time: 15 minutes • Cooking time: 25 minutes*

1 cup sugar
1 cup LAND O LAKES® Butter, cut into pieces
1 (6-ounce) package (1 cup) semi-sweet real chocolate chips
$1/4$ cup chopped walnuts

In 2-quart saucepan combine sugar and butter. Cook over low heat, stirring occasionally, until candy thermometer reaches 300°F or small amount of mixture dropped into ice water forms brittle strands (25 to 30 minutes). Spread on waxed paper-lined 15x10x1-inch jelly roll pan. Sprinkle chocolate chips over hot candy; let stand 5 minutes. Spread melted chocolate evenly over candy; sprinkle with nuts. Cool completely; break into pieces. **YIELD:** $1^1/4$ pounds (3 dozen pieces).

Microwave Directions: In 2-quart casserole combine sugar and butter. Microwave on HIGH, stirring occasionally, until microwave candy thermometer reaches 300°F or small amount of mixture dropped into ice water forms brittle strands (12 to 18 minutes). Spread on waxed paper-lined 15x10x1-inch jelly roll pan. Sprinkle chocolate chips over hot candy; let stand 5 minutes. Spread melted chocolate evenly over candy; sprinkle with nuts. Cool completely; break into pieces.

*Nutrition Facts (1 piece): Calories 100; Protein 0g; Carbohydrate 8g;*
*Fat 7g; Cholesterol 15mg; Sodium 50mg*

Cashew Butter Crunch

# Homemade Caramel Corn N' Nuts

*This best-ever caramel corn is made extra special with the addition of mixed nuts.*

*Preparation time: 45 minutes • Baking time: 45 minutes*

20 cups popped popcorn
2 cups firmly packed brown
   sugar
1 cup LAND O LAKES® Butter
$1/2$ cup dark corn syrup
$1/2$ teaspoon salt
$1/2$ teaspoon baking soda
1 cup mixed salted nuts

Heat oven to 200°. In roasting pan place popcorn; set aside.

In 2-quart saucepan combine brown sugar, butter, corn syrup and salt. Cook over medium heat, stirring occasionally, until mixture comes to a full boil (12 to 14 minutes). Continue cooking, stirring occasionally, until candy thermometer reaches 238°F or small amount of mixture dropped in ice water forms a soft ball (4 to 6 minutes). Remove from heat; stir in baking soda. Pour over popcorn; sprinkle nuts over caramel mixture. Stir until all popcorn is coated. Bake for 20 minutes; stir. Continue baking for 25 minutes. Remove from oven; immediately place caramel corn on waxed paper. Cool completely. Break into pieces. Store in tightly covered container. **YIELD:** 18 cups.

*Nutrition Facts ($1/2$ cup): Calories 140; Protein 1g; Carbohydrate 19g;*
*Fat 7g; Cholesterol 15mg; Sodium 130mg*

# Aunt Emily's Soft Caramels

*This buttery caramel recipe has been enjoyed for generations.*

*Preparation time: 10 minutes • Cooking time: 2 hours 20 minutes*

2 cups sugar
1 cup firmly packed brown
   sugar
1 cup LAND O LAKES®
   Butter, softened
1 cup milk
1 cup whipping cream
1 cup light corn syrup
1 teaspoon vanilla

In 4-quart saucepan combine all ingredients <u>except</u> vanilla. Cook over low heat, stirring occasionally, until sugar is dissolved and butter is melted (20 to 25 minutes). Continue cooking, without stirring, until candy thermometer reaches 248°F or small amount of mixture dropped into ice water forms a firm ball (about 2 hours). Remove from heat; stir in vanilla. Pour into buttered 13x9-inch pan. Cool completely; cut into $1^1/2$ x 1-inch pieces. **YIELD:** 6 dozen.

TIP: After cutting, wrap each caramel in plastic food wrap.

*Nutrition Facts (1 caramel): Calories 80; Protein 0g; Carbohydrate 12g;*
*Fat 4g; Cholesterol 10mg; Sodium 35mg*

*Homemade Caramel Corn N' Nuts*

# Old-Fashioned Soft Popcorn Balls

*These chewy popcorn balls will be a hit at Halloween or during the winter holidays.*

*Preparation time: 1 hour • Cooking time: 40 minutes*

20 cups popped popcorn
2 cups sugar
1 1/2 cups water
1/2 cup light corn syrup
1/2 teaspoon salt
1 teaspoon vinegar

1 cup candy corn, small gumdrops, raisins or salted peanuts

In large bowl or roasting pan place popcorn; set aside.

In 2-quart saucepan combine all remaining ingredients <u>except</u> candy. Cook over medium heat, stirring occasionally, until candy thermometer reaches 250°F or small amount of mixture dropped into ice water forms a hard ball (40 to 45 minutes).

Remove from heat; pour over popcorn. Stir until all popcorn is coated. Gently stir in candy. Using buttered hands shape about <u>1 cup</u> popcorn into ball. Place on waxed paper. Repeat with remaining popcorn. Cool completely; wrap in waxed paper or plastic food wrap. **YIELD:** 15 balls.

*Nutrition Facts (1 ball): Calories 260; Protein 3g; Carbohydrate 62g; Fat 1g; Cholesterol 0mg; Sodium 110mg*

# Old-Fashioned Peanut Brittle

*A favorite during the holidays, this candy brings back memories.*

*Preparation time: 15 minutes • Cooking time: 1 hour 52 minutes*

2 cups sugar
1 cup light corn syrup
1/2 cup water
1 cup LAND O LAKES® Butter, cut into pieces
2 cups raw peanuts
1 teaspoon baking soda

In 3-quart saucepan combine sugar, corn syrup and water. Cook over low heat, stirring occasionally, until sugar is dissolved and mixture comes to a full boil (20 to 30 minutes). Add butter; continue cooking, stirring occasionally, until candy thermometer reaches 280°F or small amount of mixture dropped into ice water forms a pliable strand (80 to 90 minutes).

Stir in peanuts; continue cooking, stirring constantly, until candy thermometer reaches 305°F or small amount of mixture dropped into ice water forms brittle strands (12 to 14 minutes).

Remove from heat; stir in baking soda. Pour mixture onto 2 buttered cookie sheets; spread about 1/4 inch thick. Cool completely; break into pieces.
**YIELD:** 2 pounds (6 dozen pieces).

<u>Microwave Directions</u>: In 3-quart casserole combine sugar, corn syrup and water. Microwave on HIGH, stirring after half the time, until sugar is dissolved and mixture comes to a full boil (5 to 8 minutes). Add butter; microwave on HIGH, stirring after half the time, until microwave candy thermometer reaches 280°F or small amount of mixture dropped into ice water forms a pliable strand (15 to 20 minutes). Stir in peanuts. Microwave on HIGH, stirring after half the time, until microwave candy thermometer reaches 305°F or small amount of mixture dropped into ice water forms brittle strands (6 to 8 minutes). Stir in baking soda. Pour mixture onto 2 buttered cookie sheets; spread about 1/4 inch thick. Cool completely; break into pieces.

*Nutrition Facts (1 piece): Calories 90; Protein 1g; Carbohydrate 10g; Fat 5g; Cholesterol 5mg; Sodium 45mg*

Old-Fashioned Soft Popcorn Balls

# Dark Chocolate Fudge

*This dark fudge can be flavored 4 luscious ways.*

*Preparation time: 10 minutes • Cooking time: 7 minutes • Chilling time: 2 hours*

2 cups miniature marshmallows

3 (6-ounce) packages (3 cups) semi-sweet real chocolate chips

1 (14-ounce) can sweetened condensed milk

$1^1/2$ teaspoons vanilla

In 2-quart saucepan combine marshmallows, chocolate chips and sweetened condensed milk. Cook over low heat, stirring often, until melted and smooth (7 to 9 minutes). Remove from heat; stir in vanilla. Pour into greased 8 or 9-inch square pan. Refrigerate until firm (at least 2 hours). Cut into squares. **YIELD:** 2 pounds (64 candies).

VARIATIONS

Peanut Butter Swirl Fudge: Reduce $1^1/2$ teaspoons vanilla to 1 teaspoon. Prepare fudge as directed above; stir in $^1/2$ cup chopped salted peanuts and $^1/2$ cup peanut butter until peanut butter just begins to melt. (Swirls of peanut butter will be visible.) Pour into greased 8 or 9-inch square pan. Continue as directed above.

Almond Fudge: Reduce $1^1/2$ teaspoons vanilla to 1 teaspoon. Prepare fudge as directed above; stir in 1 teaspoon almond extract. Pour into greased 8 or 9-inch square pan. Continue as directed above.

Macadamia Nut Fudge: Prepare fudge as directed above. Stir in $^1/2$ cup coarsely chopped macadamia nuts. Pour into greased 8 or 9-inch square pan. Continue as directed above.

Microwave Directions: In $1^1/2$-quart casserole or medium glass bowl combine marshmallows, chocolate chips and sweetened condensed milk. Microwave on HIGH, stirring after half the time, until melted (3 to 4 minutes). Stir until smooth; stir in vanilla. Pour into greased 8 or 9-inch square pan. Refrigerate at least 2 hours or until firm. Cut into squares.

*Nutrition Facts (1 candy): Calories 70; Protein 1g; Carbohydrate 9g;*
*Fat 3g; Cholesterol 2mg; Sodium 9mg*

# Candy Making Questions & Answers

### Can I double my candy recipes?

No. We do not recommend doubling any candy recipe. Follow candy recipe directions carefully to ensure success.

### Is pan size important when making candy?

Yes. Always use the recommended size of heavy cooking pan to prevent candy from boiling over.

### What fat should I use in my candies?

We recommend butter be used when making candy, especially candy made from a boiled sugar syrup. Margarine and low fat spreads do not create the correct texture in the final candy because of the emulsifiers added to their formulas. Butter also gives the best flavor to candy.

### How do I know when my candy is at the correct temperature?

It is essential to use a candy thermometer when making candies from a cooked syrup. Stand the thermometer upright in the pan with the candy syrup completely covering the bulb. Take care that the thermometer is not resting on the bottom of the pan.

If you do not have a candy thermometer, use the cold water test. Drop a small amount of the candy mixture into a cupful of very cold water. Remove the candy drop from the water and form into a ball with fingers. The firmness of the ball determines the candy temperature and is an indication of doneness.

### Candy Temperature Definitions

- ◆ Thread - 223 to 234°F
  Forms a 2-inch soft thread.

- ◆ Soft Ball - 234 to 240°F
  Forms a soft ball which flattens when removed from water.

- ◆ Firm Ball - 242 to 248°F
  Forms a firm ball which does not flatten when removed from water.

- ◆ Hard Ball - 250 to 268°F
  Forms a hard, but pliable, ball.

- ◆ Soft Crack - 270 to 290°F
  Separates into hard, but pliable, strands.

- ◆ Hard Crack - 300 to 310°F
  Separates into hard, brittle strands.

# Breads

To "break bread"
means to offer
hospitality—and what
better way to
welcome friends and family
to the table than
with fresh-baked bread.
Try Festive Orange
Nut Bread or
Spiced Pumpkin Muffins
for a special treat.

*Apricot Cardamom Wreath, see page 88*

# Apricot Cardamom Wreath

*Brandied apricots are tucked inside a sweet cardamom bread that's shaped in a wreath and sprinkled with sugar crystals.*

*Preparation time: 1 hour • Rising time: 1 hour 30 minutes • Baking time: 30 minutes*

## Bread

|   |   |
|---|---|
| 1 | cup sugar |
| 1 | teaspoon ground cardamom |
| $1/2$ | cup LAND O LAKES® Butter |
| 1 | (12-ounce) can evaporated milk |
| 2 | teaspoons salt |
| 2 | ($1/4$-ounce) packages active dry yeast |
| $1/4$ | cup warm water (105 to 115°F) |
| $1/2$ | cup LAND O LAKES® Sour Cream (Regular, Light or No•Fat) |
| 3 | eggs |
| $6^{1}/_{2}$ to $7^{1}/_{2}$ | cups all-purpose flour |

## Filling

|   |   |
|---|---|
| 2 to $2^{1}/_{2}$ | cups water |
| $1/4$ | cup brandy or water |
| 1 | (6-ounce) package (2 cups) dried apricots |
|   |   |
| 1 | egg, slightly beaten |
| 2 | tablespoons milk |
|   | Large crystal sugar |

In 2-quart saucepan stir together sugar and cardamom; add butter, evaporated milk and salt. Cook over medium heat, stirring occasionally, until butter is melted (5 to 8 minutes). Cool to warm (105 to 115°F). In large mixer bowl dissolve yeast in $1/4$ cup warm water; stir in warm milk mixture, sour cream, eggs and 3 cups flour. Beat at medium speed, scraping bowl often, until smooth (1 to 2 minutes). By hand, stir in enough remaining flour to make dough easy to handle. Turn dough onto lightly floured surface; knead until smooth and elastic (about 5 minutes). Place in greased bowl; turn greased side up. Cover; let rise in warm place until double in size (about 1 to $1^{1}/2$ hours). Dough is ready if indentation remains when touched.

Meanwhile, in 2-quart saucepan combine 2 cups water, brandy and apricots. Cook over low heat, stirring occasionally and adding small amounts of additional water if necessary, until apricots are tender and mixture is thickened (40 to 45 minutes); set aside.

Punch down dough; divide in half. Let rest 10 minutes. On lightly floured surface roll one half of dough to 20x9-inch rectangle; cut into 3 (3-inch) strips. Spread each strip with $1/4$ cup apricot mixture to within $1/2$ inch of edges. Bring 20-inch sides up together; pinch sides and ends tightly to seal well. Gently braid filled strips together. Place on greased large cookie sheet; form into wreath. Pinch ends to seal well. Repeat with remaining dough and apricot mixture. Cover; let rise 30 minutes.

Heat oven to 350°. Bake for 25 to 30 minutes or until lightly browned. In small bowl stir together 1 egg and milk. Brush breads with egg mixture; sprinkle with large crystal sugar. Continue baking for 5 to 10 minutes or until golden brown. Remove from cookie sheets; cool on wire racks. **YIELD:** 2 wreaths (24 servings).

TIP: For best results, bake one wreath at a time.

*Nutrition Facts (1 serving): Calories 260; Protein 6g; Carbohydrate 42g; Fat 7g; Cholesterol 60mg; Sodium 250mg*

# Banana Macadamia Nut Bread

*Bake this flavorful banana bread and serve for holiday breakfasts, coffees or teas.*

*Preparation time: 20 minutes • Baking time: 35 minutes*

2 cups all-purpose flour
$^3/_4$ cup sugar
$^1/_2$ cup LAND O LAKES® Butter, softened
2 eggs
1 teaspoon baking soda
$^1/_2$ teaspoon salt
1 tablespoon grated orange peel
1 teaspoon vanilla
1 cup (2 medium) mashed ripe bananas
$^1/_4$ cup orange juice
1 cup flaked coconut
1 ($3^1/_2$-ounce) jar ($^3/_4$ cup) coarsely chopped macadamia nuts or walnuts

Heat oven to 350°. In large mixer bowl combine all ingredients <u>except</u> bananas, orange juice, coconut and nuts. Beat at low speed, scraping bowl often, until well mixed (2 to 3 minutes). Add bananas and orange juice. Continue beating, scraping bowl often, until well mixed (1 minute). By hand, stir in coconut and nuts. (Batter will be thick.) Spread into 3 greased $5^1/_2$x3-inch mini loaf pans or 1 greased 9x5-inch loaf pan. Bake mini loaves for 35 to 45 minutes or 9x5-inch loaf for 60 to 65 minutes or until toothpick inserted in center comes out clean. Cool 10 minutes; remove from pans. Cool completely. **YIELD:** 3 ($5^1/_2$x3-inch) loaves or 1 (9x5-inch) loaf (24 servings).

*Nutrition Facts (1 serving): Calories 160; Protein 2g; Carbohydrate 19g; Fat 9g; Cholesterol 30mg; Sodium 140mg*

# Sweet Cream Holiday Rolls

*These rolls will be a favorite no matter which variation you use.*

*Preparation time: 45 minutes • Rising time: 1 hour • Baking time: 20 minutes*

**Dough**
2 (approximately 1-pound) loaves frozen bread dough <u>or</u> sweet roll dough, thawed

**Filling**
2 tablespoons LAND O LAKES® Butter, softened
$^1/_4$ teaspoon ground cloves

**Glaze**
$^1/_2$ cup sugar
$^1/_2$ cup LAND O LAKES® Sour Cream (Regular, Light <u>or</u> No•Fat)
$^1/_4$ cup LAND O LAKES® Butter, softened
2 tablespoons orange juice

On lightly floured surface roll each loaf of dough into 12x6-inch rectangle. Spread each rectangle with <u>1 tablespoon</u> butter; sprinkle each with <u>$^1/_8$ teaspoon</u> cloves. Roll each rectangle up jelly roll fashion beginning with 6-inch side. Pinch edge of dough into roll to seal well. Cut into 1-inch slices; place 6 slices in each of 2 greased 9-inch round cake pans. Cover; let rise in warm place until dough is double in size (about 1 hour).

<u>Heat oven to 350°</u>. Bake for 20 to 25 minutes or until golden brown. Cover rolls with aluminum foil during last 10 minutes of baking if browning too quickly.

Meanwhile, in 2-quart saucepan combine all glaze ingredients. Cook over medium heat, stirring occasionally, until mixture comes to a full boil (5 to 6 minutes); boil 3 minutes. Pour warm glaze over warm rolls. **YIELD:** 1 dozen.

VARIATIONS
<u>Candied Fruit</u>: Sprinkle $^1/_4$ cup chopped dried candied fruit mix over each 12x6-inch rectangle. Continue as directed above.

<u>Almond</u>: <u>Omit cloves</u>. Sprinkle $^1/_4$ cup slivered almonds and 1 tablespoon sugar over each 12x6-inch rectangle. Continue as directed above. Glaze: <u>Omit orange juice</u>. Stir in $^1/_4$ teaspoon almond extract just before pouring glaze over rolls. If desired, garnish with maraschino cherries.

*Nutrition Facts (1 roll): Calories 300; Protein 6g; Carbohydrate 46g; Fat 10g; Cholesterol 20mg; Sodium 430mg*

# Cranberry Sour Cream Crumble

*A layer of cranberries makes this coffee cake extra special.*

*Preparation time: 30 minutes • Baking time: 1 hour 10 minutes*

$^1/_4$ cup chopped almonds

### Topping
$^1/_2$ cup all-purpose flour
$^1/_3$ cup sugar
$^1/_4$ cup chopped almonds
$^1/_4$ cup LAND O LAKES® Butter, melted
$^1/_4$ teaspoon vanilla

### Coffee Cake
1 cup sugar
$^1/_2$ cup LAND O LAKES® Butter, softened
1 teaspoon vanilla
2 eggs
2 cups all-purpose flour
1$^1/_4$ teaspoons baking powder
$^1/_2$ teaspoon baking soda
$^1/_4$ teaspoon salt
1 cup LAND O LAKES® Sour Cream (Regular, Light or No•Fat)
1 cup whole cranberry sauce

Heat oven to 350°. Sprinkle $^1/_4$ cup chopped almonds on bottom of greased 9-inch springform pan or 10-inch tube pan; set aside.

In medium bowl stir together all topping ingredients until crumbly; set aside.

In large mixer bowl combine 1 cup sugar, $^1/_2$ cup butter and 1 teaspoon vanilla. Beat at medium speed, scraping bowl often, until creamy (1 to 2 minutes). Add eggs; continue beating, scraping bowl often, until well mixed (1 to 2 minutes). Continue beating, adding 2 cups flour, baking powder, baking soda and salt alternately with sour cream, until well mixed (1 to 2 minutes). Spoon <u>half</u> of batter into prepared pan; spread to cover bottom. Spread cranberry sauce over batter; spread to edges. Spread remaining batter over cranberry sauce to cover. Sprinkle topping over batter. Bake for 70 to 85 minutes or until toothpick inserted in center comes out clean. Cool 10 minutes; remove side of pan. **YIELD:** 12 servings.

*Nutrition Facts (1 serving): Calories 390; Protein 5g; Carbohydrate 53g; Fat 18g; Cholesterol 70mg; Sodium 290mg*

*Cranberry Sour Cream Crumble*

# Festive Orange Nut Bread

*Make this flavorful bread in mini loaf pans for an easy hostess gift.*

*Preparation time: 20 minutes • Baking time: 50 minutes*

2 cups all-purpose flour
$^3/_4$ cup sugar
$^1/_2$ cup milk
$^1/_2$ cup orange juice
1 egg, slightly beaten
2 tablespoons
   LAND O LAKES®
   Butter, melted
2 tablespoons grated orange
   peel
1 teaspoon baking powder
$^1/_2$ teaspoon baking soda
$^1/_4$ teaspoon salt
$^1/_2$ cup chopped walnuts

Heat oven to 350°. In large bowl combine all ingredients <u>except</u> walnuts; stir just until moistened. Stir in walnuts. Pour into greased 8x4-inch loaf pan. Bake for 50 to 60 minutes or until toothpick inserted in center comes out clean. Cool 10 minutes; remove from pan. **YIELD:** 1 loaf (12 servings).

TIP: 4 greased $5^1/_2$ x 3-inch mini loaf pans can be substituted for 8 x 4-inch loaf pan. Bake for 35 to 42 minutes.

*Nutrition Facts (1 serving): Calories 190; Protein 4g; Carbohydrate 31g; Fat 6g; Cholesterol 30mg; Sodium 150mg*

# Orange Almond Braided Coffee Cake

*Tender pastry encloses the moist orange almond filling.*

*Preparation time: 1 hour • Rising time: 2 hours • Baking time: 20 minutes*

**Coffee Cake**
1 cup milk
$^1/_4$ cup LAND O LAKES®
   Butter
1 ($^1/_4$-ounce) package
   active dry yeast
$^1/_4$ cup warm water
   (105 to 115°F)
$3^1/_2$ to $4^1/_2$ cups all-purpose flour
$^1/_4$ cup sugar
1 egg
1 teaspoon salt

**Filling**
1 ($3^1/_2$-ounce) package
   almond paste
$^1/_4$ cup firmly packed
   brown sugar
$^1/_4$ cup LAND O LAKES®
   Butter, softened
$^1/_4$ teaspoon grated
   orange peel

**Glaze**
1 cup powdered sugar
2 to 3 tablespoons milk
$^1/_2$ teaspoon almond
   extract
$^1/_4$ teaspoon grated
   orange peel

In 1-quart saucepan heat milk over medium heat until just comes to a boil (5 to 7 minutes); stir in $^1/_4$ cup butter until melted. Cool to warm (105 to 115°F). In large mixer bowl dissolve yeast in warm water. Add cooled milk mixture, <u>2 cups</u> flour, sugar, egg and salt. Beat at medium speed, scraping bowl often, until smooth (1 to 2 minutes). Stir in enough remaining flour to make dough easy to handle. Turn dough onto lightly floured surface; knead until smooth and elastic (about 10 minutes). Place in greased bowl; turn greased side up. Cover; let rise in warm place until double in size (about $1^1/_2$ hours). Dough is ready if indentation remains when touched. Punch down dough.

In small mixer bowl combine all filling ingredients. Beat at medium speed, scraping bowl often, until well mixed (1 to 2 minutes). Divide dough into 2 equal portions. On lightly floured surface roll one portion into 10-inch square; cut square into 3 (10x3-inch) rectangles. Spread about <u>2 tablespoons</u> filling down center of each rectangle to within $^1/_2$ inch of edge on all sides. Bring long sides together over filling; pinch sides and ends tightly to seal. Gently braid 3 filled pieces together to make 1 coffee cake. Pinch ends together to seal; tuck ends under braid. Repeat with remaining portion of dough to make second coffee cake. Transfer both coffee cakes to greased cookie sheet. Cover; let rise until double in size (30 to 40 minutes).

<u>Heat oven to 350°</u>. Bake for 20 to 30 minutes or until golden brown. In small bowl stir together all glaze ingredients. Drizzle over warm coffee cakes. **YIELD:** 2 coffee cakes (16 servings).

*Nutrition Facts (1 serving): Calories 250; Protein 5g; Carbohydrate 37g Fat 9g; Cholesterol 35mg; Sodium 210mg*

Festive Orange Nut Bread

# Orange Sugared Scones

*Orange and currants add extra flavor to traditional scones.*

*Preparation time: 25 minutes • Baking time: 25 minutes*

$2^1/2$ cups all-purpose flour
2 teaspoons baking powder
$^1/2$ teaspoon baking soda
$^1/2$ teaspoon salt
$^1/2$ teaspoon cinnamon
$^1/2$ cup LAND O LAKES® Butter
$^1/2$ cup sugar
$^1/2$ cup currants or raisins
1 tablespoon grated orange
   peel
1 cup LAND O LAKES®
   Sour Cream (Regular,
   Light or No•Fat)
1 egg, separated
4 teaspoons lemon juice
2 tablespoons sugar

Heat oven to 375°. In large bowl combine flour, baking powder, baking soda, salt and cinnamon; cut in butter until crumbly. In small bowl combine $^1/2$ cup sugar, currants and orange peel. Stir into flour mixture. In medium bowl, with wire whisk, stir together sour cream, egg yolk and lemon juice until smooth. Stir sour cream mixture into flour mixture. (Mixture will be dry.) Knead about 5 to 8 times to combine all ingredients. Divide dough in half. Pat each half into 6-inch circle. Place both 6-inch circles on greased large cookie sheet. Cut each circle into 6 wedges.

In small bowl beat egg white with fork until frothy. Brush top of each scone with egg white; sprinkle with 2 tablespoons sugar. Bake for 25 to 30 minutes or until toothpick inserted in center of scone comes out clean and scones are lightly browned. Cool on wire rack. To serve, separate into individual scones. **YIELD:** 1 dozen.

*Nutrition Facts (1 scone): Calories 240; Protein 4g; Carbohydrate 34g;*
*Fat 10g; Cholesterol 45mg; Sodium 280mg*

*Orange Sugared Scones*

# Glazed Chocolate Mini Loaves

*Mini loaves of rich chocolate bread are glazed with additional chocolate.*

*Preparation time: 40 minutes • Baking time: 35 minutes*

## Bread

- $2/3$ cup firmly packed brown sugar
- $1/2$ cup LAND O LAKES® Butter, softened
- 1 cup miniature semi-sweet real chocolate chips, melted
- 2 eggs
- $2^1/2$ cups all-purpose flour
- $1^1/2$ cups applesauce
- 1 teaspoon baking powder
- 1 teaspoon baking soda
- 2 teaspoons vanilla
- $1/2$ cup miniature semi-sweet real chocolate chips

## Glaze

- $1/2$ cup miniature semi-sweet real chocolate chips
- 1 tablespoon LAND O LAKES® Butter
- 5 teaspoons water
- $1/2$ cup powdered sugar
- $1/4$ teaspoon vanilla
  Pinch of salt

Heat oven to 350°. In large mixer bowl combine brown sugar and $1/2$ cup butter. Beat at medium speed, scraping bowl often, until creamy (1 to 2 minutes). Add 1 cup melted chocolate chips and eggs; continue beating until well mixed (1 to 2 minutes). Add flour, applesauce, baking powder, baking soda and 2 teaspoons vanilla. Beat at low speed, scraping bowl often, until creamy (1 to 2 minutes). By hand, stir in $1/2$ cup chocolate chips. Spoon batter into 5 greased $5^1/2$x 3-inch mini loaf pans or aluminum foil pans. Bake for 35 to 42 minutes or until center crack is dry when touched. Cool 10 minutes. Remove from pans; do not remove if using aluminum foil pans. (Bread can be frozen unfrosted. Remove from freezer; bring to room temperature before frosting.)

Meanwhile, in 2-quart saucepan combine $1/2$ cup chocolate chips, 1 tablespoon butter and water. Cook over low heat, stirring constantly, until melted and smooth. Remove from heat. Stir in powdered sugar, $1/4$ teaspoon vanilla and salt; drizzle over each loaf. Cool completely. **YIELD:** 5 mini loaves (25 servings).

VARIATION
Glazed Chocolate Mint Mini Loaves: Omit 1 teaspoon vanilla in bread and $1/4$ teaspoon vanilla in glaze. Add $1/2$ teaspoon mint extract to bread and $1/4$ teaspoon mint extract to glaze.

*Nutrition Facts (1 serving): Calories 190; Protein 2g; Carbohydrate 27g; Fat 10g; Cholesterol 35mg; Sodium 110mg*

*Glazed Chocolate Mini Loaves*

# Spiced Pumpkin Muffins

*During the fall harvest enjoy tender pumpkin muffins subtly spiced with cinnamon and ginger.*

*Preparation time: 10 minutes • Baking time: 15 minutes*

2 cups all-purpose flour
$^2/_3$ cup firmly packed brown
    sugar
$^1/_3$ cup sugar
1 tablespoon baking powder
1 teaspoon salt
1 teaspoon cinnamon
$^1/_4$ teaspoon baking soda
$^1/_4$ teaspoon ground ginger
$^1/_2$ cup LAND O LAKES®
    Butter, melted
$^1/_2$ cup cooked pumpkin*
$^1/_3$ cup buttermilk**
2 eggs, slightly beaten

Heat oven to 400°. In large bowl stir together all ingredients <u>except</u> butter, pumpkin, buttermilk and eggs. In medium bowl stir together all remaining ingredients; stir into flour mixture just until moistened. Spoon into paper-lined or greased muffin pan. Bake for 15 to 20 minutes or until lightly browned. Cool 5 minutes; remove from pan. **YIELD:** 1 dozen.

<u>Microwave Directions</u>: Mix muffins as directed above. Spoon <u>one-third</u> of batter into microwave-proof 6-cup paper-lined muffin pan, filling cups <u>half</u> full. Microwave on HIGH, turning after half the time, until muffins are dry on top ($2^1/_2$ to $3^1/_2$ minutes). Repeat with remaining batter. **YIELD:** 18 muffins.

\* $^1/_2$ cup canned pumpkin can be substituted for $^1/_2$ cup cooked pumpkin.

\*\* 1 teaspoon vinegar plus enough milk to equal $^1/_3$ cup can be substituted for $^1/_3$ cup buttermilk.

*Nutrition Facts (1 muffin): Calories 230; Protein 4g; Carbohydrate 35g;*
*Fat 9g; Cholesterol 60mg; Sodium 380mg*

*Spiced Pumpkin Muffins*

# Pumpkin Banana Chocolate Chip Bread

*Miniature chocolate chips add color and flavor to this moist pumpkin banana bread.*

*Preparation time: 20 minutes • Baking time: 40 minutes*

$1\frac{1}{2}$ cups firmly packed brown sugar

$\frac{3}{4}$ cup LAND O LAKES® Butter, softened

3 eggs

1 cup cooked pumpkin

2 medium (1 cup) ripe bananas, mashed

3 cups all-purpose flour

2 teaspoons baking soda

$1\frac{1}{2}$ teaspoons pumpkin pie spice*

$\frac{1}{2}$ teaspoon baking powder

$\frac{1}{2}$ teaspoon salt

$\frac{1}{2}$ cup miniature semi-sweet chocolate chips**

Heat oven to 350°. In large mixer bowl combine brown sugar, butter and eggs. Beat at medium speed, scraping bowl often, until mixture is creamy (1 to 2 minutes). Add pumpkin and bananas. Continue beating until well mixed (1 to 2 minutes). (Mixture will have curdled appearance.) Add all remaining ingredients <u>except</u> chocolate chips. Continue beating just until moistened (about 1 minute). By hand, stir in chocolate chips. Spread into 4 greased $5\frac{1}{2}$x3-inch mini loaf pans or 1 greased 9x5-inch loaf pan. Bake mini loaves for 40 to 50 minutes or 9x5-inch loaf for 65 to 75 minutes or until toothpick inserted in center comes out clean. Cool 5 minutes; remove from pans. Cool completely. **YIELD:** 4 ($5\frac{1}{2}$x3-inch) loaves or 1 (9x5-inch) loaf (32 servings).

* $\frac{3}{4}$ teaspoon cinnamon, $\frac{1}{2}$ teaspoon ground ginger, $\frac{1}{4}$ teaspoon <u>each</u> ground nutmeg and ground cloves can be substituted for $1\frac{1}{2}$ teaspoons pumpkin pie spice.

** $\frac{1}{2}$ cup semi-sweet chocolate chips can be substituted for $\frac{1}{2}$ cup miniature semi-sweet chocolate chips.

*Nutrition Facts (1 serving): Calories 150; Protein 2g; Carbohydrate 23g; Fat 6g; Cholesterol 30mg; Sodium 160mg*

# Bread Making Questions & Answers

### Which breads can I freeze?

Yeast breads, coffee cakes, muffins and quick breads can be frozen at 0°F or below for up to twelve months.

### How should I freeze breads?

Cool bread completely. Do not frost or decorate. Place coffee cakes on aluminum foil-wrapped cardboard before wrapping tightly with aluminum foil or plastic food wrap.

### After freezing bread, what is the best way to thaw and serve it?

Loosen the wrap around the bread slightly; thaw at room temperature for 2 to 3 hours. Serve at room temperature or reheat. To reheat, wrap in aluminum foil; bake at 350° for 15 to 20 minutes. To reheat bread in the microwave, wrap in paper toweling and microwave on HIGH (briefly, to avoid a tough texture) 5 to 40 seconds.

### When making quick bread or muffins, how can I tell if my baking powder is still good?

Add 1 teaspoon baking powder to $^{1}/_{3}$ cup hot water. Your baking powder is still "good" if it bubbles vigorously.

### When making coffee cake, why should I use shiny pans?

Shiny pans reflect heat, resulting in a golden, delicate, tender crust.

### How can I tell when my coffee cake is done?

Follow the doneness test given with your recipe; usually a toothpick inserted in the center comes out clean when a coffee cake is done.

# Desserts

Due to America's
diverse heritage, we've
inherited desserts from
all over the world.
The holidays are the
perfect time to sample
these special treats.
Turn the page and
you'll discover desserts
that have their
beginnings in England,
Scandinavia, Germany,
China and France.

*Fruited Streusel Kuchen With Orange Cream, see page 104*

# Fruited Streusel Kuchen With Orange Cream

*Sliced apples, cranberries, dried fruits and nuts, combine with sugar
to form a streusel topping on this orange-flavored cake.*

*Preparation time: 1 hour • Baking time: 35 minutes*

## Kuchen
- 2$\frac{1}{4}$ cups all-purpose flour
- 2 teaspoons baking powder
- $\frac{1}{4}$ teaspoon salt
- $\frac{1}{3}$ cup sugar
- $\frac{1}{3}$ cup LAND O LAKES® Butter, softened
- 2 eggs
- $\frac{1}{2}$ cup milk
- $\frac{1}{2}$ cup orange juice
- 1 tablespoon orange-flavored liqueur or orange juice
- 1 teaspoon vanilla
- 1 large tart cooking apple, peeled, cored, sliced $\frac{1}{8}$-inch
- $\frac{1}{2}$ cup coarsely chopped dried apricots
- $\frac{1}{2}$ cup dried figs, quartered
- $\frac{1}{2}$ cup golden raisins
- $\frac{1}{2}$ cup coarsely chopped walnuts
- $\frac{1}{2}$ cup fresh or frozen whole cranberries

## Streusel Topping
- $\frac{1}{2}$ cup sugar
- 2 tablespoons LAND O LAKES® Butter, softened
- 1 teaspoon cinnamon
- 1 teaspoon grated orange peel

## Orange Cream
- 2 cups (1 pint) whipping cream
- $\frac{1}{4}$ cup sugar
- 2 teaspoons grated orange peel
- 1 tablespoon orange-flavored liqueur or orange juice

Heat oven to 350°. In medium bowl stir together flour, baking powder and salt; set aside.

In large mixer bowl beat together $\frac{1}{3}$ cup sugar and $\frac{1}{3}$ cup butter at medium speed, scraping bowl often, until well mixed (1 to 2 minutes). Continue beating, adding eggs one at a time, until well mixed (1 to 2 minutes). Reduce speed to low. Continue beating, scraping bowl often and gradually adding flour mixture alternately with milk and $\frac{1}{2}$ cup orange juice, until smooth (2 to 3 minutes). By hand, stir in 1 tablespoon orange-flavored liqueur and vanilla. Spread into greased 12$\frac{1}{2}$-inch removable bottom tart pan. Arrange apple slices around outside edge of surface. Sprinkle apricots, figs, raisins, walnuts and cranberries around and on top of apple slices. Gently press into batter.

In medium bowl stir together all streusel topping ingredients; sprinkle over fruit. Bake for 35 to 45 minutes or until lightly browned.

Meanwhile, in small chilled mixer bowl beat chilled whipping cream at high speed, scraping bowl often, until soft peaks form (1 to 2 minutes). Continue beating, gradually adding $\frac{1}{4}$ cup sugar and orange peel, until stiff peaks form. By hand, fold in 1 tablespoon orange-flavored liqueur. Serve with warm kuchen. **YIELD:** 12 servings.

TIP: Two (9-inch) round cake pans, lined with 12-inch square aluminum foil, leaving excess aluminum foil over edges, greased, can be substituted for 12$\frac{1}{2}$-inch tart pan. Bake for 30 to 35 minutes. Cool in pans 20 minutes. Using aluminum foil, lift out of pan; carefully remove aluminum foil.

*Nutrition Facts (1 serving): Calories 480; Protein 6g; Carbohydrate 57g; Fat 26g; Cholesterol 110mg; Sodium 200mg*

# Rum Hazelnut Fruited Cake

*A rich, moist fruitcake filled with apricots, figs, pears, cherries and raisins, then soaked in rum.*

*Preparation time: 45 minutes • Baking time: 1 hour 5 minutes • Cooling time: 30 minutes • Holding time: 3 days*

$3/4$ cup sugar

$3/4$ cup firmly packed brown sugar

1 cup LAND O LAKES® Butter, softened

3 eggs

2 cups all-purpose flour

$1/2$ cup LAND O LAKES® Sour Cream (Regular, Light or No•Fat)

$3/4$ cup dark rum*

$1/4$ cup light molasses

1 teaspoon baking powder

1 teaspoon baking soda

1 teaspoon cinnamon

1 teaspoon ground nutmeg

2 tablespoons grated orange peel

1 tablespoon grated lemon peel

2 cups coarsely chopped dried apricots

2 cups coarsely chopped hazelnuts

1 cup coarsely chopped dried figs or pitted dates

1 cup halved red candied cherries

1 cup coarsely chopped dried pears

Heat oven to 325°. In large mixer bowl combine sugar, brown sugar and butter. Beat at low speed, scraping bowl often, until creamy (2 to 3 minutes). Continue beating, adding eggs one at a time, until creamy (1 to 2 minutes). Add flour, sour cream, $1/2$ cup rum, molasses, baking powder, baking soda, cinnamon, nutmeg, orange peel and lemon peel. Continue beating, scraping bowl often, until well mixed (1 to 2 minutes). By hand, fold in all remaining ingredients <u>except</u> $1/4$ cup rum. Spread batter into 2 greased and floured 9x5-inch loaf pans. Bake for 55 to 70 minutes or until toothpick inserted in center comes out clean. Cool 30 minutes; remove from pans.

Place remaining $1/4$ cup rum in medium bowl; soak 2 (20-inch) squares of cheesecloth (large enough to completely wrap cakes) in rum. For each fruitcake spread rum-soaked cheesecloth on large sheet of aluminum foil; place cakes in center. Wrap tightly with cheesecloth and aluminum foil. Place in refrigerator to mellow for 3 days; store refrigerated. To serve, slice thinly. **YIELD:** 2 loaves (36 servings).

* $3/4$ cup water plus 2 teaspoons rum extract can be substituted for $3/4$ cup dark rum.

TIP: Fruitcake can be prepared in 8 ($5^1/2$x3-inch) mini loaf pans. Bake for 45 to 55 minutes or until toothpick inserted in center comes out clean.

*Nutrition Facts (1 serving): Calories 240; Protein 3g; Carbohydrate 34g; Fat 10g; Cholesterol 30mg; Sodium 120mg*

# Orange Mint Coffee

*Poured over mint and orange, this pleasing coffee is delicious, iced or hot.*

*Preparation time: 20 minutes • Cooling time: 1 hour • Chilling time: 2 hours*

### Iced Coffee

6 sprigs fresh mint

6 orange slices

10 cups fresh brewed coffee

$2^1/2$ cups vanilla ice cream

### Hot Coffee

6 sprigs fresh mint

6 orange slices

10 cups fresh brewed coffee

Sweetened whipped cream

For Iced Coffee: Place mint and orange slices into large heatproof pitcher; add fresh brewed coffee. Let cool 1 hour. Cover; refrigerate until chilled (about 2 hours). Into each of 6 glasses scoop $1/2$ cup ice cream; pour chilled coffee over ice cream. **YIELD:** 6 servings.

For Hot Coffee: Place 1 sprig of mint and 1 orange slice in each of 6 cups. Pour fresh brewed coffee into each cup. Serve with sweetened whipped cream. If desired, refill cups with additional coffee. **YIELD:** 6 servings.

*Nutrition Facts (1 serving Iced Coffee): Calories 120; Protein 2g; Carbohydrate 15g; Fat 6g; Cholesterol 25mg; Sodium 60mg*

# Eggnog Praline Torte

*Tender hazelnut meringue layers are filled with almond praline candy and a whipped eggnog cream in this luscious cake.*

*Preparation time: 1 hour 15 minutes • Baking time: 30 minutes • Cooling time: 45 minutes • Chilling time: 2 hours*

## Cake
- 1$\frac{1}{2}$ cups hazelnuts <u>or</u> filberts
- $\frac{1}{2}$ cup slivered almonds
- 8 eggs, separated
- 2 egg whites
- 1 cup sugar
- $\frac{1}{3}$ cup fine dried bread crumbs
- 1$\frac{1}{4}$ teaspoons baking powder
- 1 teaspoon ground nutmeg
- $\frac{1}{8}$ teaspoon salt
- 1 teaspoon vanilla

  Powdered sugar

## Praline
- $\frac{3}{4}$ cup sugar
- $\frac{3}{4}$ cup slivered almonds

## Eggnog Whipped Cream
- $\frac{3}{4}$ cup firmly packed brown sugar
- $\frac{1}{2}$ cup prepared eggnog
- 3 cups whipping cream

Heat oven to 325°. Grease 15x10x1-inch jelly roll pan. Line with piece of waxed paper long enough to extend about 1 inch over ends of pan; grease well. Set aside.

In 5-cup blender container or food processor bowl combine hazelnuts and $\frac{1}{2}$ cup almonds. Cover; blend at high speed until finely ground (do not grind into paste). In large mixer bowl beat 10 egg whites at high speed until stiff peaks form (1 to 2 minutes). Transfer to another large bowl; set aside.

In same large mixer bowl beat egg yolks at medium speed until thick and pale yellow (about 4 minutes). Add 1 cup sugar; continue beating until very thick (2 minutes). Reduce speed to low. Add ground nuts, bread crumbs, baking powder, nutmeg, salt and vanilla. Continue beating until well blended. By hand, stir about <u>1 cup</u> beaten egg whites into nut mixture. Gently stir in remaining beaten egg whites just until blended. Spread batter in prepared pan. Bake for 30 to 40 minutes or until golden brown and edges pull away from sides of pan. Lightly sprinkle top of hot cake with powdered sugar. Invert cake onto large clean cloth towel; peel off waxed paper. Cool completely.

Meanwhile, line cookie sheet with aluminum foil. In 10-inch skillet place $\frac{3}{4}$ cup sugar. Cook over medium heat, stirring occasionally, until sugar melts and turns golden brown (about 15 minutes). Quickly stir in $\frac{3}{4}$ cup slivered almonds until well coated. Pour and spread nut mixture onto aluminum foil-lined cookie sheet. Cool completely. Break praline into small pieces, <u>reserving several to use as garnish on cake</u>. In 5-cup blender container or food processor bowl place praline pieces. Cover; blend at high speed until finely ground, but leaving smaller chunks (30 seconds); set aside.

In large mixer bowl stir together brown sugar and eggnog until smooth. Beat at high speed, gradually adding whipping cream, until stiff peaks form (3 to 4 minutes).

To assemble torte cut cake crosswise into four equal (about 10x3$\frac{1}{2}$-inch) strips. Place one cake strip on serving plate. Frost with about <u>$\frac{1}{2}$ cup</u> eggnog whipped cream. Sprinkle with <u>$\frac{1}{3}$ cup</u> ground praline. Repeat stacking layers of cake, eggnog whipped cream and ground praline. Frost top and sides of cake with eggnog whipped cream. Sprinkle top with praline and pipe decorative designs with eggnog whipped cream. Refrigerate at least 2 hours or overnight. Just before serving garnish with reserved praline pieces. Store refrigerated. **YIELD:** 12 servings.

*Nutrition Facts (1 serving): Calories 630; Protein 11g; Carbohydrate 54g; Fat 43g; Cholesterol 230mg; Sodium 160mg*

*Eggnog Praline Torte*

# Holiday Fruited Pound Cake

*The traditional flavors of the holiday season are to be enjoyed in this rich butter cake.*

*Preparation time: 25 minutes • Baking time: 1 hour • Cooling time: 1 hour 30 minutes*

### Cake

| | |
|---|---|
| 1½ | cups sugar |
| 1 | cup LAND O LAKES® Butter, softened |
| 4 | ounces cream cheese, softened |
| 6 | eggs |
| 1 | tablespoon grated orange peel |
| 1 | tablespoon vanilla |
| 1 | teaspoon brandy extract |
| 1 | teaspoon rum extract |
| 3 | cups all-purpose flour |
| ½ | teaspoon baking powder |
| ½ | cup green candied cherries, coarsely chopped |
| ½ | cup red candied cherries, coarsely chopped |
| ½ | cup raisins |

### Glaze

| | |
|---|---|
| ¾ | cup powdered sugar |
| ½ | teaspoon rum extract |
| 3 to 4 | teaspoons milk |

### Garnish

Green and red candied cherries, if desired

Heat oven to 350°. In large mixer bowl combine sugar, butter and cream cheese. Beat at medium speed, scraping bowl often, until creamy (2 to 3 minutes). Add eggs, orange peel, vanilla, brandy extract and 1 teaspoon rum extract. Continue beating, scraping bowl often, until well mixed (2 to 3 minutes). Reduce speed to low; add flour and baking powder. Continue beating, scraping bowl often, until well mixed (2 to 3 minutes). By hand, stir in ½ cup green cherries, ½ cup red cherries and raisins. Spoon into greased and floured 12-cup Bundt or 10-inch tube pan. Bake for 60 to 70 minutes or until toothpick inserted in center comes out clean. Cool 10 minutes; remove from pan. Cool completely.

In small bowl combine powdered sugar, ½ teaspoon rum extract and enough milk for desired glazing consistency. Drizzle over cooled cake. Garnish with green and red cherries. **YIELD:** 16 servings.

*Nutrition Facts (1 serving): Calories 390; Protein 5g; Carbohydrate 59g; Fat 16g; Cholesterol 110mg; Sodium 220mg*

# Cranberry Apple Cobbler

*Sugar glazed cranberries and apples peek through a sweet, crisp cobbler topping.*

*Preparation time: 30 minutes • Baking time: 40 minutes*

### Cobbler

| | |
|---|---|
| ½ | cup all-purpose flour |
| ½ | cup sugar |
| ½ | cup firmly packed brown sugar |
| ½ | teaspoon cinnamon |
| ½ | teaspoon ground nutmeg |
| 2 | cups fresh or frozen whole cranberries, thawed |
| 4 | medium (4 cups) tart cooking apples, peeled, cored, sliced ¼-inch |

### Crumb Topping

| | |
|---|---|
| ⅔ | cup all-purpose flour |
| ½ | cup sugar |
| ½ | cup LAND O LAKES® Butter Vanilla |
| 4 | cups vanilla ice cream |

Heat oven to 400°. In large bowl combine all cobbler ingredients <u>except</u> cranberries and apples. Add cranberries and apples; toss to coat with flour mixture. Place in 2-quart casserole.

In medium bowl stir together ⅔ cup flour and ½ cup sugar; cut in butter until crumbly. Sprinkle over fruit mixture. Bake for 40 to 45 minutes or until golden brown. Serve warm with ice cream. **YIELD:** 8 servings.

*Nutrition Facts (1 serving): Calories 500; Protein 5g; Carbohydrate 79g; Fat 19g; Cholesterol 60mg; Sodium 180mg*

*Holiday Fruited Pound Cake*

# Raspberry Filled Tarts

*Raspberry preserves fill these lemon-flavored pastries.*

*Preparation time: 1 hour • Baking time: 11 minutes*

2¾ cups all-purpose flour
1 cup LAND O LAKES®
    Butter, softened
1 cup LAND O LAKES®
    Sour Cream (Regular,
    Light or No•Fat)
2 tablespoons grated lemon
    peel

1 cup raspberry preserves*

Powdered sugar, if desired

Heat oven to 400°. In large mixer bowl combine 1 cup flour, butter, sour cream and lemon peel. Beat at medium speed, scraping bowl often, until well mixed (2 to 3 minutes). By hand, stir in remaining flour until well mixed. On well floured surface roll out dough, one third at a time, to 12x9-inch rectangle. With sharp knife, cut into 12 (3-inch) squares. Place squares on cookie sheets. Repeat with remaining dough. Place about 1 teaspoonful preserves in center of each square. Bring together 4 corners of each square and pinch to hold together. Bake for 11 to 14 minutes or until lightly browned. Cool completely; sprinkle with powdered sugar. **YIELD:** 3 dozen.

*1 cup your favorite flavor preserves can be substituted for 1 cup raspberry preserves.

*Nutrition Facts (1 tart): Calories 110; Protein 1g; Carbohydrate 14g;
Fat 6g; Cholesterol 15mg; Sodium 60mg*

---

# Frozen Lemon Souffle With Sparkling Strawberry Sauce

*This tangy lemon fluff is a breeze to mix up and can be done ahead. Garnish with
candied lemon peel, whipped cream and a drizzle of strawberry sauce sparkling with champagne.*

*Preparation time: 20 minutes • Freezing time: 12 hours • Chilling time: 30 minutes*

**Strawberry Sauce**
1 (10-ounce) package frozen
    loose pack strawberries,
    thawed
3 tablespoons powdered
    sugar
⅓ cup champagne or
    sparkling catawba juice, if
    desired

**Souffle**
1 (8-ounce) package cream
    cheese, softened
1 (14-ounce) can sweetened
    condensed milk
1 (6-ounce) can frozen
    lemonade concentrate,
    thawed
2 to 3 drops yellow food coloring
1½ cups whipping cream

**Garnish**
    Whipped cream,
      if desired
    Lemon slices, if desired

In 5-cup blender container or food processor bowl combine all sauce ingredients. Cover; blend at high speed until smooth (30 to 45 seconds). Cover; refrigerate until ready to serve.

In large mixer bowl beat cream cheese at low speed until fluffy. Continue beating, gradually adding sweetened condensed milk, lemonade and food coloring, until smooth (2 to 3 minutes). In chilled small mixer bowl beat 1½ cups chilled whipping cream at high speed, scraping bowl often, until stiff peaks form (1 to 2 minutes). By hand, fold whipped cream into lemonade mixture. Spoon lemonade mixture into 1½-quart souffle dish or bowl. Cover; freeze at least 12 hours or up to 3 days.

Place in refrigerator 30 minutes before serving. Garnish with additional whipped cream and lemon slices. Serve with Strawberry Sauce. **YIELD:** 10 servings (2⅓ cups sauce).

TIP: To keep souffle firm while on a buffet table, fill punch bowl with crushed ice; set souffle dish on top of ice in punch bowl.

*Nutrition Facts (1 serving): Calories 440; Protein 7g; Carbohydrate 46g;
Fat 26g; Cholesterol 90mg; Sodium 150mg*

*Raspberry Filled Tarts*

# Gingerbread With Fruited Compote

*Winter fruits simmer with fresh gingerroot for a warm accompaniment to this moist gingerbread.*

*Preparation time: 45 minutes • Baking time: 30 minutes • Standing time: 15 minutes*

## Gingerbread
1 3/4 cups all-purpose flour
1/3 cup firmly packed brown sugar
1/2 cup LAND O LAKES® Butter, softened
1/2 cup light molasses
1/2 cup buttermilk*
1 egg
1 teaspoon baking soda
1/2 teaspoon salt
1/4 teaspoon ground cloves
1/4 teaspoon ground nutmeg
2 teaspoons finely chopped fresh gingerroot**
1 teaspoon grated lemon peel

## Fruit Compote
2 tablespoons LAND O LAKES® Butter
1 large (1 1/2 cups) tart cooking apple, sliced 1/8-inch
1 large (1 1/2 cups) ripe pear, sliced 1/8-inch
1/2 cup orange marmalade
2 teaspoons grated lemon peel
1 teaspoon finely chopped fresh gingerroot***
1 teaspoon lemon juice
1 seedless orange, pared, sectioned

Heat oven to 350°. In large mixer bowl combine all gingerbread ingredients. Beat at low speed, scraping bowl often, until well mixed (1 to 2 minutes). Pour into greased and floured 9-inch round cake pan. Bake for 30 to 40 minutes or until top springs back when touched lightly in center. Let stand 15 minutes.

Meanwhile, in 2-quart saucepan melt 2 tablespoons butter; add all remaining fruit compote ingredients except orange sections. Cook over medium heat, stirring occasionally, until fruit is tender (3 to 4 minutes). (Compote sauce will be thin.) Stir in orange sections. Serve over warm gingerbread. **YIELD:** 9 servings.

\* 1 1/2 teaspoons vinegar plus enough milk to equal 1/2 cup can be substituted for 1/2 cup buttermilk.

\*\* 1/2 teaspoon ground ginger can be substituted for 2 teaspoons finely chopped fresh gingerroot.

\*\*\* 1/4 teaspoon ground ginger can be substituted for 1 teaspoon finely chopped fresh gingerroot.

*Nutrition Facts (1 serving): Calories 370; Protein 4g; Carbohydrate 59g; Fat 14g; Cholesterol 60mg; Sodium 410mg*

*Gingerbread With Fruited Compote*

# Gingersnap Pumpkin Cream Tart

*A light and creamy pumpkin filling tops a crunchy gingersnap crust.*

*Preparation time: 20 minutes • Baking time: 12 minutes • Cooling time: 30 minutes • Chilling time: 3 hours*

## Crust

1½  cups crushed gingersnap
      cookies
¼   cup sugar
¼   cup chopped pecans
⅓   cup LAND O LAKES®
      Butter, melted

## Filling

1   cup powdered sugar
1   (8-ounce) package cream
    cheese
1   cup cooked pumpkin
1   teaspoon cinnamon
¼   teaspoon ground nutmeg
¼   teaspoon ground ginger
½   teaspoon vanilla
1   cup whipping cream

Heat oven to 350°. In medium bowl stir together all crust ingredients until well mixed. Reserve 3 tablespoons for topping. Press mixture on bottom and up side of 10-inch tart pan. Bake for 12 to 15 minutes. Cool completely.

Meanwhile, in large mixer bowl combine all filling ingredients except whipping cream. Beat at medium speed, scraping bowl often, until light and fluffy (1 to 2 minutes). Continue beating, gradually adding whipping cream, until mixture is thick and fluffy (2 to 3 minutes). Spread filling over cooled crust. Sprinkle with reserved 3 tablespoons crust mixture. Refrigerate until set (at least 3 hours). **YIELD:** 12 servings.

*Nutrition Facts (1 serving): Calories 310; Protein 3g; Carbohydrate 27g;
Fat 22g; Cholesterol 70mg; Sodium 200mg*

*Gingersnap Pumpkin Cream Tart*

# Chocolate-Marbled Almond Cheesecake

*This rich, dark chocolate-marbled cheesecake, on an almond crust,*
*was meant for those with a passion for chocolate.*

*Preparation time: 30 minutes • Baking time: 3 hours 5 minutes • Cooling time: 1 hour • Chilling time: 8 hours*

2 cups sugar

4 (8-ounce) packages cream cheese, softened

4 eggs

1 cup LAND O LAKES® Sour Cream (Regular, Light or No•Fat)

1 tablespoon unsweetened cocoa

2 teaspoons vanilla

1 teaspoon almond extract

1 (12-ounce) package semi-sweet real chocolate chips, melted

1 (2-ounce) package (1/2 cup) blanched almonds, finely chopped

Chocolate and white chocolate leaves, if desired

Heat oven to 325°. In large mixer bowl combine sugar and cream cheese. Beat at medium speed, scraping bowl often, until light and creamy (3 to 4 minutes). Continue beating, adding eggs one at a time, until well mixed (1 to 2 minutes). Add all remaining ingredients except chocolate chips and almonds. Continue beating, scraping bowl often, until well mixed (1 to 2 minutes). By hand, gently stir in melted chocolate chips to swirl chocolate throughout batter for marbled effect. Lightly butter 9-inch springform pan; press almonds firmly on bottom of pan. Pour batter into prepared pan. Bake for 65 to 75 minutes or until just set 2 inches from edge of pan. Turn off oven; leave cheesecake in oven for 2 hours. Loosen side of cheesecake from pan by running knife around inside of pan. Cool completely. Cover; refrigerate 8 hours or overnight. Garnish with chocolate and white chocolate leaves. Store refrigerated. **YIELD:** 12 servings.

*Nutrition Facts (1 serving): Calories 610; Protein 11g; Carbohydrate 55g;*
*Fat 42g; Cholesterol 160mg; Sodium 260mg*

# Chocolate Mousse Squares

*Mousse-like dessert that's easy enough to prepare for a large group.*

*Preparation time: 30 minutes • Chilling time: 6 hours*

2 cups (about 24) finely crushed chocolate sandwich cookies

1/3 cup LAND O LAKES® Butter, melted

2 cups powdered sugar

1 cup LAND O LAKES® Butter, softened

1 (8-ounce) package cream cheese, softened

4 (1-ounce) squares unsweetened baking chocolate, melted, cooled

1 cup refrigerated pasteurized liquid eggs

2 teaspoons vanilla

1 cup flaked coconut

1 cup chopped walnuts

1 1/2 cups whipping cream

In medium bowl stir together crushed cookies and 1/3 cup melted butter. Reserve 1/4 cup crumb mixture; set aside.

Press remaining crumb mixture on bottom of 13x9-inch pan. In large mixer bowl combine powdered sugar, 1 cup butter, cream cheese, chocolate, eggs and vanilla. Beat at medium speed, scraping bowl often, until smooth and fluffy (2 to 3 minutes). By hand, stir in coconut and walnuts. In chilled small mixer bowl beat chilled whipping cream at high speed, scraping bowl often, until soft peaks form. Gently stir into chocolate mixture; pour over crumb crust. Sprinkle with reserved 1/4 cup crumb mixture. Cover; refrigerate until set (at least 6 hours). Cut into squares. Store refrigerated. **YIELD:** 15 servings.

*Nutrition Facts (1 serving): Calories 540; Protein 6g; Carbohydrate 32g;*
*Fat 46g; Cholesterol 110mg; Sodium 330mg*

*Chocolate-Marbled Almond Cheesecake*

# Chocolate Fondue

*Try the caramel raspberry or peanut butter variations*
*of this fondue — dip fresh strawberries, bananas or pound cake.*

*Preparation time: 35 minutes • Cooking time: 30 minutes*

## Choco-Caramel-Raspberry

1  (12-ounce) package (2 cups) semi-sweet real chocolate chips
1  (14-ounce) package caramels, unwrapped
1  (12-ounce) can evaporated milk
½  cup LAND O LAKES® Butter
½  cup seedless raspberry preserves

## Choco-Peanut

1  (12-ounce) package (2 cups) semi-sweet real chocolate chips
1  (10-ounce) package (1¾ cups) peanut butter-flavored chips
1  (12-ounce) can evaporated milk
½  cup LAND O LAKES® Butter

Cubed pound cake, angel food cake and/or cut-up fresh fruit

In 2-quart saucepan combine all ingredients for desired flavor. Cook over low heat, stirring occasionally, until melted and smooth (30 to 35 minutes for Choco-Caramel-Raspberry; 20 to 25 minutes for Choco-Peanut). Pour fondue into fondue pot, chafing dish or small crockery cooker and keep warm. Serve pound cake, angel food cake and/or fresh fruit to dip in fondue. **YIELD:** 4 cups.

*Nutrition Facts (1 tablespoon Choco-Caramel-Raspberry): Calories 80; Protein 1g; Carbohydrate 10g; Fat 4g; Cholesterol 5mg; Sodium 35mg*

*Chocolate Fondue*

# Pumpkin Cheesecake With Gingersnaps

*A dollop of nutmeg-sprinkled whipped cream and a gingersnap cookie garnish this rich, moist cheesecake.*

*Preparation time: 30 minutes • Baking time: 1 hour 20 minutes • Cooling time: 1 hour • Chilling time: 8 hours*

## Crust

- 1/3 cup crushed gingersnap cookies
- 1 tablespoon LAND O LAKES® Butter, melted

## Cheesecake

- 2 cups firmly packed brown sugar
- 4 (8-ounce) packages cream cheese, softened
- 4 eggs
- 1 (16-ounce) can pumpkin
- 1 1/2 teaspoons cinnamon
- 1 teaspoon ground nutmeg
- 1/4 teaspoon ground cloves
- 1/4 teaspoon ground ginger

## Garnish

- Sweetened whipped cream, if desired
- Ground nutmeg, if desired
- 16 (1 1/2-inch) gingersnap cookies

Heat oven to 325°. In small bowl stir together crushed gingersnap cookies and melted butter; sprinkle on bottom of 9-inch springform pan (will just lightly coat bottom).

In large mixer bowl combine brown sugar and cream cheese. Beat at medium speed, scraping bowl often, until creamy (3 to 4 minutes). Continue beating, adding eggs one at a time, until creamy (1 to 2 minutes). Add all remaining cheesecake ingredients. Continue beating, scraping bowl often, until well mixed (1 to 2 minutes). Pour batter into prepared pan. Bake for 1 hour 20 minutes to 1 hour 40 minutes or until set. Turn off oven; leave cheesecake in oven for 2 hours. Loosen side of cheesecake from pan by running knife around inside of pan. Cool completely.

Cover; refrigerate 8 hours or overnight. Store refrigerated. To serve, pipe sweetened whipped cream on each serving; sprinkle with nutmeg. Garnish with gingersnaps. **YIELD:** 16 servings.

*Nutrition Facts (1 serving): Calories 350; Protein 6g; Carbohydrate 32g; Fat 22g; Cholesterol 120mg; Sodium 210mg*

# Garnishing Desserts

To make desserts dazzle, your recipes need to do more than just taste great, they must look special too. An attractive garnish will enhance the appearance and add that extra special touch. A garnish can be as simple as fresh mint leaves or raspberries, or as ornate as an intricate caramel filigree. Choose a garnish that complements or reflects the flavors in your dessert. Be careful not to go overboard with garnishes. Following are some suggestions that will dress up your desserts for any occasion.

◆ Pipe whipped cream or frosting with a pastry bag or resealable plastic food bag. After filling plastic food bag, take care to snip off only one small corner for piping.

◆ Flavor 1 cup whipped cream with $1/2$ teaspoon extract or 1 tablespoon liqueur and dollop or pipe onto pies, cakes, tortes, cheesecakes, etc.

◆ Chocolate Curls—warm a bar or block of chocolate or white chocolate in microwave on HIGH until slightly warm (10 to 30 seconds). Using even pressure, pull vegetable peeler across chocolate. (Pressure will determine thickness.) Refrigerate until firm.

◆ Use cookie cutters as stencils and fill design with jelly or candy sprinkles to decorate frosted cakes.

◆ Place paper doily over unfrosted spice, gingerbread or chocolate cake. Sift powdered sugar over doily, then carefully lift off. Cocoa powder can be substituted for powdered sugar for white or yellow cakes.

◆ To make caramel filigree, heat $1/4$ cup sugar in a heavy saucepan over medium heat, stirring constantly, until sugar melts. Remove from heat. Using a fork, drizzle melted sugar onto waxed paper-lined pan forming a web. Be careful, because sugar is very hot! When cool carefully remove waxed paper. Place on cake.

◆ To make a strawberry fan, cut strawberry into slices starting at tip and ending close to stem, but not cutting all the way through. Spread slices into fan shape. Use to garnish desserts.

◆ Caramelize nuts by melting 2 table-spoons sugar in an 8-inch skillet over low heat. Stir in $1/4$ cup nuts such as slivered almonds or pecan halves. Continue cooking, stirring constantly, until coated and golden brown. Remove nuts to waxed paper and let cool. Break apart and use to garnish.

◆ Pull a knife or fork tines though frosting on top and/or sides of cake or torte to create a design.

# Gifts

*Enjoy this special time of year by sharing homemade gifts of food. Included in this treasury of delicious foods are Triple Nut Chocolate Butter Toffee, Cranberry Maple Walnut Pound Cake and Sugar & Spice Assorted Nuts.*

*Chocolate Mint Mallow Cups, see page 124; Decadent Chocolate Ganache, see page 125; Swirled Chocolate Spoons, see page 125*

# Chocolate Mint Mallow Cups

*A little extra time is needed for these individual mint delights, but everyone will praise the results.*

*Preparation time: 45 minutes • Cooking time: 13 minutes • Chilling time: 3 hours 30 minutes*

1 (6-ounce) package (1 cup) semi-sweet real chocolate chips
8 paper baking cups

$^1/_2$ cup milk
24 large marshmallows
$^1/_8$ teaspoon salt
1 teaspoon vanilla
$^1/_8$ teaspoon peppermint extract
6 drops red food coloring
1 cup ($^1/_2$ pint) whipping cream
$^1/_3$ cup crushed starlight peppermint candies, reserve 1 tablespoon

In 1-quart saucepan melt chocolate chips over low heat, stirring occasionally, until chips are melted (4 to 5 minutes). Place 8 paper baking cups in muffin pan. With pastry brush coat inside of each cup evenly with melted chocolate, about $^1/_8$ inch thick, bringing coating almost to top of cup but not over edge. Refrigerate until firm (at least 30 minutes).

Meanwhile, in 2-quart saucepan combine milk and marshmallows. Cook over low heat, stirring occasionally, until marshmallows are melted (9 to 12 minutes). Remove from heat; stir in salt, vanilla, peppermint extract and red food coloring. Refrigerate until mixture mounds slightly when dropped from a spoon (about 1 hour).

Meanwhile, in chilled mixer bowl beat chilled whipping cream at high speed, scraping bowl often, until stiff peaks form. Stir marshmallow mixture until smooth. Fold marshmallow mixture and crushed peppermint candies into whipped cream. Spoon about $^1/_3$ cup marshmallow whipped cream mixture into each chocolate cup. Refrigerate until set (at least 2 hours).

Carefully remove paper liners from chocolate cups. To serve, sprinkle with reserved 1 tablespoon crushed candies. Store refrigerated. **YIELD:** 8 servings.

Microwave Directions: In small bowl microwave chocolate chips on HIGH, stirring every 30 seconds, until chips are melted (1$^1/_2$ to 2$^1/_2$ minutes). Prepare chocolate cups as directed above. In medium bowl microwave milk and marshmallows on HIGH, stirring every minute, until marshmallows are melted (1$^1/_2$ to 2$^1/_2$ minutes). Continue as directed above.

TIP: Use silver or gold foil baking cups for a more festive appearance.

*Nutrition Facts (1 serving): Calories 300; Protein 2g; Carbohydrate 35g; Fat 19g; Cholesterol 40mg; Sodium 60mg*

# Decadent Chocolate Ganache

*A versatile recipe for chocolate lovers! Serve this thick spread on
pound cake or shortbread, use as a cake filling or heat and pour over ice cream.*

*Preparation time: 15 minutes • Chilling time: 2 hours*

8 ounces high quality semi-
   sweet real chocolate, very
   finely chopped
3 tablespoons
   LAND O LAKES®
   Butter, softened
6 tablespoons whipping
   cream
1 to 2 tablespoons liqueur
   (hazelnut, almond,
   orange, coffee or mint)*

In medium bowl stir together chocolate and butter. In 2-quart saucepan heat whipping cream over low heat until very hot but not boiling (5 to 6 minutes). Remove from heat. Stir chocolate mixture into whipping cream until smooth. Stir in liqueur. Pour ganache into one or two small containers or decorative crocks. Cover; refrigerate at least 2 hours before serving. If refrigerated longer, before serving let stand at room temperature until spreading consistency (about 1 hour). Store airtight in refrigerator for up to 6 weeks. Serve as a spread on pound cake or cookies, use as a filling for cakes or heat and serve over ice cream. **YIELD:** $1^1/3$ cups.

\* 1 teaspoon mint, brandy or rum extract can be substituted for 1 to 2 tablespoons liqueur.

*Nutrition Facts (1 tablespoon): Calories 90; Protein 4g; Carbohydrate 7g;
Fat 7g; Cholesterol 10mg; Sodium 20mg*

# Swirled Chocolate Spoons

*Make these chocolate spoons for someone special to eat or to stir into hot coffee. By dipping spoons in white and
dark chocolate, a marbled effect can be achieved. Be sure to use good quality chocolate.*

*Preparation time: 30 minutes • Standing time: 3 hours*

  Water
6 ounces high quality semi-
   sweet real chocolate,
   chopped
$^1/2$ cup vanilla milk chips*
12 heavy plastic spoons

  Colored cellophane and
   ribbon, if desired

In 10-inch skillet place 1 inch water; bring to a full boil. Reduce heat to low. In 2-cup measure place semi-sweet chocolate; place in skillet. In 1-cup measure place vanilla milk chips; place in skillet. Stir chocolate and vanilla milk chips constantly until melted and smooth (5 to 10 minutes). Remove from skillet. Making one spoon at a time, dip spoon into semi-sweet chocolate, just coating front and back of bowl of spoon. Drizzle about 1 teaspoon melted vanilla milk chips on front of spoon bowl. Using toothpick, swirl together to create marbled look. Set spoons on waxed paper-lined cookie sheet. Let stand at room temperature until set (2 to 3 hours). Wrap each spoon in cellophane and tie with ribbon. **YIELD:** 12 spoons.

\* 3 ounces white chocolate, chopped, can be substituted for $^1/2$ cup vanilla milk chips.

TIP: Semi-sweet chocolate and vanilla milk chips can be melted in microwave.
   Place in 2-cup measures. Microwave on HIGH 1 minute. Stir vigorously until smooth.

TIP: Eat the chocolate right off the spoons or stir into hot coffee or cocoa.

*Nutrition Facts (1 serving): Calories 110; Protein 1g; Carbohydrate 12g;
Fat 7g; Cholesterol 5mg; Sodium 5mg*

# Chocolate Chip & Almond Caramel Corn

*This chocolate caramel corn is so good it's almost addictive.*

*Preparation time: 20 minutes • Baking time: 45 minutes*

3 quarts (12 cups) popped popcorn
1 cup firmly packed brown sugar
1/3 cup sugar
3/4 cup LAND O LAKES® Butter
1/2 cup light corn syrup
1/2 teaspoon baking soda
1/2 teaspoon vanilla
1/2 cup toasted slivered almonds, chopped
1 (12-ounce) package (2 cups) semi-sweet chocolate chips*

Heat oven to 250°. Spray 2 (13x9-inch) baking pans with no stick cooking spray. Divide popcorn between pans. In 3-quart saucepan combine brown sugar, sugar, butter and corn syrup. Cook over medium high heat, stirring occasionally, until mixture comes to a full boil (7 to 9 minutes). Reduce heat to medium low. Continue cooking, without stirring, until candy thermometer reaches 234°F or small amount of mixture dropped into ice water forms a soft ball (4 to 6 minutes). (If heat is too high, sugar will scorch; too low and sugar will not caramelize.)

Remove from heat; stir in baking soda and vanilla. Pour caramel mixture over popcorn in both pans. Sprinkle nuts evenly over both pans. Sprinkle each pan with 1/2 cup chocolate chips. Stir popcorn to coat kernels with caramel. Bake 45 minutes, stirring every 15 minutes. Immediately place caramel corn on waxed paper. Sprinkle evenly with remaining chocolate chips. Cool completely. Break into pieces. Store in airtight containers. **YIELD:** 15 cups.

\* 1 (11 1/2-ounce) package (2 cups) milk chocolate chips can be substituted for 1 (12-ounce) package (2 cups) semi-sweet chocolate chips.

*Nutrition Facts (1/2 cup): Calories 160; Protein 1g; Carbohydrate 21g; Fat 9g; Cholesterol 10mg; Sodium 70mg*

# Coconut Candies

*Cut out fun shaped candies and decorate with candy coating, or roll candies into balls and dip into candy coating.*

*Preparation time: 1 hour • Chilling time: 1 hour*

**Candy**
2 1/2 cups powdered sugar
2 cups shredded coconut
1/2 cup cold plain mashed potatoes (no salt, butter or milk)
1 teaspoon almond extract
1/2 teaspoon vanilla

**Decorations**
Chocolate or vanilla candy coating, melted
Prepared frosting

In large mixer bowl combine all candy ingredients. Beat at low speed, scraping bowl often, until well mixed (2 to 3 minutes). Press coconut mixture onto waxed paper or parchment-lined 15x10x1-inch jelly roll pan. Roll flat and even with rolling pin. Cover; freeze 1 hour.

Remove from freezer; invert onto surface lightly dusted with powdered sugar. With 1 1/2 to 2-inch assorted cookie cutters, cut into desired shapes or roll into 1-inch balls. Dip candies into or decorate with melted candy coating. Decorate with frosting. Store frozen. **YIELD:** 15 candies.

*Nutrition Facts (1 candy): Calories 130; Protein 0g; Carbohydrate 26g; Fat 3g; Cholesterol 0mg; Sodium 25mg*

*Chocolate Chip & Almond Caramel Corn, see page 126; Coconut Candies, see page 126; Triple Nut Chocolate Butter Toffee, see page 128*

# Buttery Pistachio Brittle

*This buttery candy makes a great holiday gift.*

*Preparation time: 10 minutes • Cooking time: 1 hour 30 minutes*

2 cups sugar
1 cup light corn syrup
$1/2$ cup water
1 cup LAND O LAKES® Butter
2 cups salted pistachio nuts
1 teaspoon baking soda

In 3-quart saucepan combine sugar, corn syrup and water. Cook over low heat, stirring occasionally, until sugar is dissolved and mixture comes to a full boil (15 to 25 minutes). Add butter. Continue cooking, stirring occasionally, until candy thermometer reaches 280°F or small amount of mixture dropped into ice water forms a pliable strand (60 to 80 minutes).

Stir in pistachios. Continue cooking, stirring constantly, until candy thermometer reaches 305°F or small amount of mixture dropped into ice water forms a brittle strand (15 to 20 minutes).

Remove from heat; stir in baking soda. Pour mixture onto 2 buttered cookie sheets; spread about $1/4$ inch thick. Cool completely; break into pieces. **YIELD:** 2 pounds (6 dozen pieces).

*Nutrition Facts (1 piece): Calories 80; Protein <1g; Carbohydrate 10g; Fat 4g; Cholesterol 5mg; Sodium 45mg*

# Triple Nut Chocolate Butter Toffee

*Just the right recipe for a true candy lover!*

*Preparation time: 10 minutes • Cooking time: 30 minutes • Cooling time: 1 hour*

$1^1/2$ cups real milk chocolate chips
$1^1/2$ cups semi-sweet real chocolate chips
$1/4$ cup chopped almonds, toasted
$1/4$ cup chopped pecans, toasted
$1/4$ cup chopped walnuts, toasted
2 cups sugar
2 cups LAND O LAKES® Butter
$1/2$ cup water
1 teaspoon salt
2 teaspoons vanilla

Butter 13x9-inch pan; line with parchment paper or waxed paper. Butter paper. Sprinkle $3/4$ cup milk chocolate chips, $3/4$ cup semi-sweet chocolate chips, 2 tablespoons almonds, 2 tablespoons pecans and 2 tablespoons walnuts over parchment paper; set aside.

In Dutch oven combine sugar, butter, water and salt. Cook over medium high heat, stirring constantly, until mixture comes to a full boil (10 to 12 minutes). Boil, stirring often, until candy thermometer reaches 305°F or small amount of mixture dropped into ice water forms hard brittle strands (20 to 25 minutes).

Remove from heat; stir in vanilla. Pour into prepared pan. Immediately sprinkle with remaining almonds, pecans and walnuts; with knife swirl into toffee. Sprinkle remaining milk chocolate chips and semi-sweet chocolate chips evenly over toffee, pressing gently into toffee. Cool completely. (Refrigerate to speed cooling process, if desired.) Break into pieces. **YIELD:** $3^1/2$ pounds (5 dozen pieces).

*Nutrition Facts (1 piece): Calories 130; Protein 1g; Carbohydrate 12g; Fat 9g; Cholesterol 20mg; Sodium 100mg*

*Swirled Chocolate Spoons, see page 125; Homemade Caramel Sauce, see page 141; Festive Julekage, see page 140; Buttery Pistachio Brittle, see page 128; Buttery Butterscotch Cutouts, see page 12; Chocolate Cherry Snowballs, see page 14*

# Mascarpone Fudge With Almond

*Rich and creamy mascarpone cheese gives a satin-like texture to this holiday favorite.*

*Preparation time: 20 minutes • Cooking time: 30 minutes • Chilling time: 2 hours*

6 cups sugar
1 cup LAND O LAKES® Butter
1 (12-ounce) can evaporated milk
1 (8-ounce) tub mascarpone cheese*
1 (11$^1$/2-ounce) package (2 cups) real milk chocolate chips**
1 (12-ounce) package (2 cups) semi-sweet real chocolate chips***
4 ounces bittersweet chocolate
1 (13-ounce) jar marshmallow creme
1 tablespoon almond extract
1 tablespoon vanilla

In Dutch oven combine sugar, butter, evaporated milk and mascarpone cheese. Cook over medium heat, stirring with wire whisk often, until mixture comes to a full boil (20 to 30 minutes). Boil, stirring constantly, until candy thermometer reaches 234°F or small amount of mixture dropped into ice water forms a soft ball (10 to 13 minutes).

Remove from heat; whisk in all chocolate and marshmallow creme. Beat until smooth and glossy. Stir in almond extract and vanilla. Pour into buttered 15x10x1-inch jelly roll pan. Refrigerate until firm (at least 2 hours). Cut into pieces. Store refrigerated. **YIELD:** 150 pieces.

* 1 (8-ounce) package cream cheese can be substituted for 1 (8-ounce) tub mascarpone cheese.

** 12 ounces real milk chocolate, coarsely chopped, can be substituted for 1 (11$^1$/2-ounce) package (2 cups) real milk chocolate chips.

***12 ounces semi-sweet real chocolate can be substituted for 1 (12-ounce) package (2 cups) semi-sweet real chocolate chips.

*Nutrition Facts (1 piece): Calories 80; Protein 1g; Carbohydrate 13g; Fat 4g; Cholesterol 5mg; Sodium 25mg*

# Sugar & Spice Assorted Nuts

*Sugar and spice and everything nice — that's what these nuts are!*

*Preparation time: 10 minutes • Cooking time: 8 minutes • Cooling time: 30 minutes*

$^1$/4 cup LAND O LAKES® Butter
1 cup blanched whole almonds
1 cup pecan halves
1 cup walnut halves
$^1$/2 cup sugar

3 tablespoons sugar
1 tablespoon cinnamon
$^1$/2 teaspoon ground ginger
$^1$/2 teaspoon ground nutmeg
$^1$/4 teaspoon ground cardamom

In 10-inch skillet melt butter; stir in almonds, pecans, walnuts and $^1$/2 cup sugar. Cook over medium heat, stirring occasionally, until sugar is melted and nuts are browned (8 to 12 minutes).

Meanwhile, in large bowl combine all remaining ingredients. Stir in nuts. Spread on waxed paper; cool completely (30 minutes). Break into pieces. Store in tightly covered container. **YIELD:** 3 cups (24 servings).

*Nutrition Facts (1 serving): Calories 140; Protein 2g; Carbohydrate 8g; Fat 10g; Cholesterol 10mg; Sodium 20mg*

*Mascarpone Fudge With Almond*

# Almond Filled Stollens

*This German holiday specialty is great sliced and toasted, then served with butter.*

*Preparation time: 50 minutes • Rising time: 2 hours 15 minutes • Baking time: 35 minutes • Cooling time: 1 hour*

## Stollen

- 4 (¼-ounce) packages quick-rise active dry yeast
- ½ cup warm water (105 to 115°F)
- 1 teaspoon sugar
- 5 to 6 cups all-purpose flour
- ½ cup sugar
- 1½ cups LAND O LAKES® Butter, softened
- 1 cup LAND O LAKES® Sour Cream (Regular, Light or No•Fat)
- 3 egg yolks
- 1 teaspoon salt
- 1 tablespoon grated lemon peel
- 2 teaspoons lemon juice
- 2 teaspoons almond extract
- 1 teaspoon vanilla
- 1½ cups currants or raisins
- 1 cup candied fruit mix
- ⅓ cup dried cranberries or dried cherries
- 3 tablespoons brandy, almond-flavored liqueur or apple juice
- ½ cup chopped almonds, toasted

## Filling

- 1 (7-ounce) tube almond paste
- 3 tablespoons LAND O LAKES® Butter, softened
- ½ cup chopped almonds, toasted

## Glaze

- 1 egg
- 1 teaspoon sugar
- 1 tablespoon milk

- 1 tablespoon powdered sugar

In large mixer bowl dissolve yeast in warm water; stir in 1 teaspoon sugar. Add 2 cups flour, ½ cup sugar, 1½ cups butter, sour cream, egg yolks, salt, lemon peel, lemon juice, almond extract and vanilla. Beat at medium speed, scraping bowl often, until smooth (1 to 2 minutes). By hand, stir in enough remaining flour to make dough easy to handle. Turn dough onto well floured surface; knead until smooth and elastic (8 to 10 minutes). Place in greased bowl; turn greased side up. Cover; let rise in warm place until double in size (about 1½ hours). Dough is ready if indentation remains when touched. Punch down dough.

Meanwhile, in medium bowl combine currants, candied fruit mix and cranberries. Pour brandy over fruit; let stand 15 minutes.

Place dough on lightly floured surface. Knead fruit and brandy mixture and ½ cup almonds into dough just until fruit is thoroughly distributed. Divide dough in half. On lightly floured surface roll out half into 14x10-inch oval approximately ½ inch thick.

In small bowl stir together almond paste and 3 tablespoons butter. Spread half of mixture lengthwise on half of oval. Sprinkle with ¼ cup almonds; press into filling. Fold oval lengthwise so top edge is within 1 inch from bottom edge. Pinch edges gently to seal. Place on greased cookie sheet. Repeat with remaining dough. Cover; let rise 45 minutes. (Stollens will not double in size.)

Heat oven to 350°. In small bowl, with fork, beat together all glaze ingredients except powdered sugar; brush on stollens. Bake for 35 to 45 minutes or until golden brown. Cool completely. Sift powdered sugar over top of stollens.
**YIELD:** 2 stollens (36 servings).

TIP: To freeze stollen, do not sift with powdered sugar. Wrap tightly in plastic food wrap; freeze. Before serving, thaw; sift powdered sugar over top.

*Nutrition Facts (1 serving): Calories 270; Protein 4g; Carbohydrate 32g; Fat 14g; Cholesterol 50mg; Sodium 170mg*

*Almond Filled Stollens*

# Fruited Pound Cake

*This buttery pound cake is filled with candied fruit.*

*Preparation time: 20 minutes • Baking time: 45 minutes*

2$\frac{1}{4}$ cups all-purpose flour
1$\frac{1}{2}$ cups sugar
1 cup LAND O LAKES® Butter, softened
1 (8-ounce) package cream cheese, softened
4 eggs
1$\frac{1}{2}$ teaspoons baking powder
1$\frac{1}{2}$ teaspoons vanilla
1$\frac{1}{2}$ cups chopped mixed candied fruit
$\frac{1}{2}$ cup chopped walnuts

Heat oven to 350°. In large mixer bowl combine 1$\frac{1}{4}$ cups flour and all remaining ingredients <u>except</u> candied fruit and walnuts. Beat at medium speed, scraping bowl often, until well mixed (2 to 3 minutes). By hand, stir in remaining 1 cup flour, candied fruit and nuts. Pour into 6 greased 5$\frac{1}{2}$x3-inch mini loaf pans. Bake for 45 to 55 minutes or until toothpick inserted in center comes out clean. Cool 10 minutes; remove from pan. Cool completely. **YIELD:** 6 loaves (60 servings).

TIP: 2 greased 8x4-inch loaf pans can be substituted for mini loaf pans. Bake for 50 to 60 minutes.

*Nutrition Facts (1 serving): Calories 100; Protein 1g; Carbohydrate 11g; Fat 5g; Cholesterol 30mg; Sodium 60mg*

# Cranberry Maple Walnut Pound Cake

*Perfect for holiday giving or to serve as a tea bread or simple dessert, this cake brings traditional American flavors together in a deliciously moist dessert.*

*Preparation time: 20 minutes • Baking time: 1 hour 10 minutes • Cooling time: 1 hour 15 minutes*

### Pound Cake

2 cups sugar
1 cup LAND O LAKES® Butter, softened
5 eggs
$\frac{1}{4}$ cup LAND O LAKES® Sour Cream (Regular, Light <u>or</u> No•Fat)
$\frac{1}{4}$ cup maple syrup <u>or</u> maple-flavored syrup
1 teaspoon grated orange peel
1 teaspoon vanilla
2$\frac{1}{4}$ cups all-purpose flour
$\frac{1}{2}$ teaspoon salt
1$\frac{1}{2}$ cups fresh <u>or</u> frozen cranberries, coarsely chopped
1 cup toasted chopped walnuts

### Glaze

1 cup powdered sugar
1 tablespoon LAND O LAKES® Butter, softened
2 tablespoons maple syrup <u>or</u> maple-flavored syrup
1 to 2 tablespoons milk

Heat oven to 350°. In large mixer bowl beat sugar and 1 cup butter on medium speed, scraping bowl often, until creamy (2 to 3 minutes). Continue beating, adding eggs 1 at a time, until well mixed (1 to 2 minutes). Add sour cream, $\frac{1}{4}$ cup maple syrup, orange peel and vanilla; continue beating, scraping bowl often, until well mixed (1 to 2 minutes). Reduce speed to low; add flour and salt. Continue beating just until flour is blended. By hand, fold in cranberries and walnuts. Pour batter into greased and floured 10-inch tube pan. Tap pan on counter to release any air bubbles. Bake for 70 to 85 minutes or until toothpick inserted in center comes out clean. Cool 15 minutes on wire rack; remove from pan. Cool completely.

Meanwhile, in small bowl stir together powdered sugar, 1 tablespoon butter and 2 tablespoons maple syrup. Stir in milk until desired consistency. Drizzle over cooled pound cake. **YIELD:** 16 servings.

TIP: For easy chopping of cranberries, freeze cranberries and chop in blender.

TIP: Cranberry Maple Walnut Pound Cake can be prepared in 2 greased and floured 8x4-inch loaf pans or 4 greased and floured 5$\frac{1}{2}$x3-inch mini loaf pans. Bake 8x4-inch loaves for 60 to 75 minutes and 5$\frac{1}{2}$x3-inch loaves for 50 to 65 minutes.

*Nutrition Facts (1 serving): Calories 390; Protein 5g; Carbohydrate 53g; Fat 19g; Cholesterol 100mg; Sodium 220mg*

*Fruited Pound Cake*

# Rich Snowflake Bread

*This unique shaped bread is very tender and rich, with a touch of anise.*

*Preparation time: 45 minutes • Rising time: 1 hour 30 minutes • Baking time: 25 minutes*

### Bread

| | |
|---|---|
| $^3/_4$ | cup milk |
| $^1/_2$ | cup LAND O LAKES® Butter |
| $^1/_2$ | teaspoon salt |
| 1 | ($^1/_4$-ounce) package active dry yeast |
| $^1/_4$ | cup warm water (105 to 115°F) |
| $4^1/_2$ to 5 | cups all-purpose flour |
| $^1/_4$ | cup honey |
| 2 | eggs |
| 2 | teaspoons crushed anise seed |
| 2 | teaspoons vanilla |

### Glaze

| | |
|---|---|
| 1 | egg |
| 1 | tablespoon water |
| 1 | tablespoon honey |

In 1-quart saucepan stir together milk, butter and salt. Cook over medium heat, stirring occasionally, until butter is melted (5 to 7 minutes). Cool to warm (105 to 115°F). In large bowl dissolve yeast in warm water; add warm milk mixture, 2 cups flour, $^1/_4$ cup honey, eggs, anise and vanilla. Beat at low speed until smooth (1 to 2 minutes). By hand, stir in enough remaining flour to make dough easy to handle. Turn dough onto lightly floured surface; knead until smooth and elastic (about 5 minutes). Place in greased bowl; turn greased side up. Cover; let rise in warm place until double in size (about 1 hour). Dough is ready if indentation remains when touched.

Punch down dough; divide in half. Form each half into ball. Place each ball in center of greased cookie sheet. Form dough into $7^1/_2$-inch round loaves. Cover; let rise until almost double (30 to 40 minutes).

Heat oven to 350°. After shaped dough has risen, with serrated knife, make cuts to resemble snowflake. Bake for 20 minutes. Remove from oven. In small bowl stir together all glaze ingredients; brush on loaves. Continue baking for 5 to 10 minutes or until deep golden brown. Remove from cookie sheets; cool on wire racks. **YIELD:** 2 loaves (24 servings).

*Nutrition Facts (1 serving): Calories 150; Protein 4g; Carbohydrate 22g; Fat 5g; Cholesterol 40mg; Sodium 100mg*

# Fruit Preserve Butter

*Flavored butter goes well with holiday breads, pancakes and waffles.*

*Preparation time: 10 minutes*

| | |
|---|---|
| $^1/_3$ | cup powdered sugar |
| $^1/_2$ | cup LAND O LAKES® Butter, softened |
| 1 | tablespoon your favorite flavor fruit preserves (strawberry, blackberry, pineapple, raspberry, etc.) |

In small mixer bowl combine all ingredients. Beat at low speed, scraping bowl often, until well mixed (1 to 2 minutes). **YIELD:** $^3/_4$ cup.

*Nutrition Facts (1 tablespoon): Calories 80; Protein 0g; Carbohydrate 4g; Fat 8g; Cholesterol 20mg; Sodium 80mg*

# Fruit Preserve Cream Cheese

*Spread this flavored cream cheese on your favorite breads and toasted bagels.*

*Preparation time: 10 minutes*

| | |
|---|---|
| $^1/_4$ | cup your favorite flavor fruit preserves (apricot, raspberry, peach, etc.) |
| 1 | (8-ounce) package cream cheese, softened |
| 2 | tablespoons powdered sugar |

In small mixer bowl combine all ingredients. Beat at low speed, scraping bowl often, until well mixed (1 to 2 minutes). **YIELD:** 1 cup.

*Nutrition Facts (1 tablespoon): Calories 70; Protein 1g; Carbohydrate 4g; Fat 5g; Cholesterol 15mg; Sodium 40mg*

*Rich Snowflake Bread, Fruit Preserve Butter*

# Savory Nuts

*Three types of nuts and Parmesan cheese combine for an extra special treat.*

*Preparation time: 15 minutes • Baking time: 10 minutes*

2 cups pecan halves
1 cup blanched almonds
1 cup hazelnuts or filberts
1/4 cup LAND O LAKES® Butter, melted
1/4 cup freshly grated Parmesan cheese
1 teaspoon seasoned salt

Heat oven to 325°. In small bowl stir together pecans, almonds, hazelnuts and melted butter. Spread into 13x9-inch baking pan. Bake for 10 to 12 minutes or until lightly toasted. Sprinkle with Parmesan cheese and seasoned salt; stir until well coated. Cool completely. Store in airtight container. **YIELD:** 4 cups (32 servings).

*Nutrition Facts (1 serving): Calories 110; Protein 2g; Carbohydrate 3g; Fat 11g; Cholesterol 5mg; Sodium 80mg*

# Cinnamon Sugar Tortilla Crispies

*This unique snack idea originated south of the border.*

*Preparation time: 30 minutes • Frying time: 35 seconds*

10 (8-inch) flour tortillas
3 cups vegetable oil

1/4 cup sugar
2 teaspoons cinnamon

Cut each tortilla into 8 wedges. In deep 10-inch skillet heat oil to 400°F. Fry, 10 wedges at a time, turning occasionally, until very lightly browned (35 to 45 seconds). Using slotted spoon, remove chips from oil.

In large plastic food bag combine sugar and cinnamon; add warm tortillas. Shake until chips are well coated. Store in tightly covered container. **YIELD:** 80 crispies.

*Nutrition Facts (5 crispies): Calories 140; Protein 2g; Carbohydrate 19g; Fat 6g; Cholesterol 0mg; Sodium 130mg*

# Spicy Mexican Popcorn

*The popular flavors of Mexico come alive in this spicy, buttery popcorn.*

*Preparation time: 15 minutes*

12 cups plain popped popcorn
1/4 cup LAND O LAKES® Butter
1 teaspoon chili powder
1/4 teaspoon garlic salt
1/2 teaspoon hot pepper sauce

In large bowl place popcorn. In 2-quart saucepan melt butter over low heat (4 to 5 minutes). Stir in all remaining ingredients. Pour over popped popcorn; toss to combine. **YIELD:** 12 cups.

TIP: To reheat and crisp leftover popcorn, place on 15x10x1-inch jelly roll pan. Bake at 350° for 10 to 15 minutes or until crisp.

*Nutrition Facts (1/2 cup): Calories 30; Protein 0g; Carbohydrate 2g; Fat 2g; Cholesterol 5mg; Sodium 40mg*

*Savory Nuts, Cinnamon Sugar Tortilla Crispies, Spicy Mexican Popcorn*

# Festive Julekage

*This Scandinavian holiday bread is filled with candied fruit, raisins and almonds.*

*Preparation time: 45 minutes • Rising time: 2 hours 30 minutes • Baking time: 35 minutes • Cooling time: 1 hour*

## Bread

1 ($^1$/4-ounce) package active dry yeast
$^1$/4 cup warm water (105 to 115°F)
3$^1$/4 to 3$^3$/4 cups all-purpose flour
$^2$/3 cup chopped mixed candied fruit
$^1$/2 cup golden raisins
$^1$/3 cup slivered almonds
$^1$/4 cup sugar
$^3$/4 cup milk
$^1$/4 cup LAND O LAKES® Butter, softened
1 egg
$^1$/2 teaspoon salt
$^1$/2 teaspoon cardamom
$^1$/2 teaspoon grated lemon peel

LAND O LAKES® Butter, melted

## Glaze

1 cup powdered sugar
1 to 2 tablespoons milk

Candied cherries, if desired

In large mixer bowl dissolve yeast in warm water. Add 2 cups flour, candied fruit, raisins, almonds, sugar, milk, butter, egg, salt, cardamom and lemon peel. Beat at medium speed, scraping bowl often, until smooth (1 to 2 minutes). By hand, stir in enough remaining flour to make dough easy to handle. Turn dough onto lightly floured surface; knead until smooth and elastic (about 5 minutes). Place in greased bowl; turn greased side up. Cover; let rise in warm place until double in size (about 1$^1$/2 hours). Dough is ready if indentation remains when touched.

Punch down dough; shape into round loaf. Place in greased 9-inch round cake pan. Brush top of bread with melted butter. Cover; let rise until double in size (about 1 hour).

Heat oven to 350°. Bake for 35 to 45 minutes or until golden brown. Remove from pan immediately. Cool completely.

In small bowl stir together powdered sugar and 1 to 2 tablespoons milk to reach desired consistency. Spread over cooled bread. Garnish with candied cherries.
**YIELD:** 1 loaf (24 servings).

*Nutrition Facts (1 serving): Calories 150; Protein 3g; Carbohydrate 27g; Fat 4g; Cholesterol 15mg; Sodium 80mg*

# Caramel Hot Fudge Sauce

*Two all time favorites, chocolate and caramel, combine in a rich sauce for topping ice cream or cake.*

*Preparation time: 10 minutes • Cooking time: 18 minutes*

1⅓ cups firmly packed brown
    sugar
½ cup LAND O LAKES® Butter
⅔ cup whipping cream
½ cup light corn syrup
1 tablespoon honey
4 ounces high quality
    bittersweet chocolate,
    chopped
1 tablespoon vanilla

In 2-quart saucepan combine brown sugar, butter, whipping cream, corn syrup and honey. Cook over medium heat, stirring constantly, until candy thermometer reaches 234°F or small amount of mixture dropped into ice water forms a soft ball (18 to 22 minutes). Remove from heat; with wire whisk stir in chocolate and vanilla until smooth. Store refrigerated. **YIELD:** 2⅔ cups.

VARIATION
<u>Caramel Sauce</u>: Omit bittersweet chocolate.

TIP: For holiday gift giving this sauce, with or without chocolate, makes a delightful, quick gift for teachers, neighbors, etc. Pour sauce into jars; write recipe on decorative card and tie onto jar with festive ribbon.

*Nutrition Facts (1 tablespoon): Calories 80; Protein 0g; Carbohydrate 9g;*
*Fat 5g; Cholesterol 10mg; Sodium 30mg*


# Homemade Caramel Sauce

*Serve this rich dessert sauce over ice cream, gingerbread or pound cake.*

*Preparation time: 15 minutes • Cooking time: 5 minutes*

¾ cup firmly packed brown
    sugar
¾ cup sugar
⅓ cup LAND O LAKES® Butter
½ cup light corn syrup
⅔ cup whipping cream

In 2-quart saucepan combine all ingredients <u>except</u> whipping cream. Cook over medium heat, stirring occasionally, until mixture comes to a full boil (5 to 8 minutes). Cool 5 minutes. Stir in whipping cream. Serve warm or divide sauce into 3 (¾ cup) portions and prepare variations as directed below. Store refrigerated. **YIELD:** 2¼ cups.

<u>Microwave Directions</u>: In 2-quart casserole combine all ingredients <u>except</u> whipping cream. Microwave on HIGH, stirring every minute, until mixture comes to a full boil (4 to 5 minutes). Cool 5 minutes. Stir in whipping cream. Serve warm or divide sauce into 3 (¾ cup) portions and prepare variations as directed below. Store refrigerated.

VARIATIONS
<u>Rum Raisin Sauce</u>: While still warm, stir ¼ cup raisins and ¼ teaspoon rum extract into ¾ cup sauce.

<u>Banana Sauce</u>: Cool ¾ cup sauce completely. Cut 1 banana into cubes; stir into cooled sauce.

<u>Praline Sauce</u>: While still warm, stir ½ cup toasted pecan halves into ¾ cup sauce.

*Nutrition Facts (1 tablespoon): Calories 80; Protein 0g; Carbohydrate 12g;*
*Fat 3g; Cholesterol 10mg; Sodium 25mg*

# Buttery Pecan Caramels

*These buttery caramels are topped with a crown of chocolate and a crunchy pecan half.*

*Preparation time: 20 minutes • Cooking time: 42 minutes • Chilling time: 1 hour 30 minutes*

2 cups sugar
2 cups half-and-half
¾ cup light corn syrup
½ cup LAND O LAKES® Butter
½ cup semi-sweet real
    chocolate chips, melted
64 pecan halves

In 4-quart saucepan combine sugar, <u>1 cup</u> half-and-half, corn syrup and butter. Cook over medium heat, stirring occasionally, until mixture comes to a full boil (7 to 8 minutes). Add remaining half-and-half. Continue cooking, stirring often, until candy thermometer reaches 245°F or small amount of mixture dropped into ice water forms a firm ball (35 to 40 minutes).

Pour into buttered 8-inch square pan. Cover; refrigerate just until firm (1 to 1½ hours).

Cut into 64 pieces. Drop ¼ teaspoon melted chocolate on top of each caramel; press pecan half into chocolate. <u>Cover; store</u> refrigerated. **YIELD:** 64 caramels.

*Nutrition Facts (1 caramel): Calories 70; Protein 0g; Carbohydrate 11g;*
*Fat 3g; Cholesterol 5mg; Sodium 25mg*

# Gift Giving Ideas With Food

◆ Use empty round cardboard oatmeal containers to package cookies, caramel corn, peanut brittle or snack mixes. Cover containers with colored tissue paper, contact paper, wrapping paper or iridescent Mylar®. Or, cover with plain paper and decorate with rubber stamps, stenciling or sponge painting. Add a bow made from ribbon, raffia or silk cording for an extra festive touch.

◆ Make your own "window" gift bags. Cut out a diamond or square window from brown paper lunch bags or brightly colored gift bags. Tape a piece of clear acetate or cellophane across the inside of the bag covering the window. Fill bags with cookies, spiced nuts or candies.

◆ Design your own gift basket around your favorite food gift. For example, a coffee or tea basket can be made by lining a basket with a colorful kitchen towel or cloth napkin. Arrange small tins of special teas or bags of flavored coffee beans in the basket. Include a couple of pretty teacups and saucers or coffee mugs to complete the gift.

◆ Prepare your favorite scones or muffins and place them on a cloth napkin-lined tray along with a copy of the recipe written on an attractive card. Include a jar of homemade or purchased fruit preserves. If desired, also include a bread stone or butter crock.

◆ Keep an eye out for fun and unusual cookie cutters throughout the year. Check craft stores, antique or collectible shops, grocery, cookware and hardware stores. Bake cutout cookies using these interesting cookie cutters. To present the cookies as a gift, place on a holiday plate and wrap in plastic food wrap. With ribbon, tie one of the cookie cutters onto the gift.

◆ Make your holiday gifts of food really sparkle by dusting them with edible glitter or silver and gold dust. Available at specialty cooking shops and bakery supply stores, edible glitter and dust add an elegant touch to your delicious gifts.

◆ Personalized cutout cookies will delight children and adults alike. Cut out cookies in a shape that represents something special to each person. Decorate cookies and write their names with frosting. Use cookies as "gift cards" on their packages or as place cards at your holiday table.

◆ When giving gifts of food, make interesting gift tags using recipe cards. Write the recipe on the card along with "to" and "from." Now the receiver can enjoy your gift all year long.

# Menus

The enjoyment of family and friends sharing a meal can be the highlight of the holidays. Use this special collection of menus for inspiration this season. You'll find some traditional favorites as well as many new ideas.

## Thanksgiving Dinner Menu

Pureed Sweet Potato Soup

Roasted Turkey

Corn Bread Stuffing
or
Bread Sage Stuffing

Grandma's Cream Gravy
or
Brown Turkey Gravy

Cranberry Orange Relish

Crusty Hard Rolls

Festive Vegetable Sauté

Maple Pecan Pumpkin Pie

Roasted Turkey, see page 146; Corn Bread Stuffing, see page 147; Cranberry Orange Relish, see page 149

# Roasted Turkey

*The perfect oven-roasted turkey!*

### To Prepare Turkey:

1. Thaw turkey in original plastic wrapper according to chart below.

### Approximate Thawing Times:

| Weight | In Cold Water* | In Refrigerator |
|---|---|---|
| 10 - 14 pounds | 5 - 6 hours | 2 - 3 days |
| 14 - 18 pounds | 6 - 7 hours | 2 - 3 days |
| 18 - 22 pounds | 7 - 8 hours | 3 - 4 days |

\* Change water frequently to keep cold.
  Keep thawed turkey refrigerated. Do not stuff until ready to roast. Roast within 24 hours after thawing. Refreezing is not recommended.

2. Remove turkey from plastic bag. Remove neck and giblets from cavities.

3. Rinse turkey thoroughly in cold water and drain well.

4. Stuff neck and body cavities lightly (about $3/4$ cup stuffing per pound of turkey).

5. Fold neck skin to back of bird and secure. Fold wing tips under back or tie to body. Tuck tail into body cavity. Tie legs together.

6. If using a standard meat thermometer, insert into thigh muscle next to body, not touching bone. Turkey is done when meat thermometer reaches 180 to 185°F.

### To Roast Turkey:

1. Place turkey, breast side up, in shallow pan and brush with melted butter.

2. Roast turkey in 325° oven according to chart below. If roasting turkey unstuffed, subtract 3 minutes per pound.

3. Giblets, <u>except</u> liver, may be simmered in salted water for 2 to $2^{1}/_2$ hours; add liver for last half hour. Use cooked, chopped giblets in gravy or dressing.

### Approximate Roasting Times in 325° oven:

| Weight | In Shallow Open Pan | In Loose Foil Tent |
|---|---|---|
| 10 - 14 pounds | 3 - $4^1/_2$ hours | $3^1/_2$ - 5 hours |
| 14 - 18 pounds | 4 - 5 hours | $4^1/_2$ - $5^1/_2$ hours |
| 18 - 22 pounds | $4^1/_2$ - 6 hours | 5 - $6^1/_2$ hours |

Roasting time will be shorter or longer than indicated on the chart if the turkey is warmer or colder than refrigerator temperature.

# Corn Bread Stuffing

*Corn bread and bacon are mixed for a one-of-a-kind country-style stuffing.*

*Preparation time: 30 minutes*

4 cups crumbled corn bread*
1/4 cup LAND O LAKES® Butter, melted
1/4 cup chicken broth
8 slices crisply cooked bacon, crumbled, reserve drippings
4 stalks (2 cups) celery, sliced 1/2-inch
1 medium (1/2 cup) onion, chopped
1 teaspoon salt
1/4 teaspoon pepper
3 tablespoons reserved bacon drippings

In large bowl stir together all ingredients. Use to stuff 12 to 14-pound turkey. **YIELD:** 6 1/2 cups (8 servings).

*9-inch square baking pan of corn bread will make 4 cups crumbled corn bread.

TIP: Prepare half of recipe to stuff 4 to 5-pound roasting chicken, duck or goose.

*Nutrition Facts (1 serving): Calories 310; Protein 7g; Carbohydrate 25g; Fat 20g; Cholesterol 80mg; Sodium 990mg*

# Bread Sage Stuffing

*Traditional old-fashioned sage stuffing with ideas for new variations.*

*Preparation time: 20 minutes*

4 cups dried bread cubes
1/2 cup LAND O LAKES® Butter, melted
1/2 cup chicken broth
4 stalks (2 cups) celery, sliced 1/2-inch
2 medium (1 cup) onions, chopped
1 tablespoon dried sage leaves, crushed
1 teaspoon salt
1/8 teaspoon pepper

In large bowl stir together all ingredients. Use to stuff 12 to 14-pound turkey. **YIELD:** 9 cups (12 servings).

VARIATIONS
Oyster Stuffing: Reduce salt to 1/2 teaspoon. Add 2 cups rinsed, drained oysters.

Raisin-Nut Stuffing: Add 1 cup pecans or walnut halves and 1 cup raisins.

TIP: Prepare half of recipe to stuff 4 to 5-pound roasting chicken, duck or goose.

*Nutrition Facts (1 serving): Calories 130; Protein 2g; Carbohydrate 12g; Fat 8g; Cholesterol 20mg; Sodium 400mg*

# Pureed Sweet Potato Soup

*When guests arrive, serve this rich, flavorful soup with crusty bread.*

*Preparation time: 40 minutes • Cooking time: 22 minutes*

4 cups water
2 pounds (4 medium) sweet potatoes <u>or</u> yams, peeled, cut into 1-inch pieces
$1/4$ cup LAND O LAKES® Butter
1 medium (1 cup) leek, quartered lengthwise, sliced $1/4$-inch
1 ($14^1/2$-ounce) can chicken broth
$1^3/4$ cups whipping cream
1 teaspoon chopped fresh thyme leaves*
$1/2$ teaspoon coarsely ground pepper
$1/4$ teaspoon salt

$1/4$ cup whipping cream
Leek greens, chopped, if desired

In 3-quart saucepan bring water to a full boil; add sweet potatoes. Continue cooking over medium heat until sweet potatoes are fork tender (10 to 15 minutes). Drain; place in food processor bowl. In same saucepan melt butter until sizzling; stir in leek. Cook over medium heat, stirring occasionally, until leek is tender (2 to 3 minutes).

Meanwhile, process sweet potatoes until smooth (1 to 2 minutes). Continue processing, gradually adding chicken broth through feed tube, until well blended (30 to 60 seconds). Add leek mixture; continue processing 30 seconds. Pour back into saucepan; stir in $1^3/4$ cups whipping cream, thyme, pepper and salt. Cook over medium heat, stirring occasionally, until heated through (10 to 15 minutes).

To serve, in individual bowls ladle soup; with spoon swirl about <u>2 teaspoons</u> whipping cream on surface of each serving of soup. Garnish with leek greens. **YIELD:** 8 servings.

* $1/4$ teaspoon dried thyme leaves can be substituted for 1 teaspoon chopped fresh thyme leaves.

TIP: Soup can be prepared in blender. Place one-fourth potato mixture, one-fourth chicken broth and leek mixture in 5-cup blender container. Cover; blend on high until mixture is creamy (1 to 2 minutes). Pour back into saucepan. Repeat three more times with remaining ingredients until all are blended. Continue as directed above.

*Nutrition Facts (1 serving): Calories 400; Protein 5g; Carbohydrate 33g; Fat 29g; Cholesterol 100mg; Sodium 330mg*

# Crusty Hard Rolls

*These rolls have a crusty outside with a chewy texture inside.*

*Preparation time: 1 hour • Rising time: 1 hour 30 minutes • Baking time: 20 minutes*

$2^1/2$ cups warm water (105 to 115°F)
2 ($1/4$-ounce) packages active dry yeast
1 tablespoon LAND O LAKES® Butter, softened
5 to 6 cups all-purpose flour
2 teaspoons salt
1 egg white
1 tablespoon water

In medium bowl stir together $2^1/2$ cups warm water and yeast until dissolved; stir in butter until melted. In large bowl stir together <u>3 cups</u> flour and salt. Stir in yeast mixture. Stir in remaining flour, $1/2$ cup at a time, until soft dough forms. Turn dough onto lightly floured surface; knead until smooth and elastic (about 8 minutes). Place in greased bowl; turn greased side up. Cover; let rise in warm place until double in size (about 1 hour). Dough is ready if indentation remains when touched.

Punch down dough; divide in half. With floured hands divide each half into 9 pieces. Shape into 4x2-inch individual rolls; place on greased cookie sheets. With serrated knife slit center of each roll. Cover; let rise until double in size (about 30 minutes).

<u>Heat oven to 400°</u>. Bake for 15 to 20 minutes or until lightly browned.

Meanwhile, in small bowl stir together egg white and 1 tablespoon water. Remove rolls from oven; brush tops with egg white mixture. Return to oven; continue baking for 5 minutes or until golden brown. Remove from cookie sheets; cool on wire racks. **YIELD:** $1^1/2$ dozen.

*Nutrition Facts (1 roll): Calories 140; Protein 4g; Carbohydrate 27g; Fat 1g; Cholesterol 2mg; Sodium 250mg*

# Cranberry Orange Relish

*This traditional relish, with the crunch of pecans, is the perfect accompaniment to turkey.*

*Preparation time: 20 minutes • Chilling time: 2 hours*

1 orange
4 cups fresh <u>or</u> frozen
   cranberries, thawed
$^2/_3$ cup sugar
$^1/_1$ cup chopped pecans
2 tablespoons chopped
   crystallized ginger

Peel orange; reserve fruit for other use. Cut up peel into 1-inch pieces. In food processor bowl finely grind orange peel (about 15 seconds). Add half of cranberries; process slightly. Add remaining cranberries and process until coarsely chopped. Place in large bowl; stir in sugar, pecans and ginger. Cover; refrigerate until flavors are blended (at least 2 hours). **YIELD:** 24 servings.

TIP: A blender or grinder can be used in place of food processor.

*Nutrition Facts (1 serving): Calories 45; Protein 0g; Carbohydrate 9g; Fat 1g; Cholesterol 0mg; Sodium 1mg*

# Festive Vegetable Sauté

*These crisp, colorful vegetables are the perfect accompaniment for roasted meat.*

*Preparation time: 30 minutes • Cooking time: 21 minutes*

5 cups water
4 medium (2 cups) carrots,
   3x$^1/_4$x$^1/_4$-inch strips
4 medium (2 cups) parsnips,
   peeled, cut lengthwise into
   3x$^1/_2$x$^1/_2$-inch strips
$^1/_2$ pound fresh green beans,
   trimmed
1 medium red pepper, cut into
   $^1/_4$-inch strips
1 yellow summer squash, cut
   into 3x$^1/_4$x$^1/_4$-inch strips
3 tablespoons
   LAND O LAKES® Butter
$^1/_4$ teaspoon salt
$^1/_4$ teaspoon coarsely ground
   pepper

In 3-quart saucepan bring water to a full boil. To blanch vegetables add one kind at a time to boiling water; cook 1 minute for all vegetables <u>except</u> 7 minutes for green beans. Drain; set aside.

In 10-inch skillet melt butter until sizzling; stir in salt, pepper and blanched vegetables. Cook over medium high heat, stirring occasionally, until vegetables are crisply tender (10 to 12 minutes). **YIELD:** 8 servings.

TIP: Vegetables can be blanched up to 1 day ahead; store refrigerated.

<u>Microwave Directions</u>: <u>Reduce 5 cups water to $^1/_2$ cup</u>. In 3-quart casserole place beans and water. Cover; microwave on HIGH until beans begin to cook (3 to 5 minutes). Stir in carrots and parsnips. Cover; microwave on HIGH, stirring after half the time, until vegetables are crisply tender (9 to 12 minutes). Stir in red pepper and squash. Cover; microwave on HIGH until squash is crisply tender (2 to 3 minutes). Stir in butter, salt and pepper.

*Nutrition Facts (1 serving): Calories 100; Protein 2g; Carbohydrate 16g; Fat 5g; Cholesterol 10mg; Sodium 130mg*

# Grandma's Cream Gravy

*Smooth creamy gravy, just like Grandma makes.*

*Preparation time: 5 minutes • Cooking time: 7 minutes*

$1/4$ cup water
Milk
3 tablespoons all-purpose
    flour
Salt
Cracked pepper

Deglaze pan by stirring water into pan with drippings. Heat, stirring and scraping pan, 2 to 3 minutes. Strain pan juices into 2-cup measure; remove excess fat, <u>reserving 2 tablespoons fat</u>. Add enough milk to equal 2 cups liquid; set aside.

In 2-quart saucepan cook reserved 2 tablespoons fat over medium heat until bubbly (1 to $1^{1}/2$ minutes). Stir in flour. Continue cooking, stirring constantly, 1 minute. Stir in pan juice mixture. Continue cooking, stirring constantly, until thickened (3 to 5 minutes). Season to taste. **YIELD:** 2 cups (8 servings).

<u>Microwave Directions</u>: Deglaze pan as directed above. Strain pan juices into 2-cup measure; remove excess fat, <u>reserving 2 tablespoons fat</u>. Add enough milk to equal 2 cups liquid; set aside. In 4-cup glass measure combine reserved 2 tablespoons fat and flour. Microwave on HIGH until bubbly (1 to $1^{1}/2$ minutes). Stir in pan juice mixture. Microwave on HIGH, stirring twice during last half of time, until thickened ($3^{1}/2$ to $4^{1}/2$ minutes). Season to taste.

*Nutrition Facts (1 serving): Calories 70; Protein 2g; Carbohydrate 5g;*
*Fat 4g; Cholesterol 5mg; Sodium 25mg*


# Brown Turkey Gravy

*This gravy method works for chicken, beef or pork gravy, too.*

*Preparation time: 5 minutes • Cooking time: 7 minutes*

$3/4$ cup water
Chicken broth <u>or</u> water
$1/4$ cup all-purpose flour
Salt
Cracked pepper

Deglaze pan by stirring <u>$1/4$ cup</u> water into pan with drippings. Heat, stirring and scraping pan, 2 to 3 minutes. Strain pan juices into 4-cup measure; remove excess fat, <u>reserving 3 tablespoons fat</u>. Add enough chicken broth or water to equal 3 cups liquid. In 3-quart saucepan combine 3 cups pan juice mixture and 3 tablespoons reserved fat; cook over medium heat until mixture comes to a full boil (3 to 5 minutes).

Meanwhile, in jar with lid combine remaining $1/2$ cup water and flour; shake well to mix. Slowly stir into hot pan juice mixture. Continue cooking, stirring constantly, until mixture comes to a full boil; boil 1 minute. Season to taste. **YIELD:** 3 cups (12 servings).

<u>Microwave Directions</u>: Deglaze pan as directed above. Strain pan juices into 8-cup measure; remove excess fat, <u>reserving 3 tablespoons fat</u>. Add enough chicken broth or water to equal 3 cups liquid; add reserved 3 tablespoons fat. Microwave on HIGH until mixture comes to a full boil (3 to 5 minutes). Meanwhile, in jar with lid combine $1/2$ cup water and flour; shake well to mix. Slowly stir into hot pan juice mixture. Microwave on HIGH, stirring twice, until mixture comes to a full boil ($3^{1}/2$ to $4^{1}/2$ minutes). Season to taste.

*Nutrition Facts (1 serving): Calories 45; Protein 1g; Carbohydrate 2g;*
*Fat 4g; Cholesterol 5mg; Sodium 180mg*

# Maple Pecan Pumpkin Pie

*A hint of maple in the filling, a drizzling over the pecans and
a touch in the whipped cream makes traditional pumpkin pie extraordinary.*

*Preparation time: 30 minutes • Baking time: 55 minutes*

**Single crust pie pastry**

- 1 (16-ounce) can pumpkin
- 1/4 cup sugar
- 2 eggs, slightly beaten
- 1 cup whipping cream
- 1/2 cup pure maple syrup <u>or</u> maple-flavored syrup
- 1 teaspoon cinnamon
- 1/2 teaspoon ground nutmeg
- 1/4 teaspoon ground ginger
- 1/4 teaspoon ground cloves

- 1/2 cup pecan halves
- 2 tablespoons pure maple syrup <u>or</u> maple-flavored syrup

- 1/2 cup whipping cream
- 1 tablespoon pure maple syrup <u>or</u> maple-flavored syrup

Heat oven to 375°. Line 9-inch pie pan with pastry; crimp or flute crust. Set aside.

In large bowl stir together pumpkin, sugar and eggs. Stir in all remaining ingredients <u>except</u> pecans, 2 tablespoons maple syrup, 1/2 cup whipping cream and 1 tablespoon maple syrup. Pour into prepared pie shell. Cover edge of crust with 2-inch strip of aluminum foil. Bake for 40 minutes. Remove aluminum foil. Bake for 15 to 25 minutes or until knife inserted in center comes out clean.

Arrange pecan halves on top of pie; drizzle or brush 2 tablespoons maple syrup over pecans.

In chilled small mixer bowl beat chilled whipping cream at high speed, scraping bowl often, until soft peaks form. Gradually add 1 tablespoon maple syrup; continue beating until stiff peaks form (1 to 2 minutes). Serve pie with whipped cream.
**YIELD:** 8 servings.

*Nutrition Facts (1 serving): Calories 460; Protein 5g; Carbohydrate 44g;
Fat 30g; Cholesterol 140mg; Sodium 150mg*

## Autumn Harvest Thanksgiving Menu

Turkey Breast With
Sausage-Apricot Stuffing

Sweet Potatoes With Apples

Pistachio Sprinkled Green Beans

Caramelized Onion Relish

Old-Fashioned Spoon Bread
With Maple Butter

Harvest Nut Tart

*Turkey Breast With Sausage-Apricot Stuffing, see page 154; Sweet Potatoes With Apples, see page 155; Pistachio Sprinkled Green Beans, see page 155; Caramelized Onion Relish, see page 156; Harvest Nut Tart, see page 157*

# Turkey Breast With Sausage-Apricot Stuffing

*Sausage, combined with apricots and pecans, delights the senses when roasted with turkey.*

*Preparation time: 30 minutes • Baking time: 2 hours*

12 ounces pork sausage
 2 cups dried bread cubes
 1 cup pecan halves
 $^{1}/_{2}$ cup chopped dried apricots
 $^{1}/_{4}$ cup LAND O LAKES®
  Butter, melted
 $^{1}/_{3}$ cup chicken broth
 2 stalks (1 cup) celery, sliced
  $^{1}/_{2}$-inch
 1 medium ($^{1}/_{2}$ cup) onion,
  chopped
 $^{1}/_{2}$ teaspoon salt
 $^{1}/_{4}$ teaspoon dried sage leaves,
  crushed
 $^{1}/_{8}$ teaspoon pepper

 1 (5 to 7-pound) bone-in
  turkey breast
 3 tablespoons
  LAND O LAKES®
  Butter, melted

Heat oven to 350°. In 10-inch skillet brown sausage over medium heat; drain off fat. In large bowl stir together browned sausage and all remaining ingredients except turkey breast and 3 tablespoons butter. Gently loosen skin from turkey in neck area to make large area to stuff. Stuff with sausage mixture; secure skin flap with toothpicks. Place remaining sausage mixture in 1-quart covered casserole; refrigerate. During last 30 minutes of turkey breast baking time, bake remaining stuffing for 25 to 30 minutes or until heated through. Place stuffed turkey breast, breast side up, on rack in roasting pan. Brush with 3 tablespoons melted butter. Bake, basting occasionally, for 2 to 2$^{1}/_{2}$ hours or until meat thermometer reaches 170 to 175°F and turkey breast is fork tender. Let stand 10 minutes. **YIELD:** 8 servings.

Microwave Directions: Reduce $^{1}/_{4}$ cup butter to 3 tablespoons. In 2-quart casserole microwave sausage on HIGH, stirring twice during last half of time, until sausage is cooked through (4$^{1}/_{2}$ to 5 minutes). Stir in all remaining ingredients except turkey breast and 3 tablespoons butter. Stuff as directed above. Place remaining sausage mixture in same 2-quart covered casserole; refrigerate. Place turkey breast, breast side down, in 12x8-inch baking dish. Brush with melted 3 tablespoons butter. Sprinkle with paprika. Cover with vented plastic food wrap; microwave on HIGH 10 minutes. Reduce power to MEDIUM (50% power); microwave, turning dish $^{1}/_{4}$ turn after half the time, 25 minutes. Turn turkey breast, breast side up. Baste. Sprinkle with paprika. Cover; microwave on MEDIUM (50% power), turning dish $^{1}/_{4}$ turn after half the time, until meat thermometer reaches 170 to 175°F and turkey breast is fork tender (22 to 25 minutes). Place turkey breast on serving platter. Tent with aluminum foil; let stand 5 to 10 minutes. Meanwhile, microwave remaining stuffing on HIGH, stirring after half the time, until heated through (5$^{1}/_{2}$ to 6$^{1}/_{2}$ minutes).

*Nutrition Facts (1 serving): Calories 410; Protein 33g; Carbohydrate 17g; Fat 23g; Cholesterol 110mg; Sodium 620mg*

# Sweet Potatoes With Apples

*Twice-baked sweet potatoes, subtly flavored with orange peel and nutmeg.*

*Preparation time: 30 minutes • Baking time: 1 hour 15 minutes*

8 medium sweet potatoes <u>or</u> yams

$^1/_3$ cup firmly packed brown sugar

$^1/_2$ cup LAND O LAKES® Butter, softened

$^1/_4$ teaspoon ground nutmeg

$^1/_2$ teaspoon grated orange peel

2 medium (2 cups) tart cooking apples, peeled, cored, coarsely chopped

Heat oven to 350°. Prick sweet potatoes with fork to allow steam to escape. Bake for 55 to 65 minutes or until fork tender. Cut thin lengthwise slice from top of each sweet potato; scoop out inside, leaving thin shell. Place shells on 15x10x1-inch jelly roll pan; set aside.

In large mixer bowl place hot sweet potato and all remaining ingredients <u>except</u> apple. Beat at medium speed, scraping bowl often, until well mixed and no lumps remain (2 to 3 minutes). By hand, stir in apples. Fill reserved shells with sweet potato mixture. Bake for 20 to 25 minutes or until heated through. **YIELD:** 8 servings.

TIP: If desired, do not stuff shells. Spoon hot sweet potato mixture into serving bowl.

*Nutrition Facts (1 serving): Calories 290; Protein 2g; Carbohydrate 44g; Fat 12g; Cholesterol 30mg; Sodium 140mg*

# Pistachio Sprinkled Green Beans

*Pistachio nuts are a great flavor complement to green beans or Brussels sprouts.*

*Preparation time: 15 minutes • Cooking time: 13 minutes*

$1^1/_2$ pounds green beans <u>or</u> Brussels sprouts, trimmed*

3 tablespoons LAND O LAKES® Butter

$^1/_4$ teaspoon pepper

$^1/_4$ cup (2 ounces) coarsely chopped salted pistachio nuts <u>or</u> toasted pine nuts

In 3-quart saucepan place green beans; add enough water to cover. Bring to a full boil. Cook over medium heat until green beans are crisply tender (12 to 15 minutes); drain. Return to pan; add butter and pepper. Cook over medium heat, stirring occasionally, until butter is melted (1 to 2 minutes). Sprinkle with pistachio nuts. **YIELD:** 8 servings.

* 3 (10-ounce) packages frozen green beans or Brussels sprouts can be substituted for $1^1/_2$ pounds green beans or Brussels sprouts. Cook according to package directions.

*Nutrition Facts (1 serving): Calories 110; Protein 4g; Carbohydrate 9g; Fat 8g; Cholesterol 10mg; Sodium 120mg*

# Caramelized Onion Relish

*A rich sweet condiment that complements poultry or grilled meats.*
*Be sure to cook the onions to a deep golden brown.*

*Preparation time: 5 minutes • Cooking time: 35 minutes*

2 tablespoons
  LAND O LAKES® Butter
3 large yellow onions, sliced
1/2 teaspoon dried thyme leaves
1/4 teaspoon salt
1/4 teaspoon rubbed sage
1/8 teaspoon pepper
2 teaspoons white wine
  vinegar

In 12-inch skillet melt butter over medium high heat until sizzling; add onions. Cook, stirring occasionally, until onions are tender and deep golden brown (35 to 40 minutes). Stir in thyme, salt, sage, pepper and vinegar. Serve warm or at room temperature with poultry or meat. **YIELD:** 8 servings.

*Nutrition Facts (1 serving): Calories 60; Protein 1g; Carbohydrate 6g;*
*Fat 3g; Cholesterol 10mg; Sodium 100mg*

# Old-Fashioned Spoon Bread With Maple Butter

*This souffle-like spoonable bread is delicious served with ham.*

*Preparation time: 45 minutes • Baking time: 40 minutes*

**Spoon Bread**
2 cups milk
1 cup yellow cornmeal
2 tablespoons
  LAND O LAKES®
  Butter, softened
1 teaspoon baking powder
1/2 teaspoon salt
1 cup milk
3 eggs, separated

**Maple Butter**
1/2 cup LAND O LAKES®
  Butter, softened
2 tablespoons maple syrup or
  maple-flavored syrup
1/8 teaspoon cinnamon

Heat oven to 350°. In 2-quart saucepan combine 2 cups milk and cornmeal. Cook over medium heat, stirring constantly, until all milk is absorbed and mixture is of cooked cereal consistency (8 to 11 minutes). Remove from heat. Add 2 tablespoons butter, baking powder and salt; stir until well mixed and butter is melted. With wire whisk beat in milk and egg yolks until smooth. Transfer to large bowl; set aside.

In small mixer bowl beat egg whites at high speed, scraping bowl often, until stiff peaks form (1 to 2 minutes). Fold into cornmeal mixture until uniform and no lumps are visible. Carefully pour into 2-quart greased casserole. Bake for 40 to 50 minutes or until golden brown and top springs back when touched lightly in center.

In small bowl stir together all maple butter ingredients; serve with warm spoon bread. **YIELD:** 8 servings (1/2 cup maple butter).

*Nutrition Facts (1 serving plus 1 tablespoon maple butter): Calories 270; Protein 7g;*
*Carbohydrate 19g; Fat 19g; Cholesterol 150mg; Sodium 390mg*

# Harvest Nut Tart

*Take advantage of the autumn abundance of nuts in this caramel nut tart.*
*A drizzle of chocolate and touch of brandy flavor are delicious accents.*

*Preparation time: 45 minutes • Baking time: 20 minutes • Cooking time: 18 minutes • Cooling time: 30 minutes*

## Nut Crust

- $1^{1}/2$ cups mixed nuts (pecans, hazelnuts and/or macadamia nuts)
- $^{1}/3$ cup whole or slivered almonds
- 3 tablespoons sugar
- $^{1}/3$ cup LAND O LAKES® Butter, softened
- 1 teaspoon vanilla

## Caramel Nut Topping

- 28 caramels, unwrapped
- $^{1}/3$ cup half-and-half
- $1^{1}/2$ cups mixed toasted nuts (pecan halves, hazelnuts and/or macadamia nuts)
- 1 teaspoon brandy extract

- 3 tablespoons real milk chocolate or semi-sweet real chocolate chips
- 1 teaspoon vegetable oil

- Unsweetened whipped cream, if desired
- Chocolate dipped nuts, if desired

Heat oven to 350°. In 5-cup blender container or food processor bowl combine $1^{1}/2$ cups nuts, almonds and sugar. Cover; blend at high speed until finely ground (do not grind into paste). In medium bowl stir together butter and vanilla until very soft. Add ground nut mixture; stir just until dough holds together. Press on bottom of 9-inch tart pan with removable bottom. Place on cookie sheet. Bake for 20 to 25 minutes or until golden brown.

In 2-quart saucepan combine caramels and half-and-half. Cook over low heat, stirring often, until caramels are melted and mixture is smooth (15 to 20 minutes). Remove from heat; gently stir $1^{1}/2$ cups nuts and brandy extract into caramel mixture. Spoon into cooled crust; push nuts to evenly cover. Cool 30 minutes.

In 1-quart saucepan melt chocolate chips and oil over low heat until melted and smooth (3 to 5 minutes). Drizzle over tart. Serve with whipped cream and garnish with chocolate dipped nuts. **YIELD:** 12 servings.

*Nutrition Facts (1 serving): Calories 400; Protein 5g; Carbohydrate 28g;*
*Fat 33g; Cholesterol 15mg; Sodium 110mg*

## A Thanksgiving Feast Menu

Walnut Cranberry Stuffed Brie

Blueberry & Mandarin
Orange Salad

Cranberry-Orange
Stuffed Turkey

Garden Vegetable Sauté

Sweet Potato Crescent Rolls

Johnny Appleseed Cake
With Caramel Sauce

*Cranberry-Orange Stuffed Turkey, see page 160; Garden Vegetable Sauté, see page 160; Sweet Potato Crescent Rolls, see page 161*

# Cranberry - Orange Stuffed Turkey

*Picture perfect turkey, filled with cranberry and orange bread stuffing, ready for a special holiday.*

*Preparation time: 45 minutes • Baking time: 5 hours • Cooling time: 15 minutes*

## Stuffing
- 3 cups fresh <u>or</u> frozen cranberries
- ³/4 cup sugar
- 1¹/2 cups orange juice
- 9 cups dried bread cubes
- 1 cup LAND O LAKES® Butter, melted
- 6 stalks (3 cups) celery, sliced ¹/2-inch
- 2 medium (1 cup) onions, chopped
- 2 teaspoons salt
- ¹/2 teaspoon pepper
- ¹/4 teaspoon allspice

## Turkey
- 1 (18 to 22-pound) fresh <u>or</u> frozen turkey, thawed

## Sauce
- 2 (10-ounce) packages frozen cranberry-orange sauce
- ¹/2 cup orange juice

In 3-quart saucepan stir together cranberries, sugar and 1¹/2 cups orange juice. Cook over medium high heat, stirring occasionally, until cranberries pop and sugar dissolves (9 to 11 minutes); cool 15 minutes.

Meanwhile, in large bowl stir together all remaining stuffing ingredients. Stir in cranberry mixture. <u>Heat oven to 325°.</u> Stuff turkey with stuffing. Place turkey on rack in roasting pan. Bake as directed on turkey package or approximately 5 to 6 hours for 18 to 22-pound stuffed turkey. Meat thermometer should read 180°F in thigh.

Meanwhile, in 2-quart saucepan stir together sauce ingredients. Cook over medium high heat, stirring occasionally, until melted (2 to 3 minutes). Baste turkey with sauce during last 30 minutes of baking time. Loosely cover turkey with aluminum foil if browning too quickly. Heat remaining sauce; serve over turkey. **YIELD:** 18 servings.

*Nutrition Facts (1 serving): Calories 870; Protein 100g; Carbohydrate 40g; Fat 30g; Cholesterol 400mg; Sodium 730mg*

# Garden Vegetable Sauté

*Basil and oregano spice up this medley of fresh garden vegetables.*

*Preparation time: 25 minutes • Cooking time: 12 minutes*

- ¹/2 cup LAND O LAKES® Butter
- 2 teaspoons dried basil leaves
- 1 teaspoon dried oregano leaves
- 1 teaspoon finely chopped fresh garlic
- 4 medium (2 cups) carrots, sliced diagonally ¹/4-inch
- 2 cups broccoli flowerets
- 2 medium onions, cut into ¹/4-inch rings
- 1 (8-ounce) package (2 cups) fresh mushrooms, sliced ¹/4-inch
- 2 red <u>or</u> green peppers, cut into strips
- 2 medium (2 cups) zucchini, sliced ¹/8-inch
- 1 cup (4 ounces) LAND O LAKES® Shredded Cheddar Cheese
- 1 cup (4 ounces) LAND O LAKES® Shredded Mozzarella Cheese

In Dutch oven melt butter until sizzling; stir in basil, oregano and garlic. Add carrots, broccoli and onions. Cook over medium heat, stirring often, until vegetables are crisply tender (7 to 9 minutes). Stir in mushrooms, red pepper and zucchini. Continue cooking, stirring constantly, until vegetables are crisply tender (5 to 6 minutes). Place in serving dish; sprinkle with cheeses. Cover; let stand 1 to 2 minutes or until cheeses are melted. **YIELD:** 12 servings.

*Nutrition Facts (1 serving): Calories 170; Protein 7g; Carbohydrate 8g; Fat 13g; Cholesterol 35mg; Sodium 200mg*

# Sweet Potato Crescent Rolls

*Serve traditional sweet potatoes in a new way, in a tender, delicious crescent roll.*

*Preparation time: 45 minutes • Rising time: 50 minutes • Baking time: 10 minutes*

## Dough

| | |
|---|---|
| 4 to 4$\frac{1}{2}$ | cups all-purpose flour |
| $\frac{1}{4}$ | cup sugar |
| 1 | ($\frac{1}{4}$-ounce) package quick rise active dry yeast |
| 1 | teaspoon salt |
| 1 | teaspoon cinnamon |
| $\frac{1}{2}$ | teaspoon ground nutmeg |
| $\frac{1}{4}$ | teaspoon ground ginger |
| $\frac{1}{8}$ | teaspoon ground cloves |
| 1 | cup mashed sweet potatoes |
| $\frac{1}{4}$ | cup LAND O LAKES® Butter |
| 1 | cup milk |
| 1 | egg, slightly beaten |

## Filling

| | |
|---|---|
| $\frac{1}{3}$ | cup firmly packed brown sugar |
| 2 | tablespoons sugar |
| 1 | teaspoon cinnamon |
| 2 | tablespoons LAND O LAKES® Butter, melted |
| | LAND O LAKES® Butter, melted, if desired |

In large mixer bowl combine 1$\frac{1}{2}$ cups flour, $\frac{1}{4}$ cup sugar, yeast, salt, 1 teaspoon cinnamon, nutmeg, ginger and cloves. In 2-quart saucepan combine sweet potatoes, $\frac{1}{4}$ cup butter and milk. Cook over medium heat, stirring occasionally, until butter is melted and mixture is very warm (120 to 130°F). Add to flour mixture. Beat at low speed, scraping bowl often, until moistened (1 to 2 minutes). Add egg. Beat at medium speed, scraping bowl often, 3 minutes. By hand, stir in enough remaining flour to make dough easy to handle. Turn dough onto lightly floured surface; knead until smooth and elastic (6 to 9 minutes). Place in greased bowl; turn greased side up. Cover; let rise in warm place until double in size (about 30 minutes). Dough is ready if indentation remains when touched.

Meanwhile, in small bowl combine brown sugar, 2 tablespoons sugar and 1 teaspoon cinnamon; set aside.

Punch down dough; divide dough in half. On lightly floured surface roll <u>half</u> of dough into 12-inch circle. Brush with <u>1 tablespoon</u> melted butter; sprinkle with <u>half</u> of brown sugar mixture. Cut into 12 wedges. Roll up each wedge tightly from wide end to point forming crescent. Place crescents, point side down, on greased cookie sheet; curve slightly. Repeat with remaining dough. Cover; let rise until double in size (about 20 minutes).

<u>Heat oven to 375°</u>. Bake for 10 to 12 minutes or until golden brown. Brush warm rolls with melted butter. **YIELD:** 1 dozen.

VARIATION
<u>Almond & Currant Filled Crescent Rolls</u>: Sprinkle each 12-inch circle of dough with 2 tablespoons toasted chopped almonds and 2 tablespoons currants or raisins before rolling up. Gently pat toppings into dough.

*Nutrition Facts (1 roll): Calories 310; Protein 7g; Carbohydrate 52g;*
*Fat 8g; Cholesterol 35mg; Sodium 270mg*

# Walnut Cranberry Stuffed Brie

*Served warm this appetizer will delight the palate.*

*Preparation time: 30 minutes • Baking time: 38 minutes*

$1/2$ cup cranberry preserves <u>or</u> jam

$1/2$ cup chopped walnuts, toasted

$1/3$ cup dried cranberries

$1/3$ cup currants

1 ($17^1/4$-ounce) package frozen puff pastry sheets, thawed

1 (8-ounce) $4^1/4$-inch diameter round Brie cheese

1 tablespoon milk

1 tablespoon water

1 egg

Apple slices
Crackers

Heat oven to 400°. In small bowl combine preserves, walnuts, dried cranberries and currants; set aside.

On lightly floured surface place pastry sheets, one on top of the other; roll to 13-inch square. Cut to 13-inch circle. Place circle on greased 15x10x1-inch jelly roll pan. Using paring knife, remove center of Brie in as large a piece as possible, leaving $1/4$-inch shell around outside edge and bottom. Set center of Brie aside.

Evenly press walnut cranberry mixture into hollowed Brie. Gently place removed Brie center on top of walnut cranberry mixture. (Do not push down or edges may crack.) Place filled Brie in center of pastry circle. Gather pastry up around Brie, holding firmly at top; pinch edges of pastry to seal. Check for holes in pastry, patching with extra dough if needed. Decorate top with star shaped pastry cutouts.

In small bowl, with fork, beat together milk, water and egg; brush over pastry. Bake for 38 to 42 minutes or until medium golden brown. (Brie may leak when baking.) Let stand 15 minutes to allow Brie to set; serve with apple slices or crackers. **YIELD:** 12 servings.

*Nutrition Facts (1 serving stuffed Brie only): Calories 380; Protein 8g; Carbohydrate 32g; Fat 25g; Cholesterol 35mg; Sodium 230mg*

# Blueberry & Mandarin Orange Salad

*The tangy flavor of dried fruit brings excitement to this easy salad.*

*Preparation time: 20 minutes*

**Dressing**

$1/2$ cup olive <u>or</u> vegetable oil

3 tablespoons sugar

$1/2$ teaspoon salt

$1/2$ teaspoon coarsely ground pepper

$1/4$ teaspoon beef bouillon granules

$1/4$ teaspoon dried basil leaves

3 tablespoons white wine vinegar

1 tablespoon reserved mandarin orange juice

**Salad**

$3/4$ cup fresh blueberries

$1/3$ to $1/2$ cup dried cranberries*

$1/3$ cup chopped green onions

$1/3$ cup salted sunflower nuts

$1/3$ cup toasted slivered almonds

2 (10-ounce) packages (8 cups) fancy mixed salad greens

1 (11-ounce) can mandarin orange segments, drained, <u>reserve juice</u>

In jar with tight-fitting lid combine all dressing ingredients; shake well.

In large salad bowl toss together all salad ingredients. Pour dressing over salad; toss to coat. **YIELD:** 12 servings.

* $1/3$ to $1/2$ cup dried cherries or dried blueberries can be substituted for $1/3$ to $1/2$ cup dried cranberries.

*Nutrition Facts (1 serving): Calories 180; Protein 3g; Carbohydrate 14g; Fat 13g; Cholesterol 0mg; Sodium 140mg*

*Walnut Cranberry Stuffed Brie*

# Johnny Appleseed Cake With Caramel Sauce

*Apples and walnuts are complemented by spices in this hearty cake served with a rich caramel sauce.*

*Preparation time: 35 minutes • Baking time: 40 minutes • Cooling time: 1 hour • Cooking time: 3 minutes*

## Cake

1¼ cups all-purpose flour
1 cup whole wheat flour
¾ cup sugar
¾ cup firmly packed brown sugar
1 tablespoon cinnamon
2 teaspoons baking powder
1 teaspoon salt
1 teaspoon ground nutmeg
½ teaspoon baking soda
¼ teaspoon curry powder
¾ cup vegetable oil
3 eggs, slightly beaten
2 teaspoons vanilla
2 large (2½ cups) tart cooking apples, cubed ½-inch
¾ cup finely chopped walnuts

## Sauce

1 cup firmly packed brown sugar
½ cup whipping cream
3 tablespoons LAND O LAKES® Butter
1 teaspoon vanilla

## Garnish

Sweetened whipped cream, if desired

Heat oven to 350°. In large mixer bowl combine flour, whole wheat flour, sugar, ¾ cup brown sugar, cinnamon, baking powder, salt, nutmeg, baking soda and curry powder. Beat at low speed until well mixed (1 to 2 minutes). Add oil, eggs and 2 teaspoons vanilla. Beat at medium speed, scraping bowl often, until well mixed (1 to 2 minutes). By hand, stir in apples and walnuts. Spread in greased and floured 13x9-inch baking pan. Bake for 40 to 45 minutes or until top springs back when touched lightly in center. Cool completely.

Just before serving, in 1-quart saucepan combine 1 cup brown sugar, whipping cream and butter. Cook over medium heat, stirring constantly, until sugar is dissolved (3 to 4 minutes). Stir in vanilla. Drizzle sauce over each piece of cake; dollop with whipped cream. **YIELD:** 15 servings.

TIP: Curry powder is used to intensify the apple flavor.

*Nutrition Facts (1 serving): Calories 380; Protein 4g; Carbohydrate 45g; Fat 21g; Cholesterol 60mg; Sodium 280mg*

*Johnny Appleseed Cake With Caramel Sauce*

*Thanksgiving*
*Leftovers*
*Weekend Menu*

Herb Garden Salad

Curried Turkey With
Dried Fruit

Multi Grain Pilaf

Creme Caramel
Coconut Custard

*Multi Grain Pilaf*

# Curried Turkey With Dried Fruit

*Curry powder adds a mild, sweet flavor to turkey and dried fruit.*

*Preparation time: 30 minutes • Cooking time: 21 minutes*

3 tablespoons
LAND O LAKES® Butter

2 teaspoons finely chopped
fresh garlic

3 cups bite-size pieces cooked
turkey

$^1/_2$ cup golden raisins

$1^1/_2$ cups chicken broth

$^1/_2$ cup sherry <u>or</u> apple juice

2 stalks (1 cup) celery, sliced
$^1/_2$-inch

1 medium ($^1/_2$ cup) onion,
chopped

1 (8-ounce) package whole
mixed dried fruit, each
piece cut in half

$1^1/_2$ teaspoons curry powder

$^1/_2$ teaspoon salt

2 teaspoons cornstarch

2 teaspoons water

Multi Grain Pilaf
(see below) <u>or</u>
hot cooked rice
Salted peanuts

In 10-inch skillet melt butter until sizzling; add garlic. Cook over medium high heat 1 minute. Stir in all remaining ingredients <u>except</u> cornstarch, water, pilaf and peanuts. Continue cooking until mixture comes to a full boil; reduce heat to low. Cover; continue cooking, stirring occasionally, until vegetables are crisply tender (15 to 20 minutes). In small bowl stir together cornstarch and water. Stir into hot turkey mixture. Continue cooking, stirring occasionally, until thickened (5 to 7 minutes). Serve over Multi Grain Pilaf; top with peanuts. **YIELD:** 6 servings.

*Nutrition Facts (1 serving without pilaf): Calories 370; Protein 24g; Carbohydrate 40g; Fat 12g; Cholesterol 70mg; Sodium 530mg*

# Multi Grain Pilaf

*Kasha and bulgur wheat combine with orange peel to make a new type of pilaf.*

*Preparation time: 15 minutes • Cooking time: 28 minutes*

3 tablespoons olive <u>or</u>
vegetable oil

2 medium (1 cup) onions,
chopped

1 bay leaf

$^1/_2$ cup bulgur

$^1/_2$ cup medium buckwheat
groats (kasha)

2 cups water

1 teaspoon salt

$^1/_4$ teaspoon pepper

2 teaspoons grated orange
peel

2 tablespoons orange juice

$^1/_2$ cup chopped fresh parsley

In 10-inch skillet heat oil; add onions and bay leaf. Cook over medium heat, stirring occasionally, until onion is soft (5 to 8 minutes). Add bulgur and groats. Continue cooking, stirring occasionally, until toasted (6 to 8 minutes). Add all remaining ingredients <u>except</u> parsley. Continue cooking, stirring occasionally, until mixture just comes to a boil (2 to 4 minutes). Reduce heat to low. Cover; continue cooking, stirring occasionally, until tender and liquid is absorbed (15 to 18 minutes). Remove bay leaf. Add parsley; stir with fork to fluff. **YIELD:** 6 servings.

*Nutrition Facts (1 serving): Calories 160; Protein 4g; Carbohydrate 23g; Fat 7g; Cholesterol 0mg; Sodium 360mg*

# Herb Garden Salad

*Cool and crisp, this garden-fresh salad is enhanced with herbs fresh from the garden.*

*Preparation time: 30 minutes*

## Salad

- 4 cups torn lettuce
- 1 cup sliced $1/4$-inch fresh mushrooms
- 1 cup sliced $1/8$-inch red onion, separated into rings
- $1/2$ cup torn fresh basil leaves, parsley, mint leaves <u>or</u> lemon balm
- 2 medium ripe tomatoes, each cut into 12 wedges
- $3/4$ pound green beans, blanched

## Dressing

- $1/3$ cup olive <u>or</u> vegetable oil
- $1/2$ teaspoon coarsely ground pepper
- $1/4$ teaspoon salt
- 2 tablespoons red wine vinegar
- 1 teaspoon finely chopped fresh garlic
- 1 teaspoon country-style Dijon mustard

In large bowl toss together all salad ingredients. In small bowl stir together all dressing ingredients. Pour dressing over salad; toss to coat. **YIELD:** 6 servings.

TIP: To blanch green beans, place in boiling water for 7 to 9 minutes. Rinse in cold water.

*Nutrition Facts (1 serving): Calories 150; Protein 3g; Carbohydrate 10g; Fat 12g; Cholesterol 110mg; Sodium 10mg*

*Herb Garden Salad*

# Creme Caramel Coconut Custard

*Easy but elegant! A creamy coconut custard tops creme caramel for a delightful flavor combination.*

*Preparation time: 20 minutes • Baking time: 50 minutes*

### Caramel
1/2 cup sugar

### Custard
1/4 cup sugar
6 egg yolks
1 1/2 cups half-and-half
1/2 cup cream of coconut
1 teaspoon vanilla
3/4 cup toasted flaked coconut

### Garnish
Toasted flaked coconut,
if desired

Heat oven to 325°. In 10-inch skillet cook 1/2 cup sugar over medium heat just until sugar melts and begins to turn brown (9 to 12 minutes). Do not burn. Pour about 1 1/2 teaspoons into each of 6 (6-ounce) custard cups or ramekins.

Meanwhile, in medium bowl, with wire whisk, gradually stir 1/4 cup sugar into egg yolks. Gradually whisk all remaining custard ingredients into egg mixture. Pour on top of caramel in custard cups. Place custard cups in 13x9-inch baking pan; fill around custard cups with 1 inch warm water. Bake for 50 to 60 minutes or until knife inserted in center comes out clean.

To serve, turn custards out onto individual dessert plates; garnish with toasted coconut. Serve warm or cool. Store refrigerated. **YIELD:** 6 servings.

*Nutrition Facts (1 serving): Calories 370; Protein 3g; Carbohydrate 36g;*
*Fat 23g; Cholesterol 240mg; Sodium 50mg*

*Creme Caramel Coconut Custard*

A Festival
Of Lights
Celebration Menu

Mushroom Barley Soup

Brisket With
Stone-Ground Mustard

Potato-Apple Latkes

Julienne Vegetable Salad

Sufganiyot

*Brisket With Stone-Ground Mustard, see page 173; Potato-Apple Latkes, see page 174*

# Brisket With Stone-Ground Mustard

*A tantalizing sauce of sweet, sour and spice is served over tender, boiled brisket.*

*Preparation time: 30 minutes • Cooking time: 2 hours 36 minutes*

## Brisket

- 1 (3-pound) beef brisket
- 6 cups water
- $^1/_4$ cup chopped fresh parsley
- 4 stalks celery, cut into 2-inch pieces
- 4 medium carrots, cut into 2-inch pieces
- 2 medium onions, cut into 2-inch pieces
- 1 teaspoon salt
- 1 teaspoon coarsely ground pepper
- 1 teaspoon dried thyme leaves
- 2 bay leaves

## Sauce

- 3 tablespoons all-purpose flour
- $^1/_2$ cup country-style Dijon mustard
- $^1/_2$ cup currant jelly
- $^1/_2$ cup whipping cream
- 1 teaspoon Worcestershire sauce

In Dutch oven place brisket; cover with water. Add all remaining brisket ingredients; bring to a full boil. Cover; cook over medium low heat until brisket is fork tender ($2^1/_2$ to 3 hours). Remove bay leaves. Place brisket and vegetables on serving platter; reserve broth.

In same pan or 2-quart saucepan place $1^1/_2$ cups reserved broth; with wire whisk, stir in flour. Cook over medium heat, stirring occasionally, until smooth and bubbly (2 to 3 minutes). Stir in all remaining sauce ingredients. Continue cooking, stirring occasionally, until sauce is thickened (4 to 5 minutes). Serve over carved brisket and vegetables. **YIELD:** 8 servings.

*Nutrition Facts (1 serving): Calories 350; Protein 26g; Carbohydrate 24g;*
*Fat 17g; Cholesterol 100mg; Sodium 360mg*

# Mushroom Barley Soup

*Dried and fresh mushrooms and barley combine to provide a full-bodied first course soup with a rich taste.*

*Preparation time: 1 hour • Standing time: 1 hour • Cooking time: 1 hour 17 minutes*

$7/8$ to 1 ounce dried mushrooms*

1 cup boiling water

1 tablespoon olive or vegetable oil

1 cup sliced fresh mushrooms

$1/3$ cup finely chopped carrot

1 medium (1 cup) leek, halved lengthwise, sliced $1/4$-inch

$1/2$ teaspoon finely chopped fresh garlic

$1/2$ cup barley

3 ($14^1/2$-ounce) cans low-sodium chicken broth

2 large sprigs fresh dill, if desired

2 tablespoons chopped fresh dill**

$1/2$ teaspoon salt

$1/2$ teaspoon pepper

In medium bowl place dried mushrooms. Pour boiling water over dried mushrooms; let soak 1 hour. Drain; reserve soaking liquid. Slice soaked mushrooms if whole. In Dutch oven heat oil; add soaked mushrooms, fresh mushrooms, carrot, leek and garlic. Cook over medium high heat, stirring occasionally, 7 minutes. Stir in mushroom soaking liquid, barley, chicken broth and 2 sprigs dill. Continue cooking until mixture comes to a full boil (10 to 15 minutes). Reduce heat to low. Cover; continue cooking until barley is tender (about 1 hour). Remove dill sprigs; stir in chopped dill, salt and pepper. Serve hot. **YIELD:** 8 servings.

\* Use porcini, morel, chanterelle, oyster or any Polish mushroom. Avoid shiitake as they take longer to rehydrate.

\*\* 2 teaspoons dried dill weed can be substituted for 2 tablespoons chopped fresh dill.

*Nutrition Facts (1 serving): Calories 100; Protein 4g; Carbohydrate 15g; Fat 2g; Cholesterol 0mg; Sodium 180mg*

# Potato-Apple Latkes
## (Potato-Apple Pancakes)

*No need to serve applesauce with these latkes. Shredded apple sweetens the pancakes—serve with a dollop of sour cream.*

*Preparation time: 30 minutes • Frying time: 6 minutes*

2 large (4 cups) baking potatoes, shredded

1 large (1 cup) Golden Delicious apple, shredded

1 small ($1/2$ cup) onion, grated

2 eggs

$1/4$ cup all-purpose flour

$1/2$ teaspoon salt

$1/4$ teaspoon baking powder

$1/4$ teaspoon ground coriander

$1/8$ teaspoon pepper

Vegetable oil

LAND O LAKES®
Sour Cream (Regular, Light or No•Fat), if desired
Honey, if desired

In large bowl stir together all ingredients except oil, sour cream and honey. In 10-inch skillet heat $1/4$ inch oil over medium high heat. Drop about $1/4$ cupfuls potato mixture into hot oil, flattening each mound slightly. Fry, turning once, until crisply brown (6 to 8 minutes). Drain well on paper towels. Serve warm with dollop of sour cream; drizzle with honey. **YIELD:** 16 pancakes.

*Nutrition Facts (2 pancakes): Calories 180; Protein 3g; Carbohydrate 19g; Fat 11g; Cholesterol 50mg; Sodium 370mg*

# Julienne Vegetable Salad

*Fine, julienne strips of beets, carrots and cucumber are presented on tender lettuce leaves with a dill dressing.*

*Preparation time: 45 minutes*

## Vegetables

- 2 medium (1 cup) beets, peeled, cut into very thin julienne strips
- 2 medium (1 cup) carrots, cut into very thin julienne strips
- 1 medium (1 cup) cucumber, peeled, halved lengthwise, seeded, sliced $1/2$-inch

## Dressing

- $1/4$ cup olive <u>or</u> vegetable oil
- $1/4$ cup lime juice
- $1/2$ teaspoon coarsely ground pepper
- $1/4$ teaspoon salt
- 1 tablespoon chopped fresh dill*
- 2 teaspoons grated lime peel

## Salad

- 16 leaves (2 heads) Boston lettuce
- 24 leaves (2 heads) Belgian endive
- $1/2$ cup thinly sliced red onion

Place beets, carrots and cucumbers each in their own medium size bowl. In small bowl stir together all dressing ingredients. Pour <u>2 tablespoons</u> dressing over each vegetable. On individual salad plates arrange <u>2</u> leaves Boston lettuce and <u>3</u> leaves Belgian endive. Place about <u>2 tablespoons</u> of each vegetable on lettuce leaves; garnish with red onion. **YIELD:** 8 servings.

*1 teaspoon dried dill weed can be substituted for 1 tablespoon chopped fresh dill.

*Nutrition Facts (1 serving): Calories 110; Protein 1g; Carbohydrate 7g; Fat 9g; Cholesterol 0mg; Sodium 120mg*

*Sufganiyot*

# Sufganiyot
## (Jelly Donuts)

*This spiced version of the traditional Hanukkah donut
is sure to please — great hot from the fryer, but can be made ahead.*

*Preparation time: 1 hour • Rising time: 1 hour 45 minutes • Frying time: 2 minutes*

### Donuts

- 3/4 cup milk or non-dairy liquid creamer
- 1/4 cup LAND O LAKES® Butter or Margarine
- 2 (1/4-ounce) packages active dry yeast
- 1/2 cup warm water (105 to 115°F)
- 4 1/4 to 4 3/4 cups all-purpose flour
- 1/2 cup firmly packed brown sugar
- 2 eggs
- 1 teaspoon salt
- 1 teaspoon cinnamon
- 1 teaspoon ground nutmeg

- 1/2 cup jelly or preserves (plum, apricot or raspberry)
- 1 to 2 egg whites, beaten

    Vegetable oil
    Powdered sugar or glaze (see below)

### Glaze

- 2 cups powdered sugar
- 1/3 cup hot water
- 2 teaspoons jelly or preserves (plum, apricot or raspberry)

In 1-quart saucepan heat milk over medium heat until just comes to a boil (5 to 7 minutes); stir in butter until melted. Cool to warm (105 to 115°F). In large bowl dissolve yeast in warm water. Add cooled milk mixture, 2 1/2 cups flour and sugar. Beat by hand until smooth. Stir in eggs, salt, cinnamon and nutmeg. Stir in enough remaining flour to form soft, but manageable, dough. Turn dough onto lightly floured surface, sprinkling additional flour on dough if needed to prevent dough from sticking to hands (dough should be softer than bread dough). Knead lightly 2 minutes. Place in greased bowl; turn greased side up. Cover; let rise in warm place until double in size (about 1 hour). Dough is ready if indentation remains when touched.

Punch down dough. On lightly floured surface roll dough to 1/4-inch thickness. With lightly floured 3-inch round cookie cutter cut out rounds. Put 1/2 teaspoon jelly in center of half of rounds. Brush edges with egg white; top with remaining plain rounds, sealing edges well. Place on greased cookie sheet. Cover; let rise until nearly double in size (about 45 minutes).

Heat 3 inches oil in deep fat fryer or Dutch oven to 360 to 375°F. Place donuts, no more than 3 at a time, into hot oil. Fry, turning once, until golden brown (2 minutes). Drain well on paper towels. Sprinkle with powdered sugar or cool and dip in glaze.

For glaze, in medium bowl stir together all glaze ingredients until smooth. Dip donuts into glaze; place on cooling rack to set. **YIELD:** 1 dozen.

TIP: The temperature of the oil is very important when frying donuts. Use a thermometer to reach and maintain the proper temperature.

TIP: If glaze thickens, stir in 1 to 2 teaspoons hot water.

*Nutrition Facts (1 donut): Calories 340; Protein 7g; Carbohydrate 70g;
Fat 10g; Cholesterol 45mg; Sodium 250mg*

# Top-Your-Own Pizzas

*A perennial favorite, these individual pizzas can be custom-made to suit everyone's taste at your table. An easy homemade garlic-herb crust is a fresh alternative to plain pizza crust.*

*Preparation time: 40 minutes • Standing time: 15 minutes • Baking time: 17 minutes*

## Dough

1¾ cups whole wheat flour

1 (¼-ounce) package active dry yeast

2 teaspoons dried Italian herb seasoning*

1 teaspoon salt

1¼ cups hot water (120 to 130°F)

2 tablespoons olive or vegetable oil

½ teaspoon finely chopped fresh garlic

1 cup all-purpose flour

Cornmeal

1 (6-ounce) can Italian tomato paste or ¾ cup prepared pesto

## Toppings

Chopped onion; sliced mushrooms; chopped green, yellow or red pepper; sliced ripe tomato; sliced zucchini; broccoli flowerets; chopped chilies; sliced olives; cooked sausage; sliced pepperoni; cooked shrimp; chopped marinated artichoke hearts, etc.

LAND O LAKES® Shredded Mozzarella Cheese, crumbled feta cheese, your favorite LAND O LAKES® Shredded Cheese

Heat oven to 425°. In medium bowl combine 1 cup whole wheat flour, yeast, Italian herb seasoning and salt. Stir in water, oil and garlic. Gradually stir in remaining ¾ cup whole wheat flour and all-purpose flour to make a firm dough. Cover; let stand 15 minutes.

Sprinkle 2 large cookie sheets generously with cornmeal. Divide dough into six equal portions. With well-floured fingers, press each portion of dough into 7-inch rounds (3 per cookie sheet). Prick generously with fork. Bake 5 minutes. Spread dough with either tomato paste or pesto; top as desired, ending with cheese. Bake for 12 to 18 minutes or until cheese is melted and crust begins to brown around edges.
**YIELD:** 6 (7-inch) pizzas.

* ½ teaspoon dried oregano leaves, dried marjoram leaves and dried basil leaves and ¼ teaspoon rubbed sage can be substituted for 2 teaspoons dried Italian herb seasoning.

*Nutrition Facts (1 pizza without toppings): Calories 270; Protein 9g; Carbohydrate 49g; Fat 6g; Cholesterol 0mg; Sodium 580mg*

# Sweet N' Tart Coleslaw

*A great way to have a tossed salad, this coleslaw brings cabbage, carrot, apple,
cucumber, radish and green onion together in a light sweet n' sour vinaigrette.*

*Preparation time: 20 minutes • Chilling time: 30 minutes*

### Salad

- 4 cups finely shredded green <u>and/or</u> red cabbage
- 4 radishes, sliced
- 1 green onion, sliced
- 1 medium carrot, shredded
- 1 small Granny Smith apple, shredded
- 1/2 small cucumber, halved lengthwise, thinly sliced

### Dressing

- 1 tablespoon sugar
- 1/4 teaspoon celery seed
- 1/8 teaspoon cumin
- 1/2 teaspoon Dijon-style mustard
- 2 tablespoons olive <u>or</u> vegetable oil
- 2 tablespoons lemon juice
- 1 tablespoon red wine vinegar

In large bowl combine all salad ingredients. In small bowl stir together all dressing ingredients. Add dressing to salad mixture; toss to coat well. Cover; refrigerate at least 30 minutes or up to 6 hours. **YIELD:** 6 servings.

*Nutrition Facts (1 serving): Calories 80; Protein 1g; Carbohydrate 10g;
Fat 5g; Cholesterol 0mg; Sodium 20mg*

# Fruity Freezer Ices

*No need for an ice cream maker to prepare these ices — dividing the fruit mixture
between two pans makes it easier to break up and beat once it's frozen.*

*Preparation time: 40 minutes • Cooling time: 15 minutes • Freezing time: 12 hours*

- 1/2 cup sugar
- 2 cups water
- 3 cups unsweetened frozen <u>or</u> fresh fruit*
- 3/4 cup fruit juice**
- 1/4 cup lemon juice

In 1-quart saucepan combine sugar and water. Cook over medium heat, stirring occasionally, until mixture comes to a full boil and sugar is dissolved; cool 15 minutes.

In food processor bowl place fruit. Cover; process until fruit is pureed. Add fruit juices and cooled sugar syrup; continue processing until well mixed. Divide mixture evenly between 2 (13x9-inch) pans. Cover; freeze until hard (at least 8 hours).

Break into small chunks; place in food processor bowl. Cover; process until mixture is a smooth slush. Repeat with remaining frozen mixture. Return slush mixture to one of the pans. Cover; freeze until firm (about 4 hours). Scoop like ice cream to serve. Mixture can be kept frozen up to 1 month. **YIELD:** 12 servings.

*Suggested frozen or fresh fruit: raspberries, strawberries, blueberries, sliced peaches, pineapple chunks or sliced banana.

**Suggested fruit juice: apple raspberry, pineapple, white grape or orange juice.

TIP: Serve with assorted holiday cookies.

*Nutrition Facts (1 serving): Calories 70; Protein 1g; Carbohydrate 17g;
Fat 0g; Cholesterol 0mg; Sodium 4mg*

*Pumpkin Pecan Layer Cake, see page 182*

# Pumpkin Pecan Layer Cake

*Three layers of festive fall flavors create this memorable cake.*

*Preparation time: 45 minutes • Baking time: 20 minutes • Cooling time: 30 minutes*

## Cake

- 2 cups crushed vanilla wafers
- 1 cup chopped pecans
- 3/4 cup LAND O LAKES® Butter, softened

- 1 (18-ounce) package spice cake mix
- 1 (16-ounce) can pumpkin
- 1/4 cup LAND O LAKES® Butter, softened
- 4 eggs

## Filling

- 3 cups powdered sugar
- 2/3 cup LAND O LAKES® Butter, softened
- 4 ounces cream cheese, softened
- 2 teaspoons vanilla
- 1/4 cup caramel topping

- 1 cup pecan halves

Heat oven to 350°. In large mixer bowl combine wafer crumbs, chopped pecans and 3/4 cup butter. Beat at medium speed, scraping bowl often, until crumbly (1 to 2 minutes). Press mixture evenly on bottom of 3 greased and floured 9-inch round cake pans.

In same bowl combine cake mix, pumpkin, 1/4 cup butter and eggs. Beat at medium speed, scraping bowl often, until well mixed (2 to 3 minutes). Spread 1 3/4 cups batter over crumbs in each pan. Bake for 20 to 25 minutes or until toothpick inserted in center comes out clean. Cool 5 minutes; remove from pans. Cool completely.

In small mixer bowl combine powdered sugar, 2/3 cup butter, cream cheese and vanilla. Beat at medium speed, scraping bowl often, until smooth. On serving plate layer 3 cake layers, nut side down, with 1/2 cup filling spread between each layer. With remaining filling, frost sides only of cake. Spread caramel topping over top of cake, drizzling some over frosted sides. Arrange pecan halves in rings on top of cake. Store refrigerated. **YIELD:** 16 servings.

TIP: To remove cake easily from pan, place wire cooling rack on top of cake and invert; repeat with remaining layers.

*Nutrition Facts (1 serving): Calories 600; Protein 22g; Carbohydrate 60g; Fat 38g; Cholesterol 130mg; Sodium 490mg*

# Cranberry Citrus Sparkler

*Sparkling water and lime juice are added to cranberry juice for a refreshing nonalcoholic beverage.*

*Preparation time: 15 minutes*

- 1/2 cup fresh lime juice
- 1 (12-ounce) can frozen cranberry juice cocktail concentrate
- 4 cups ice cubes
- 1 1/2 cups water
- 2 (12-ounce) cans lemon <u>or</u> lime-flavored sparkling mineral water

- Lime slices

Place <u>1 tablespoon</u> lime juice into each of 8 (10 to 12-ounce) beverage glasses. In 5-cup blender container combine cranberry cocktail concentrate, ice cubes and water. Cover; blend at high speed until ice cubes are finely chopped (20 to 30 seconds). Add about 2/3 cup cranberry mixture and 1/3 cup sparkling water to each glass. Garnish with lime slices. **YIELD:** 8 servings.

TIP: Two medium limes will yield approximately 1/2 cup fresh lime juice.

*Nutrition Facts (1 serving): Calories 110; Protein 0g; Carbohydrate 28g; Fat 0g; Cholesterol 0mg; Sodium 2mg*

# Crab, Mushroom & Leek Tart

*Serve this rich, flavorful tart with fresh fruit and home baked muffins for a delicious brunch menu.*

*Preparation time: 45 minutes • Baking time: 30 minutes*

**Pastry**

| | |
|---|---|
| 1¼ | cups all-purpose flour |
| ⅛ | teaspoon salt |
| ½ | cup LAND O LAKES® Butter |
| 3 to 4 | tablespoons cold water |

**Filling**

| | |
|---|---|
| 3 | tablespoons LAND O LAKES® Butter |
| 2 | cups (8 ounces) sliced ¼-inch fresh mushrooms |
| ½ | cup sliced leeks <u>or</u> chopped onion |
| 1 | cup whipping cream |
| 1 | (6-ounce) package frozen cooked crab, thawed, well drained |
| 2 | egg yolks, slightly beaten |
| ½ | teaspoon salt |
| ¼ | teaspoon pepper |
| ⅛ to ¼ | teaspoon hot pepper sauce |

Heat oven to 400°. In small bowl combine flour and ⅛ teaspoon salt. Cut in ½ cup butter until crumbly; with fork mix in water just until moistened. Form pastry into ball. On lightly floured surface roll pastry into 14-inch circle. Place in greased 12-inch tart pan; press on bottom and up sides of pan. Cut away excess pastry; prick with fork. Bake for 12 to 14 minutes or until lightly browned.

Meanwhile, in 10-inch skillet melt 3 tablespoons butter. Add mushrooms and leeks. Cook over medium heat, stirring occasionally, until vegetables are tender (4 to 5 minutes). Remove from heat.

In small bowl stir together all remaining filling ingredients. Stir into mushroom mixture. Pour into baked pastry shell. Bake for 18 to 22 minutes or until set and golden brown. **YIELD:** 8 servings.

*Nutrition Facts (1 serving): Calories 400; Protein 8g; Carbohydrate18g; Fat 29g; Cholesterol 160mg; Sodium 520mg*

# Glazed Cranberry Citrus Compote

*A refreshing, unique blend of chilled citrus fruits and sugar-glazed cranberries.*

*Preparation time: 30 minutes • Cooking time: 3 minutes • Chilling time: 1 hour*

| | |
|---|---|
| 1 | cup fresh <u>or</u> frozen whole cranberries, thawed |
| ¼ | cup sugar |
| 1 | tablespoon grated fresh gingerroot |
| 3 | oranges, pared, sectioned, <u>reserve juice</u> |
| 2 | grapefruit, pared, sectioned, <u>reserve juice</u> |
| 1 | tablespoon grated orange peel |
| 1 | kiwi, peeled, sliced ⅛-inch |

In 2-quart saucepan place cranberries; sprinkle with sugar and gingerroot. Cover; cook over medium heat 2 minutes. Stir cranberries. Continue cooking until cranberries begin to soften but still hold their shape (1 to 2 minutes).

Meanwhile, in large bowl stir together oranges, grapefruit and reserved juices; sprinkle with orange peel. Stir in glazed cranberries. Spoon into individual fruit dishes; top each with slice of kiwi. Cover; refrigerate at least 1 hour or until served. **YIELD:** 6 servings.

<u>Microwave Directions</u>: In medium bowl combine cranberries, sugar and gingerroot. Cover with plastic food wrap; microwave on HIGH until cranberries begin to soften but still hold their shape (1½ to 2 minutes). Meanwhile, in large bowl stir together oranges, grapefruit and reserved juices; sprinkle with orange peel. Stir in glazed cranberries. Spoon into individual fruit dishes; top each with slice of kiwi. Cover; refrigerate at least 1 hour or until served.

*Nutrition Facts (1 serving): Calories 100; Protein 1g; Carbohydrate 27g; Fat 0g; Cholesterol 0mg; Sodium 0mg*

# Raisin N' Nut Pull-Apart Coffee Cake

*Perfect for a potluck or family gathering, this old-fashioned pull-apart sweet bread will serve a crowd.*

*Preparation time: 1 hour • Rising time: 2 hours 15 minutes • Baking time: 35 minutes*

| | |
|---|---|
| 1 | cup milk |
| $1/4$ | cup LAND O LAKES® Butter |
| 1 | ($1/4$-ounce) package active dry yeast |
| $1/4$ | cup warm water (105 to 115°F) |
| $3^1/2$ to 4 | cups all-purpose flour |
| $1/4$ | cup sugar |
| 1 | egg |
| $1/2$ | teaspoon salt |
| | |
| 1 | cup sugar |
| $1/2$ | cup chopped pecans |
| $1^1/2$ | teaspoons cinnamon |
| | |
| $1/2$ | cup LAND O LAKES® Butter, melted |
| $1/2$ | cup golden raisins |

In 1-quart saucepan heat milk until just comes to a boil; stir in $1/4$ cup butter until melted. Cool to warm (105 to 115°F). In large mixer bowl dissolve yeast in warm water. Add cooled milk mixture, 2 cups flour, $1/4$ cup sugar, egg and salt. Beat at medium speed, scraping bowl often, until smooth (1 to 2 minutes). By hand, stir in enough remaining flour to make dough easy to handle. Turn dough onto lightly floured surface; knead until smooth and elastic (about 10 minutes). Place in greased bowl; turn greased side up. Cover; let rise in warm place until double in size (about $1^1/2$ hours). Dough is ready if indentation remains when touched.

Punch down dough; divide in half. With floured hands shape each half into 24 balls. In small bowl stir together 1 cup sugar, pecans and cinnamon. Dip balls first in melted butter, then in sugar mixture. Place 24 balls in bottom of greased 10-inch tube pan or Bundt pan. (If removable bottom tube pan, line with aluminum foil.) Sprinkle with raisins. Top with remaining 24 balls. Cover; let rise until double in size (about 45 minutes).

Heat oven to 375°. Bake for 35 to 40 minutes or until coffee cake sounds hollow when tapped. (Cover with aluminum foil if coffee cake browns too quickly.) Immediately invert pan on heatproof serving plate. Let pan stand 1 minute to allow sugar mixture to drizzle over cake. Remove pan; serve warm. **YIELD:** 1 coffee cake (24 servings).

*Nutrition Facts (1 serving): Calories 190; Protein 3g; Carbohydrate 28g; Fat 8g; Cholesterol 25mg; Sodium 110mg*

Holiday
Brunch Menu

Spiced Hot Chocolate Mix

Wild Rice Pancakes With
Cranberry Honey Butter

Country Provence Eggs

Fresh Fruit With Orange Cream

Spiced Hot Chocolate Mix, see page 187; Wild Rice Pancakes With Cranberry Honey Butter, see page 186; Fresh Fruit With Orange Cream, see page 186

# Wild Rice Pancakes With Cranberry Honey Butter

*These pancakes make a festive brunch for the holiday season.*

*Preparation time: 45 minutes • Cooling time: 2 minutes*

### Cranberry Honey Butter
- 1 cup LAND O LAKES® Butter, softened
- 1/4 cup honey
- 1 cup whole cranberry sauce

### Pancakes
- 1/2 cup buckwheat flour*
- 1/2 cup all-purpose flour
- 1 teaspoon sugar
- 1 teaspoon baking powder
- 1/2 teaspoon baking soda
- 1/4 teaspoon salt
- 1 cup buttermilk**
- 1 egg
- 2 tablespoons LAND O LAKES® Butter, melted
- 3/4 cup cooked wild rice

In small mixer bowl beat 1 cup butter and honey at high speed until soft and fluffy (1 to 2 minutes). Reduce speed to low; add cranberry sauce. Continue beating, scraping bowl often, until well blended (2 to 3 minutes). Cover; store refrigerated.

In large mixer bowl stir together buckwheat flour, flour, sugar, baking powder, baking soda and salt. In medium bowl, with wire whisk, stir together buttermilk and egg; add to flour mixture. Beat at medium speed, scraping bowl often, until well mixed (1 to 2 minutes). Continue beating, adding 2 tablespoons melted butter in a steady stream, just until blended. By hand, stir in wild rice. Heat lightly greased griddle or frying pan to 350°F or until drops of water sizzle. For each pancake pour 1/4 cup batter onto griddle. Cook until bubbles form on top (1 to 2 minutes). Turn; continue cooking until light golden brown (1 to 2 minutes). Serve pancakes with Cranberry Honey Butter. **YIELD:** 10 pancakes (2 cups Cranberry Honey Butter).

*1/2 cup all-purpose flour can be substituted for 1/2 cup buckwheat flour.

**1 tablespoon vinegar plus enough milk to equal 1 cup can be substituted for 1 cup buttermilk.

TIP: Cranberry Honey Butter can also be served with breads.

*Nutrition Facts (1 pancake with 1 tablespoon Cranberry Honey Butter): Calories 170; Protein 3g; Carbohydrate 19g; Fat 9g; Cholesterol 45mg; Sodium 270mg*

# Fresh Fruit With Orange Cream

*Serve this flavored cream cheese topping over your favorite fresh fruits, gingerbread or pound cake.*

*Preparation time: 20 minutes*

### Orange Cream
- 1/4 cup powdered sugar
- 1 (8-ounce) package cream cheese, softened
- 1/3 cup orange juice
- 2 teaspoons grated orange peel
- 1 tablespoon orange-flavored liqueur, if desired

### Fruit
- 4 cups cut-up assorted fresh fruit (kiwi fruit, orange segments, strawberries, apples, etc.)

In small mixer bowl combine powdered sugar and cream cheese. Beat at medium speed, scraping bowl often, until smooth (1 to 2 minutes). Add all remaining orange cream ingredients; continue beating until well mixed (1 to 2 minutes).

In medium bowl gently toss together all fruit. Serve orange cream over fruit. **YIELD:** 8 servings.

*Nutrition Facts (1 serving): Calories 160; Protein 3g; Carbohydrate 15g; Fat 10g; Cholesterol 30mg; Sodium 90mg*

# Spiced Hot Chocolate Mix

*Make homemade hot chocolate in an instant with this easy to make spiced mix.*

*Preparation time: 15 minutes*

1 vanilla bean
1$^1/_3$ cups sugar
1$^1/_3$ cups nonfat dry milk
   powder
1 cup unsweetened cocoa
3 tablespoons instant espresso
   <u>or</u> coffee powder
$^1/_2$ teaspoon cinnamon
$^1/_8$ teaspoon ground cardamom

Boiling water
Sweetened whipped cream,
   if desired

Split vanilla bean lengthwise. Scrape out insides of bean creating powder; place powder in medium bowl. Stir in sugar until well blended. Stir in all remaining ingredients <u>except</u> boiling water and whipped cream.

For each serving, place $^3/_4$ cup boiling water in large mug. Stir in $^1/_4$ cup cocoa mix until dissolved. Dollop with whipped cream. Store cocoa mix in tightly covered container. **YIELD:** 3 cups (12 servings).

TIP: Use high quality unsweetened cocoa for best flavor and texture.

TIP: Spiced Hot Chocolate Mix can be made without the vanilla bean.

*Nutrition Facts (1 serving): Calories 160; Protein 6g; Carbohydrate 33g;
Fat 1g; Cholesterol 5mg; Sodium 130mg*

# Country Provence Eggs

*Sausage, potatoes and spinach are sautéed with scrambled eggs to create a hearty provincial supper.*

*Preparation time: 30 minutes • Cooking time: 28 minutes*

8 ounces bulk pork sausage
8 small (2 cups) new red
   potatoes, cubed $^1/_2$-inch
1 medium (1 cup) onion,
   thinly sliced, separated
   into rings
$^1/_4$ cup milk
8 eggs, slightly beaten
$^1/_2$ teaspoon coarsely ground
   pepper
$^1/_4$ teaspoon salt
2 cups (5 ounces) torn
   spinach leaves
4 ounces (1 cup)
   LAND O LAKES®
   Provolone <u>or</u> Mozzarella
   Cheese, shredded
2 tablespoons freshly grated
   Parmesan cheese

In 10-inch skillet place sausage; cook over medium high heat until browned (4 to 5 minutes). Remove sausage with slotted spoon; set aside.

Add potatoes and onion to same skillet; cook over medium heat, stirring occasionally, until browned and fork tender (10 to 14 minutes). Stir in sausage.

In small bowl stir together milk, eggs, pepper and salt. Pour egg mixture over sausage mixture. Continue cooking, gently lifting portions and stirring with spatula so uncooked portion flows to bottom of pan, until eggs are partially set and scrambled (5 to 6 minutes). Gradually stir in spinach; sprinkle with Provolone cheese. Continue cooking, stirring occasionally, until spinach is wilted and eggs are set (2 to 3 minutes). Sprinkle with Parmesan cheese. **YIELD:** 8 servings.

*Nutrition Facts (1 serving): Calories 210; Protein 15g; Carbohydrate 11g;
Fat 12g; Cholesterol 240mg; Sodium 420mg*

*Gingered Fruit Dip*

# Gingered Fruit Dip

*This delectable sour cream dip, flavored with peach or apricot preserves and ginger, adds sparkle to fresh fruit.*

*Preparation time: 10 minutes • Chilling time: 1 hour*

1  (16-ounce) carton (2 cups)
   LAND O LAKES®
   Sour Cream (Regular,
   Light <u>or</u> No•Fat)
2  tablespoons firmly packed
   brown sugar
2  tablespoons peach <u>or</u>
   apricot preserves
2  tablespoons finely chopped
   crystallized ginger

   Assorted fresh <u>or</u> dried fruit,
   cut up

In medium bowl stir together all ingredients <u>except</u> fruit. Cover; refrigerate to blend flavors (at least 1 hour). Serve with fresh fruit. Store refrigerated. **YIELD:** 2 cups.

*Nutrition Facts (1 tablespoon dip): Calories 25; Protein 4g; Carbohydrate 4g;*
*Fat 1g; Cholesterol 5mg; Sodium 10mg*

# Cranberry Tea

*This festive beverage is perfect for a holiday party.*

*Preparation time: 5 minutes • Cooking time: 45 minutes*

2  cups sugar
12  cups (3 quarts) water
1  (16-ounce) bag fresh <u>or</u>
   frozen cranberries
2  cinnamon sticks
2  small lemons, sliced

In Dutch oven combine all ingredients. Cover; cook over medium heat until mixture just comes to a boil (15 to 20 minutes). Reduce heat to low; continue cooking 30 minutes. Strain; discard cranberries, cinnamon sticks and lemon slices. Return cranberry tea to pan; keep warm over low heat. **YIELD:** 3 quarts (16 servings).

TIP: Refrigerate leftover tea. Reheat by the cupful or serve chilled mixed with sparkling water or ginger ale over ice.

*Nutrition Facts (1 serving): Calories 110; Protein 0g; Carbohydrate 28g;*
*Fat 0g; Cholesterol 0mg; Sodium 5mg*

# Petits Fours

*These dainty icing coated miniature cakes add a special touch to showers, open houses or teas.*

*Preparation time: 2 hours • Baking time: 20 minutes • Cooling time: 30 minutes*

## Cake
- 1 (18$\frac{1}{2}$-ounce) package white cake mix
- $\frac{1}{2}$ teaspoon almond extract

## Icing
- 3 cups sugar
- $\frac{1}{4}$ teaspoon cream of tartar
- 1$\frac{1}{2}$ cups water
- 1 cup powdered sugar, sifted
- 1 teaspoon almond extract <u>or</u> vanilla
- 3 drops food coloring

  Candy flowers, if desired
  Frosting flowers, if desired

Heat oven to 350°. Prepare cake mix according to package directions adding $\frac{1}{2}$ teaspoon almond extract with water and baking in 2 greased and floured 9-inch square baking pans. Bake for 20 to 30 minutes or until toothpick inserted in center comes out clean. Cool 10 minutes; remove from pans. Cool completely. Trim edges from cake; cut each cake into 24 pieces.

In 3-quart saucepan combine sugar, cream of tartar and water. Cook over medium heat, stirring occasionally, until mixture comes to a full boil (12 to 14 minutes). Cover; boil 3 minutes. Uncover; continue cooking until candy thermometer reaches 226°F or small amount of mixture dropped into ice water forms a thin syrup (10 to 15 minutes). Remove from heat; cool to 110°F (do not stir). Stir in powdered sugar, 1 teaspoon almond extract and food coloring.

Place wire rack on cookie sheet. Place cake pieces on wire rack. Using ladle or large spoon, carefully spoon icing over cake pieces; spread over edges if desired. Repeat, coating each piece twice. If icing becomes too thick reheat over low heat until pouring consistency (2 to 3 minutes). Scrape icing from cookie sheet; reuse if needed. Garnish each petit four with candy flowers or frosting flowers. **YIELD:** 4 dozen.

TIP: Package petits fours in a festive candy or cake box for gift giving.

*Nutrition Facts (1 petit four): Calories 100; Protein 1g; Carbohydrate 21g; Fat 2g; Cholesterol 1mg; Sodium 40mg*

*Petits Fours*

Kids' Holiday
Vacation
Lunch Menu

Hearty Vegetable & Pasta Soup

Chicken Nugget Dippers

Graham Cracker Farm

*Chicken Nugget Dippers*

# Chicken Nugget Dippers

*As an appetizer, snack or light meal, these herbed nuggets are sure to be a popular menu addition.*

*Preparation time: 30 minutes • Baking time: 10 minutes*

## Nuggets
- $^3/_4$ cup corn flake crumbs
- $^1/_2$ teaspoon cumin
- 1 teaspoon dried Italian herb seasoning*
- 1 (12-ounce) whole boneless chicken breast, skinned, cut into 1-inch pieces
- $^1/_4$ cup LAND O LAKES® Butter, melted

## Dips
- Honey
- Barbecue sauce
- Chili sauce
- Mustard
- Ketchup
- LAND O LAKES® Sour Cream (Regular, Light or No•Fat)

Heat oven to 425°. In small bowl stir together corn flake crumbs, cumin and Italian herb seasoning. Dip chicken pieces into melted butter; coat with crumb mixture. Place $^1/_2$ inch apart on 15x10x1-inch jelly roll pan. Bake for 10 to 15 minutes or until fork tender and crisp. Serve nuggets with choice of dips. **YIELD:** 6 servings.

* $^1/_4$ teaspoon <u>each</u> dried oregano leaves, dried marjoram leaves and dried basil leaves and $^1/_8$ teaspoon rubbed dried sage can be substituted for 1 teaspoon dried Italian herb seasoning.

TIP: Nuggets can be baked ahead of time and reheated at 350° for 10 minutes.

*Nutrition Facts (1 serving nuggets only):*
*Calories 140; Protein 12g; Carbohydrate 3g; Fat 9g; Cholesterol 60mg; Sodium 140mg*

# Hearty Vegetable & Pasta Soup

*This vegetable and pasta soup is sure to please everyone!*

*Preparation time: 45 minutes • Cooking time: 48 minutes*

- $^1/_4$ cup LAND O LAKES® Butter
- 2 medium (1 cup) onions, chopped
- 2 stalks (1 cup) celery, sliced $^1/_4$-inch
- 3 (14$^1/_2$-ounce) cans low-sodium chicken broth
- 1 (14$^1/_2$-ounce) can diced tomatoes
- 1 medium (1 cup) carrot, sliced $^1/_4$-inch
- 1 medium (1 cup) potato, chopped $^1/_2$-inch
- 1 small (1 cup) rutabaga, peeled, chopped $^1/_2$-inch
- 2 bay leaves
- 1 teaspoon dried marjoram leaves
- $^1/_2$ teaspoon salt
- $^1/_4$ teaspoon pepper
- $^1/_8$ teaspoon caraway seed
- 1 (7-ounce) package (1$^1/_2$ cups) dried ring pasta*
- 1 cup frozen mixed vegetables

In Dutch oven melt butter until sizzling; add onions and celery. Cook over medium heat, stirring occasionally, until onions are soft (5 to 8 minutes). Add all remaining soup ingredients <u>except</u> pasta and mixed vegetables. Cook over high heat, stirring occasionally, until mixture comes to a full boil (10 to 15 minutes). Reduce heat to low; continue cooking, stirring occasionally, until carrots are barely tender and mixture comes to a full boil (25 to 30 minutes). Add pasta and mixed vegetables. Continue cooking over medium heat, stirring occasionally, until pasta is tender (8 to 10 minutes). Season to taste. **YIELD:** 8 servings (7$^1/_2$ cups).

* 7 ounces (1$^1/_2$ cups) dried small pasta such as alphabet or small shell pasta can be substituted for 1 (7-ounce) package (1$^1/_2$ cups) dried ring pasta.

*Nutrition Facts (1 serving): Calories 210; Protein 7g; Carbohydrate 30g;*
*Fat 7g; Cholesterol 15mg; Sodium 350mg*

# Graham Cracker Farm

*Make this for a fun family activity during holiday vacation time.*

*Preparation time: 1 hour*

1 (16-ounce) box graham
   crackers
1 (16-ounce) can vanilla-
   flavored prepared frosting
2 (10$^1$/2-ounce) soup cans,
   emptied, clean
   Assorted candies
   Toasted coconut
1 (11-ounce) box farm animal
   crackers

1. Use 15x10x1-inch jelly roll pan as base of barnyard or cover heavy piece of cardboard with aluminum foil.

2. Fill pastry bag, fitted with small size star tip, with frosting. Refill as necessary.

3. Construct barn floor by laying 2 (5x2$^1$/2-inch) whole graham crackers side by side forming a 5-inch square. Glue together with frosting.

4. Pipe thick layer of frosting along outside edge of floor. Place 4 (5x2$^1$/2-inch) whole graham crackers on 5-inch sides around barn floor to form walls (now barn looks like a box without a lid). Hold walls in place until frosting sets (1 to 2 minutes).

5. To construct sloping roof and top of barn, place 1 soup can centered inside barn. This can will provide support for the sloping roof.

6. Pipe frosting along top edges of walls. Place 2 (5x2$^1$/2-inch) whole graham crackers, 5-inch edges along top edge of barn and opposite each other, sloping in slightly to leave 2$^1$/2-inch gap. Hold in place, adding additional frosting if necessary, until frosting sets (1 to 2 minutes).

7. With sharp knife, trim top two corners of 2 (5x2$^1$/2-inch) whole graham crackers to enclose ends of barn roof. Pipe with frosting and hold in place until frosting sets (1 to 2 minutes).

8. Pipe frosting along edge of gap in roof. Place 1 (5x2$^1$/2-inch) whole graham cracker along top edges to close barn. Hold in place until frosting sets (1 to 2 minutes).

9. Pipe frosting along all barn seams to help hold barn together and to decorate.

10. With sharp knife, trim pieces of graham crackers to make barn doors and windows, as desired. Attach with frosting.

11. Decorate barn with frosting and candies, as desired.

12. To make silo use 1 soup can as base. With sharp knife, carefully cut lengthwise along perforations (5-inch side) of 4 (5x2$^1$/2-inch) whole graham crackers forming 8 (5x1$^1$/4-inch) strips.

13. Pipe frosting along 5-inch edges of strips. Place 7 strips, side by side, around soup can entirely surrounding can. Hold in place, adding additional frosting if necessary, until frosting sets (about 5 minutes).

14. With sharp knife, trim edges of 1 (2$^1$/2-inch square) piece of graham cracker to form silo roof. Attach with frosting. Decorate with frosting and candies, as desired.

15. To form a trough, cut remaining 5x1$^1$/4-inch strips of graham cracker in half lengthwise to form 2 (2$^1$/2x1$^1$/4-inch) pieces. Frost to form a V-shaped trough. Fill with candies or toasted coconut.

16. To finish barnyard, place small amount of frosting on base of animal crackers; place as desired to form a farm scene.

17. Sprinkle base of barnyard with toasted coconut, as desired.

**YIELD:** 1 barn, 1 silo, 1 trough.

*Graham Cracker Farm*

## Caroling Party Menu

Winter Warm-up Beef Simmer

Crisp Marinated Vegetables

Rosemary Breadstick Twists

Tropical Fruit Cobbler

*Winter Warm-Up Beef Simmer, Rosemary Breadstick Twists*

# Winter Warm-Up Beef Simmer

*While this rich, hearty supper simmers, enjoy the brisk autumn air or the first snowflakes of the season.*

*Preparation time: 30 minutes • Baking time: 3 hours 30 minutes*

6 slices bacon, cut into $^1/_2$-inch pieces
2 medium (1 cup) onions, chopped
1 (3 pound) beef chuck roast, trimmed, cut into $2^1/_2$-inch pieces
4 medium red potatoes, halved
3 medium carrots, cut into 1-inch pieces
2 medium onions, halved
1 (8-ounce) package fresh mushrooms, halved
$^1/_2$ cup chopped fresh parsley
$^1/_2$ cup apple juice
$^1/_2$ cup beef broth
1 (6-ounce) can tomato paste
$^1/_2$ teaspoon salt
$^1/_2$ teaspoon pepper
$^1/_2$ teaspoon dried thyme leaves
1 teaspoon finely chopped fresh garlic
2 bay leaves

Heat oven to 325°. In Dutch oven place bacon, chopped onions and roast. Cook over medium high heat, stirring occasionally, until bacon and roast are browned (8 to 10 minutes). Stir in potatoes, carrots, halved onions and mushrooms. Stir in all remaining ingredients. Cover; bake for $1^1/_2$ hours. Uncover; continue baking, stirring occasionally, for 2 hours or until roast is fork tender. **YIELD:** 8 servings.

Crockery Cooker Directions: In Dutch oven place bacon, chopped onions and roast. Cook over medium high heat, stirring occasionally, until bacon and roast are browned (8 to 10 minutes). Stir in all remaining ingredients. In $3^1/_2$-quart crockery cooker place potatoes, carrots, halved onions and mushrooms; add meat mixture. Cook on High for 4 to 5 hours or until roast is fork tender. Stir mixture before serving.

*Nutrition Facts (1 serving): Calories 280; Protein 30g; Carbohydrate 20g; Fat 9g; Cholesterol 80mg; Sodium 520mg*

---

# Rosemary Breadstick Twists

*Twist these breadsticks and dip them in a rosemary garlic butter.*

*Preparation time: 20 minutes • Baking time: 20 minutes*

$^1/_3$ cup LAND O LAKES® Butter
$2^1/_4$ cups all-purpose flour
2 tablespoons freshly grated Parmesan cheese
1 tablespoon sugar
$3^1/_2$ teaspoons baking powder
1 cup milk
1 teaspoon dried rosemary, crushed
$^1/_2$ teaspoon finely chopped fresh garlic

Heat oven to 400°. In 13x9-inch baking pan melt butter in oven (3 to 5 minutes).

Meanwhile, in medium bowl stir together all remaining ingredients <u>except</u> milk, rosemary and garlic. Stir in milk just until moistened. Turn dough onto lightly floured surface; knead until smooth (1 minute). Roll dough into 12x6-inch rectangle. Cut into 12 (1-inch) strips. Stir rosemary and garlic into melted butter. Twist each strip of dough 6 times; dip into herbed butter mixture. Place in same pan. Bake for 20 to 25 minutes or until lightly browned. **YIELD:** 1 dozen.

VARIATIONS
Basil Breadstick Twists: <u>Omit 1 teaspoon dried rosemary</u>. Add 1 teaspoon dried basil leaves. Prepare as directed above.

Dill Breadstick Twists: <u>Omit 1 teaspoon dried rosemary</u>. Add 2 teaspoons dried dill weed. Prepare as directed above.

*Nutrition Facts (1 breadstick): Calories 150; Protein 4g; Carbohydrate 20g; Fat 6g; Cholesterol 15mg; Sodium 170mg*

# Crisp Marinated Vegetables

*Crisp garden vegetables are subtly pickled in an easy marinade.*

*Preparation time: 30 minutes • Cooking time: 7 minutes • Chilling time: 4 hours*

## Marinade
- $1/2$ cup chili sauce
- $1/4$ cup vegetable oil
- 2 tablespoons firmly packed brown sugar
- 3 tablespoons water
- 3 tablespoons tarragon vinegar or cider vinegar
- $1/2$ teaspoon finely chopped fresh garlic

## Vegetables
- 6 cups water
- $1/2$ pound green or yellow beans, trimmed, cut into 2-inch pieces
- $1 1/2$ cups diagonally sliced $1/2$-inch carrots
- 2 cups broccoli flowerets
- 1 cup small pitted ripe olives
- 2 stalks (1 cup) celery, sliced 1-inch

In small bowl stir together all marinade ingredients; set aside.

In 4-quart saucepan bring 6 cups water to a full boil. Add green beans; cook 2 minutes. Add carrots; continue cooking 3 minutes. Add broccoli and celery; continue cooking 2 minutes. Drain all vegetables; place in ice water to chill. Drain. Place vegetables and olives in large bowl; stir in marinade. Cover; refrigerate, stirring occasionally, for 4 hours or overnight. Serve with slotted spoon. **YIELD:** 8 servings.

Microwave Directions: Reduce 6 cups water to $1/2$ cup. In small bowl stir together all marinade ingredients; set aside. In 2-quart casserole place water and green beans. Cover; microwave on HIGH until beans begin to cook (3 to 5 minutes). Stir in carrots. Cover; microwave on HIGH, stirring after half the time, until vegetables are crisply tender (6 to 9 minutes). Stir in broccoli and celery. Cover; microwave on HIGH until vegetables are bright green and crisply tender ($1 1/2$ to $3 1/2$ minutes). Drain all vegetables; place in ice water to chill. Drain. Place vegetables and olives in large bowl; stir in marinade. Cover; refrigerate, stirring occasionally, for 4 hours or overnight. Serve with slotted spoon.

*Nutrition Facts (1 serving): Calories 70; Protein 2g; Carbohydrate 8g; Fat 4g; Cholesterol 0mg; Sodium 220mg*

# Tropical Fruit Cobbler

*Pineapple, oranges and grapefruit form the base of a biscuit topped cobbler for an unusual homemade dessert.*

*Preparation time: 45 minutes • Baking time: 17 minutes*

## Filling
- 1 (20-ounce) can pineapple chunks in pineapple juice
- 2 tablespoons LAND O LAKES® Butter
- $1/3$ cup firmly packed brown sugar
- 3 tablespoons cornstarch
- $1/3$ cup honey
- 1 teaspoon grated lime peel
- 1 teaspoon vanilla
- 4 oranges, pared, sectioned
- 1 pink or red grapefruit, pared, sectioned

## Biscuits
- $1 3/4$ cups all-purpose flour
- 2 tablespoons sugar
- 1 tablespoon baking powder
- $1/3$ cup LAND O LAKES® Butter
- $1/2$ cup half-and-half

## Topping
- 1 tablespoon sugar
- $1/4$ cup sliced almonds

Vanilla ice cream, if desired

Heat oven to 400°. Drain pineapple; reserve juice. Set pineapple and juice aside.

In 3-quart saucepan over medium heat melt butter. Meanwhile, in medium bowl combine brown sugar and cornstarch. Stir in reserved pineapple juice (about 1 cup), honey, lime peel and vanilla. Stir pineapple juice mixture into melted butter. Cook over medium heat, stirring constantly, until mixture is thick and bubbly (5 to 10 minutes). (Mixture will be very thick.) Stir in pineapple chunks and orange and grapefruit sections. Pour mixture into buttered 2-quart casserole; set aside.

Meanwhile, in medium bowl stir together flour, 2 tablespoons sugar and baking powder. Cut in butter until mixture forms coarse crumbs. With fork stir in half-and-half until dough forms. On lightly floured surface, with floured hands, knead dough 5 times. Roll out to 8-inch circle. Cut into biscuits with 2-inch biscuit cutter. Place biscuits, touching, on top of fruit.

Sprinkle top of biscuits with 1 tablespoon sugar and $1/4$ cup sliced almonds. Bake for 17 to 24 minutes or until biscuits are light golden brown and filling is bubbly. Serve warm with ice cream. **YIELD:** 8 servings.

*Nutrition Facts (1 serving): Calories 420; Protein 5g; Carbohydrate 70g; Fat 14g; Cholesterol 35mg; Sodium 230mg*

*Crisp Marinated Vegetables*

## Holiday Open House Menu

Bacon Tomato Dip

'Tis The Season Party Nibblers

Artichoke & Jack Dip
With Pita Chips

Almond Cheese Spread

Fried Tortellini with
Sun-Dried Tomato Sauce

Spinach Mushroom Turnovers

*Bacon Tomato Dip, see page 202*

# Bacon Tomato Dip

*The flavors of bacon, tomato and basil blend perfectly in this tasty dip.*

*Preparation time: 20 minutes • Chilling time: 2 hours*

1 (16-ounce) carton (2 cups) LAND O LAKES® Sour Cream (Regular, Light or No•Fat)

8 slices crisply cooked bacon, crumbled

1 medium (1 cup) ripe tomato, chopped

1 tablespoon dried basil leaves

Crackers, chips or cut-up fresh vegetables

In medium bowl stir together all ingredients <u>except</u> crackers until well mixed. Cover; refrigerate to blend flavors (at least 2 hours). Serve dip with crackers, chips or cut-up fresh vegetables. **YIELD:** $2^1/2$ cups dip.

*Nutrition Facts (1 tablespoon dip only): Calories 20; Protein 1g; Carbohydrate 2g; Fat 1g; Cholesterol 5mg; Sodium 30mg*

# 'Tis The Season Party Nibblers

*A combo of pretzels, nuts, crackers and cereal is seasoned with Parmesan cheese and herbs to be toasted for a flavorful snack.*

*Preparation time: 10 minutes • Baking time: 18 minutes*

1 cup salted cashews

1 cup salted peanuts

1 cup Cheddar-flavored crackers (1-inch squares)

1 cup bite-size shredded wheat cereal

1 cup bite-size pretzels

2 tablespoons freshly grated Parmesan cheese

$1/4$ cup LAND O LAKES® Butter, melted

1 teaspoon Worcestershire sauce

$1/2$ teaspoon celery salt

$1/2$ teaspoon garlic powder

Heat oven to 350°. In large bowl combine cashews, peanuts, crackers, cereal, pretzels and Parmesan cheese. In small bowl combine all remaining ingredients. Pour butter mixture over cereal mixture; toss to coat. Spread mixture on 15x10x1-inch jelly roll pan. Bake, stirring occasionally, for 18 to 23 minutes or until lightly browned. Cool completely; store in tightly covered container. **YIELD:** 5 cups.

*Nutrition Facts ($1/4$ cup): Calories 140; Protein 4g; Carbohydrate 10g; Fat 10g; Cholesterol 10mg; Sodium 280mg*

# Artichoke & Jack Dip With Pita Chips

*Pita chips seasoned with taco flavor make an interesting dipper for dips.*

*Preparation time: 30 minutes • Baking time: 22 minutes*

**Pita Chips**

- 1/2 cup LAND O LAKES® Butter, melted
- 1 tablespoon taco seasoning mix
- 3 (6-inch) pita breads

**Dip**

- 1/3 cup mayonnaise
- 1 (8-ounce) package cream cheese, softened
- 1/4 teaspoon garlic salt
- 4 to 5 drops hot pepper sauce
- 8 ounces (2 cups) LAND O LAKES® Monterey Jack or Cheddar Cheese, shredded
- 1 (14-ounce) can artichoke hearts, drained, coarsely chopped

- 1/2 medium ripe tomato, chopped, drained
- 2 tablespoons sliced green onions

Heat oven to 375°. In small bowl stir together butter and taco seasoning mix. Cut each pita into 6 wedges; separate each wedge in half (36 wedges total). Brush both sides of each pita wedge with butter mixture; place pita wedges, not overlapping, on 15x10x1-inch jelly roll pans. Bake 8 minutes; remove from oven. Turn each wedge over; continue baking for 2 to 5 minutes or until wedges are golden brown and crisp.

Meanwhile, in large mixer bowl beat mayonnaise, cream cheese, garlic salt and hot pepper sauce on medium speed, scraping bowl often, until smooth (1 to 2 minutes). By hand, stir in 1 1/2 cups cheese and artichoke hearts. Spread artichoke mixture in 9-inch pie pan. Sprinkle with tomato, onions and remaining cheese. Bake for 12 to 15 minutes or until heated through. Serve with pita chips. **YIELD:** 12 servings.

*Nutrition Facts (1 serving): Calories 320; Protein 9g; Carbohydrate 15g; Fat 25g; Cholesterol 60mg; Sodium 470mg*

# Almond Cheese Spread

*The crunch of almonds and the rich flavor of cheese blend together for a delicious cracker spread.*

*Preparation time: 20 minutes*

- 1 cup (4 ounces) LAND O LAKES® Shredded Cheddar Cheese
- 1/2 cup sliced almonds, toasted
- 1/4 cup chopped fresh parsley
- 1/4 cup LAND O LAKES® Butter, softened
- 1/4 cup mayonnaise
- 2 tablespoons chopped onion

- Crackers

In medium bowl stir together all ingredients except crackers. Serve at room temperature on crackers. **YIELD:** 1 1/4 cups.

TIP: Spread can be made 2 to 3 days in advance and kept covered in refrigerator. Bring to room temperature for serving.

*Nutrition Facts (1 tablespoon spread only): Calories 80; Protein 2g; Carbohydrate 10g; Fat 8g; Cholesterol 15mg; Sodium 80mg*

# Fried Tortellini With Sun-Dried Tomato Sauce

*A great appetizer! Tortellini is cooked, fried and served with an easy homemade sun-dried tomato sauce.*

*Preparation time: 30 minutes • Cooking time: 39 minutes • Frying time: 2 minutes*

## Sauce

- 1/4 cup chopped onion
- 2 teaspoons olive <u>or</u> vegetable oil
- 1/2 cup low-sodium chicken broth
- 1/2 cup sun-dried tomatoes in oil, drained
- 3 chopped ripe Roma tomatoes
- 1 tablespoon chopped fresh basil leaves*
- 1 tablespoon chopped fresh oregano leaves**
- 1/4 teaspoon salt
- 1/4 teaspoon coarsely ground pepper

## Tortellini

- 84 (about 9 ounces) small fresh tortellini, cooked, well drained***

  Vegetable oil

In 2-quart saucepan combine onion and 2 teaspoons oil. Cook over medium heat, stirring occasionally, until onion is soft (3 to 5 minutes). Add all remaining sauce ingredients. Cook over medium heat, stirring occasionally, until mixture just comes to a boil (6 to 8 minutes). Reduce heat to medium low. Cover; continue cooking, stirring occasionally, 30 minutes. Cool 10 minutes.

Pour into 5-cup blender container. Cover; blend at high speed until smooth (30 to 45 seconds).

Meanwhile, in deep fryer or Dutch oven <u>heat oil to 375°F</u>. Fry tortellini in batches of 10 or 12 until golden brown (about 2 minutes). Drain well on paper towels. Serve tortellini with sauce. **YIELD:** 14 servings (1³/₄ cups sauce).

\* 1 teaspoon dried basil leaves can be substituted for 1 tablespoon chopped fresh basil leaves.

\*\* 1 teaspoon dried oregano leaves can be substituted for 1 tablespoon chopped fresh oregano leaves.

\*\*\* 84 frozen or dried tortellini cooked, drained, can be substituted for 84 (about 9 ounces) small fresh tortellini, cooked, well drained.

TIP: Tortellini can be fried ahead of time. Reheat on cookie sheet at 350° for 6 to 8 minutes.

TIP: If desired, do not fry tortellini; serve cooked, drained, tortellini with sauce.

*Nutrition Facts (1 serving): Calories 70; Protein 3g; Carbohydrate 12g; Fat 2g; Cholesterol 15mg; Sodium 50mg*

# Spinach Mushroom Turnovers

*These crisp and delicate turnovers are stuffed with a delicious cheese, mushroom and spinach filling.*

*Preparation time: 1 hour • Baking time: 16 minutes*

- 1/4 cup LAND O LAKES® Butter
- 1 (10-ounce) package frozen chopped spinach, thawed, well drained
- 1 (4-ounce) can mushroom stems and pieces, drained
- 1/2 teaspoon dried oregano leaves
- 1/4 teaspoon garlic powder
- 1/4 teaspoon salt
- 1 1/2 cups (6 ounces) LAND O LAKES® Shredded Cheddar Cheese
- 1 egg
- 1 (17 1/4-ounce) package (2 sheets) frozen puff pastry, thawed

- 1 egg, slightly beaten
- 1 tablespoon sesame seed

Heat oven to 350°. In 10-inch skillet melt butter until sizzling; stir in spinach, mushrooms, oregano, garlic powder and salt. Cook over medium heat, stirring occasionally, until heated through (3 to 5 minutes). Remove from heat; stir in cheese and 1 egg.

Meanwhile, on lightly floured surface unfold and roll out each sheet of puff pastry to measure 15x12 inches. Cut each sheet into 20 (3-inch) squares. Place about <u>1 1/2 teaspoons</u> spinach mixture in center of each square. Fold square over to form triangle; press edges with fork to seal. Place turnovers on cookie sheets. Brush with beaten egg and sprinkle with sesame seed. Bake for 16 to 20 minutes or until lightly browned.
**YIELD:** 40 appetizers.

<u>Make Ahead</u>: Turnovers can be made ahead and frozen before baking. When ready to serve, place frozen turnovers on cookie sheets; bake at 350° for 20 to 24 minutes or until lightly browned.

*Nutrition Facts (1 appetizer): Calories 90; Protein 2g; Carbohydrate 5g; Fat 7g; Cholesterol 20mg; Sodium 120mg*

*Fried Tortellini With Sun-Dried Tomato Sauce*

# Christmas Eve Family Supper Menu

Backwoods Spinach Salad

Hearty Smoked Fish Chowder

Cranberry Orange Scones

Gingerbread Pudding Cake

Pumpkin Ice Cream

*Backwoods Spinach Salad, see page 208; Hearty Smoked Fish Chowder, see page 208; Cranberry Orange Scones, see page 209*

# Backwoods Spinach Salad

*A slightly sweet, warm bacon dressing tossed with spinach, wild rice and crispy radishes.*

*Preparation time: 45 minutes • Cooking time: 9 minutes*

1/2 cup uncooked wild rice
8 slices bacon, cut into 1/2-inch pieces
1/4 cup cider vinegar
1/4 teaspoon salt
1/4 teaspoon pepper
2 tablespoons honey
4 cups torn spinach leaves
1 cup sliced 1/4-inch fresh mushrooms
1 cup sliced 1/4-inch radishes

Cook wild rice according to package directions.

Meanwhile, in 10-inch skillet cook bacon over medium high heat, stirring occasionally, until crisp (6 to 8 minutes). Remove bacon, reserving 2 tablespoons pan drippings. In same skillet add vinegar, salt, pepper and honey to reserved drippings. Cook over medium heat, stirring occasionally, until heated through (3 to 4 minutes). In large bowl combine wild rice, bacon and all remaining ingredients. Pour warm dressing over salad; toss to coat. **YIELD:** 6 servings.

*Nutrition Facts (1 serving): Calories 180; Protein 6g; Carbohydrate 21g; Fat 9g; Cholesterol 10mg; Sodium 260mg*

# Hearty Smoked Fish Chowder

*Smoked whitefish, trout or salmon adds depth of flavor to this potato-corn chowder.*

*Preparation time: 20 minutes • Cooking time: 25 minutes*

3 tablespoons LAND O LAKES® Butter
6 medium (2 cups) new red potatoes, cubed 1/2-inch
2 medium (1 cup) onions, chopped
1 1/2 cups milk
1 cup LAND O LAKES® Sour Cream (Regular, Light or No•Fat)
1 (10 3/4-ounce) can condensed cream of chicken soup
1 (8-ounce) can whole kernel corn, drained
8 to 12 ounces smoked fish (salmon, trout, whitefish, etc.), bones removed
1/4 teaspoon pepper
1/4 teaspoon dried thyme leaves

In 3-quart saucepan melt butter until sizzling; add potatoes and onions. Cook over medium heat, stirring occasionally, until potatoes are fork tender (15 to 20 minutes). Add all remaining ingredients. Continue cooking, stirring occasionally, until heated through (10 to 12 minutes). **YIELD:** 6 servings.

*Nutrition Facts (1 serving): Calories 290; Protein 14g; Carbohydrate 27g; Fat 14g; Cholesterol 40mg; Sodium 900mg*

# Cranberry Orange Scones

*Cranberries and orange add extra flavor to this Scottish quick bread.*

*Preparation time: 30 minutes • Baking time: 10 minutes*

### Scones
1³/₄ cups all-purpose flour
3 tablespoons sugar
2¹/₂ teaspoons baking powder
2 teaspoons grated orange peel
¹/₃ cup LAND O LAKES® Butter
1 egg, beaten
¹/₂ cup dried cranberries
4 to 6 tablespoons half-and-half

1 egg, beaten
2 tablespoons sugar

### Orange Butter
¹/₂ cup LAND O LAKES® Butter, softened
2 tablespoons orange marmalade

Heat oven to 400°. In medium bowl combine flour, 3 tablespoons sugar, baking powder and orange peel. Cut ¹/₃ cup butter into flour mixture until forms fine crumbs. Stir in 1 egg, cranberries and just enough half-and-half so dough leaves sides of bowl. Turn dough onto lightly floured surface; knead lightly 10 times. Roll into 9-inch circle; cut into 12 wedges. Place on cookie sheet. Brush with beaten egg; sprinkle each with ¹/₂ teaspoon sugar. Bake for 10 to 12 minutes or until golden brown. Immediately remove from cookie sheet.

Meanwhile, in small mixer bowl beat together ¹/₂ cup butter and orange marmalade at medium speed, scraping bowl often, until well mixed. Serve with scones.
**YIELD:** 12 scones (¹/₂ cup orange butter).

*Nutrition Facts (1 scone with 2¹/₂ teaspoons orange butter): Calories 230; Protein 3g; Carbohydrate 23g; Fat 14g; Cholesterol 70mg; Sodium 210mg*

# Gingerbread Pudding Cake

*Old-fashioned pudding cake makes a comeback as gingerbread.*

*Preparation time: 30 minutes • Baking time: 40 minutes*

2½ cups all-purpose flour
1½ teaspoons baking soda
1¼ teaspoons ground ginger
1 teaspoon cinnamon
½ teaspoon salt
½ teaspoon ground allspice
¼ teaspoon ground nutmeg
½ cup LAND O LAKES® Butter, softened
½ cup sugar
1 egg
1 cup molasses
1 cup water
¾ cup firmly packed brown sugar
⅓ cup LAND O LAKES® Butter, melted
1½ cups hot water

Pumpkin Ice Cream
(see below)

Heat oven to 350°. In medium bowl combine flour, soda, ginger, cinnamon, salt, allspice and nutmeg; set aside.

In large mixer bowl beat ½ cup butter and sugar on medium speed until creamy (1 to 2 minutes). Add egg; continue beating until well mixed. Reduce speed to low. Continue beating, alternately adding flour mixture with molasses and 1 cup water, beating after each addition only until blended. Pour batter into 13x9-inch baking pan. Sprinkle batter with ¾ cup brown sugar. In medium bowl combine ⅓ cup melted butter and 1½ cups hot water; carefully pour on top of batter. Bake for 40 to 55 minutes or until gingerbread is cracked on top and toothpick inserted in center comes out clean. Serve warm with Pumpkin Ice Cream. **YIELD:** 12 servings.

*Nutrition Facts (1 serving without ice cream): Calories 360; Protein 3g; Carbohydrate 58g; Fat 14g; Cholesterol 50mg; Sodium 380mg*

# Pumpkin Ice Cream

*Serve this delicious ice cream with gingerbread or spice cake.*

*Preparation time: 15 minutes • Freezing time: 3 hours*

⅓ cup firmly packed brown sugar
½ teaspoon cinnamon
¼ teaspoon ground mace <u>or</u> ground nutmeg
1 cup cooked pumpkin
1 quart (4 cups) vanilla ice cream, slightly softened

In large bowl stir together all ingredients <u>except</u> ice cream. Add ice cream in large spoonfuls, stirring until well blended. Spoon mixture into 9-inch square pan. Cover; freeze at least 3 hours. **YIELD:** 12 servings.

*Nutrition Facts (1 serving): Calories 120; Protein 2g; Carbohydrate 18g; Fat 5g; Cholesterol 20mg; Sodium 40mg*

*Gingerbread Pudding Cake, Pumpkin Ice Cream*

# A Casual Christmas Eve Supper Menu

Hot Spiced Punch

Yuletide Oyster Stew
With Buttery Croutons

Honey Glazed Citrus Salad

Parmesan Butter Pan Biscuits

Steamed Cranberry Pudding

*Honey Glazed Citrus Salad, Yuletide Oyster Stew With Buttery Croutons*

# Honey Glazed Citrus Salad

*A refreshing combination of flavors.*

*Preparation time: 30 minutes*

2 tablespoons vegetable oil
2 tablespoons cider vinegar
2 tablespoons honey
4 cups torn lettuce
$1/2$ cup chopped red onion
$1/4$ cup chopped fresh parsley
2 oranges, pared, sectioned, drained
2 grapefruit, pared, sectioned, drained

In large bowl stir together oil, vinegar and honey. Add all remaining ingredients; toss to coat. **YIELD:** 6 servings.

*Nutrition Facts (1 serving): Calories 120; Protein 2g; Carbohydrate 20g; Fat 5g; Cholesterol 0mg; Sodium 5mg*

# Yuletide Oyster Stew With Buttery Croutons

*Homemade croutons top this creamy rich oyster stew.*

*Preparation time: 20 minutes • Baking time: 5 minutes • Cooking time: 21 minutes*

### Croutons
2 cups (3 to 4 slices) cubed $1/2$-inch bread
$1/4$ cup LAND O LAKES® Butter
2 tablespoons freshly grated Parmesan cheese

### Stew
$1/2$ cup LAND O LAKES® Butter
$1/4$ cup chopped onion
2 medium (1 cup) carrots, shredded
1 pound fresh shucked oysters, undrained
$1/4$ cup all-purpose flour
2 cups milk
2 cups (1 pint) whipping cream
$1/2$ teaspoon salt
$1/4$ teaspoon pepper

Fresh cracked pepper

Heat oven to 400°. In small bowl toss together all crouton ingredients. Place on cookie sheet. Bake for 5 to 7 minutes or until browned; set aside.

In 3-quart saucepan melt $1/2$ cup butter. Add onion, carrots and undrained oysters. Cook over medium heat, stirring occasionally, until edges of oysters curl and vegetables are crisply tender (8 to 10 minutes). With slotted spoon remove oysters and vegetables; set aside.

Gradually whisk flour into liquid in pan until smooth. Continue cooking until bubbly (1 to 3 minutes). Gradually stir in milk, cream, salt and $1/4$ teaspoon pepper. Continue cooking, stirring occasionally, until mixture comes to a full boil (10 to 12 minutes). Add oysters and vegetable mixture. Continue cooking until heated through (2 to 3 minutes).

To serve, in individual bowls ladle soup; sprinkle with croutons and cracked pepper. **YIELD:** 6 servings.

*Nutrition Facts (1 serving): Calories 450; Protein 13g; Carbohydrate 23g; Fat 57g; Cholesterol 220mg; Sodium 690mg*

# Hot Spiced Punch

*Serve this spicy punch with a spoon so no one misses the raisins and almonds at the bottom of the cup.*

*Preparation time: 10 minutes • Standing time: 4 hours • Cooking time: 40 minutes*

4 cups apple cider
2 cups grape juice <u>or</u> dry red wine
2 tablespoons chopped crystallized ginger
8 whole cloves
6 strips (3x$\frac{1}{2}$-inch) orange peel
1 cinnamon stick

$\frac{2}{3}$ cup slivered almonds
$\frac{2}{3}$ cup raisins

In 3-quart saucepan combine all ingredients <u>except</u> almonds and raisins. Let stand at room temperature 4 hours. Cook over medium heat until mixture just comes to a boil (15 to 20 minutes). Reduce heat to low; continue cooking 15 minutes.

Strain cider mixture; discard spice mixture. Return to saucepan. Add almonds and raisins. Continue cooking over low heat until raisins are tender (10 to 15 minutes). Serve hot with a spoon in each mug. **YIELD:** 1$\frac{1}{2}$ quarts (12 servings).

*Nutrition Facts (1 serving): Calories 120; Protein 2g; Carbohydrate 22g; Fat 4g; Cholesterol 0mg; Sodium 10mg*

# Parmesan Butter Pan Biscuits

*Parmesan and basil make the difference in these country-style pan biscuits.*

*Preparation time: 15 minutes • Baking time: 20 minutes*

$\frac{1}{3}$ cup LAND O LAKES® Butter
2$\frac{1}{4}$ cups all-purpose flour
2 tablespoons freshly grated Parmesan cheese
1 tablespoon sugar
3$\frac{1}{2}$ teaspoons baking powder
1 teaspoon dried basil leaves
1 tablespoon chopped fresh parsley
1 cup milk

Heat oven to 400°. In 9-inch square baking pan melt butter in oven (3 to 5 minutes).

Meanwhile, in medium bowl combine all ingredients <u>except</u> milk. Stir in milk just until moistened. Turn dough onto lightly floured surface; knead 10 times or until smooth. Roll dough into 12x4-inch rectangle. Cut into 12 (1-inch) strips. Dip each strip into melted butter. Place in same pan. Bake for 20 to 25 minutes or until lightly browned. **YIELD:** 1 dozen.

*Nutrition Facts (1 biscuit): Calories 150; Protein 4g; Carbohydrate 20g; Fat 6g; Cholesterol 15mg; Sodium 170mg*

# Steamed Cranberry Pudding

*Old-fashioned, warmly spiced steamed pudding is sure to become a family holiday tradition.*

*Preparation time: 30 minutes • Cooking time: 2 hours*

## Pudding

- 2 cups all-purpose flour
- 1 cup sugar
- 1 cup milk
- 1 egg
- 2 tablespoons LAND O LAKES® Butter, softened
- 1 teaspoon baking soda
- 1 teaspoon cinnamon
- 1 teaspoon ground nutmeg
- $1/4$ cup all-purpose flour
- 2 cups fresh or frozen whole cranberries

## Sauce

- $1/2$ cup sugar
- $1/2$ cup firmly packed brown sugar
- $1/2$ cup LAND O LAKES® Butter
- $1/2$ cup whipping cream
- 1 teaspoon vanilla

In large mixer bowl combine all pudding ingredients except $1/4$ cup flour and cranberries. Beat at medium speed, scraping bowl often, until well mixed (1 to 2 minutes). In small bowl toss together $1/4$ cup flour and cranberries. By hand, stir cranberry mixture into batter. Pour into greased $1^1/2$-quart metal mold or casserole. Cover tightly with aluminum foil.

Place rack in Dutch oven or roasting pan; add boiling water to just below rack. Place mold on rack. Cover; cook over medium heat at a low boil for about 2 hours or until toothpick inserted in center comes out clean. Add boiling water occasionally to keep water level just below rack. Remove; let stand 2 to 3 minutes. Remove aluminum foil and unmold. Serve warm or cold with warm sauce.

In 1-quart saucepan combine all sauce ingredients except vanilla. Cook over medium heat, stirring occasionally, until mixture thickens and comes to a full boil (4 to 5 minutes). Boil 1 minute. Stir in vanilla. Store sauce refrigerated. **YIELD:** 12 servings.

*Nutrition Facts (1 serving): Calories 360; Protein 4g; Carbohydrate 55g; Fat 14g; Cholesterol 60mg; Sodium 210mg*

## French Country Christmas Menu

Provencal Lentil Salad

Leg Of Lamb Roasted
With Rosemary

Potato Ratatouille

Mint Pear Chutney

Chocolate Sugar Plum Torte

*Leg Of Lamb Roasted With Rosemary, see page 217; Potato Ratatouille, see page 217; Mint Pear Chutney, see page 218*

# Leg Of Lamb Roasted With Rosemary

*Serve lamb with mint jelly, fresh peas and new potatoes for a traditional meal.*

*Preparation time: 15 minutes • Baking time: 1 hour*

1 (3 to 4-pound) leg of lamb
2 tablespoons finely chopped fresh garlic
2 teaspoons dried rosemary leaves, crushed
1 teaspoon salt
$1/2$ teaspoon pepper

Heat oven to 350°. Place lamb, fat side up, on rack in roasting pan. In small bowl stir together all remaining ingredients. Spread over lamb. Bake for 1 hour to 1 hour 30 minutes or until meat thermometer reaches desired doneness. **YIELD:** 6 servings.

Lamb Internal Cooking Temperature

Rare 140°F     Medium 160°F     Well 170°F

*Nutrition Facts (1 serving): Calories 210; Protein 31g; Carbohydrate 1g; Fat 9g; Cholesterol 100mg; Sodium 430mg*

# Potato Ratatouille

*Potatoes, eggplant, zucchini and tomatoes simmer in an herbed garlic butter.*

*Preparation time: 20 minutes • Cooking time: 18 minutes*

$1/4$ cup LAND O LAKES® Butter
6 new red potatoes, quartered
$1/2$ teaspoon finely chopped fresh garlic
2 medium (2 cups) zucchini, sliced $1/4$-inch
1 small (2 cups) eggplant, cut into $1/2$-inch pieces
1 medium (1 cup) ripe tomato, cut into $1/2$-inch pieces
1 teaspoon dried basil leaves
$1/2$ teaspoon salt
$1/2$ teaspoon coarsely ground pepper

In 10-inch skillet melt butter until sizzling; add potatoes and garlic. Cover; cook over medium high heat, stirring occasionally, until potatoes are browned and fork tender (12 to 15 minutes). Reduce heat to medium; add all remaining ingredients. Cook, stirring occasionally, until vegetables are crisply tender (6 to 8 minutes). **YIELD:** 6 servings.

Microwave Directions: In $2^1/2$-quart casserole melt butter on HIGH (50 to 60 seconds). Stir in potatoes and garlic. Cover; microwave on HIGH, stirring after half the time, until potatoes are fork tender (7 to 9 minutes). Add all remaining ingredients. Cover; microwave on HIGH, stirring after half the time, until vegetables are crisply tender (6 to 8 minutes).

*Nutrition Facts (1 serving): Calories 140; Protein 3g; Carbohydrate 17g; Fat 8g; Cholesterol 20mg; Sodium 270mg*

# Mint Pear Chutney

*Fresh mint and pear cook down to a thick sweet-tart sauce, perfect to serve alongside lamb or pork.*

*Preparation time: 10 minutes • Cooking time: 30 minutes*

3 medium pears, peeled, chopped
1 cup finely chopped fresh mint leaves
$1/3$ cup chopped onion
$1/3$ cup raisins
$1/3$ cup firmly packed brown sugar
$1/4$ cup lemon juice
2 teaspoons finely chopped fresh gingerroot*
Dash ground red pepper

In 2-quart saucepan combine all ingredients. Cook over medium heat, stirring often, until thick (30 to 35 minutes). Serve warm or cold with lamb, pork or poultry.
**YIELD:** 2 cups.

* $1/4$ teaspoon ground ginger can be substituted for 2 teaspoons finely chopped fresh gingerroot.

*Nutrition Facts (1 tablespoon): Calories 25; Protein 0g; Carbohydrate 6g; Fat 0g; Cholesterol 0mg; Sodium 0mg*

# Provencal Lentil Salad

*Dried lentils, a good source of fiber and vegetable protein, make a delicious salad.*

*Preparation time: 20 minutes • Cooking time: 35 minutes*

### Dressing

- 3 tablespoons red wine vinegar
- 4 teaspoons olive <u>or</u> vegetable oil
- $3/4$ teaspoon grated lemon peel
- $1/4$ teaspoon salt
- $1/8$ teaspoon coarsely ground pepper

### Salad

- $1^1/4$ cups ($1/2$ pound) brown lentils, sorted, rinsed*
- $1/4$ cup chopped carrot
- $1/4$ cup chopped onion
- 4 cups water
- $3/4$ teaspoon finely chopped fresh garlic
- 1 bay leaf
- $1/4$ cup chopped fresh parsley
- 1 (2-ounce) jar chopped pimiento, drained

Chopped fresh parsley

In small bowl stir together all dressing ingredients; set aside.

In 3-quart saucepan combine lentils, carrot, onion, water, $1/2$ teaspoon garlic and bay leaf. Cook over high heat until mixture comes to a full boil (10 to 12 minutes). Reduce heat to low. Cover; continue cooking, stirring occasionally, until lentils are tender (25 to 35 minutes). Drain lentils; discard bay leaf.

In large serving bowl combine warm lentil mixture, dressing, $1/4$ cup parsley, pimiento and remaining $1/4$ teaspoon garlic. Toss to coat well. Sprinkle with additional chopped parsley. Serve warm or at room temperature. **YIELD:** 6 servings.

* $1^1/4$ cups ($1/2$ pound) French green lentils, sorted, rinsed, can be substituted for $1^1/4$ cups ($1/2$ pound) brown lentils, sorted, rinsed. French green lentils are smaller then brown lentils and require nearly twice as long to cook (about 1 hour). They have a firmer texture and work well in salads.

*Nutrition Facts (1 serving): Calories 160; Protein 11g; Carbohydrate 24g; Fat 3g; Cholesterol 0mg; Sodium 100mg*

# Chocolate Sugar Plum Torte

*Brandy soaked dried fruit is hidden inside a rich, chocolate torte which is adorned with glistening sugar plums.*

*Preparation time: 2 hours • Standing time: 6 hours 15 minutes • Baking time: 45 minutes •*
*Cooling time: 1 hour • Chilling time: 8 hours 30 minutes*

### Torte
- $1/2$ cup coarsely chopped dried apricots
- $1/2$ cup coarsely chopped walnuts
- $1/2$ cup golden raisins
- $1/4$ cup $1/4$-inch pieces dried pineapple
- $1/4$ cup brandy <u>or</u> water
- $2^1/4$ cups semi-sweet real chocolate chips
- $1/4$ cup water
- 1 cup LAND O LAKES® Butter
- 6 eggs, separated
- $1^1/3$ cups sugar
- 1 cup finely ground almonds
- 9 tablespoons cake flour
  Dash salt

### Piping & Glaze
- 2 cups semi-sweet real chocolate chips
- 2 cups (1 pint) whipping cream

### Sugar Plums
- $1/4$ cup dried apricots
- $1/4$ cup walnuts
- 2 tablespoons golden raisins
- 2 tablespoons flaked coconut
- 2 tablespoons dried dates
- 1 tablespoon brandy <u>or</u> water

  Sugar
  Large crystal sugar

Butter 10-inch professional cake pan or springform pan; line bottom with waxed paper. Butter and flour waxed paper. In medium bowl place $1/2$ cup dried apricots, $1/2$ cup walnuts, $1/2$ cup raisins, dried pineapple and $1/4$ cup brandy. Cover; let stand 6 hours or overnight.

<u>Heat oven to 350°.</u> In 2-quart saucepan cook $2^1/4$ cups chocolate chips, water and butter over low heat, stirring occasionally, until melted (5 to 7 minutes). In large bowl, with wire whisk, beat egg yolks with sugar until creamy (1 to 2 minutes). Whisk in melted chocolate mixture until blended (2 to 3 minutes). Whisk in almonds and cake flour. Fold in brandied fruit mixture (do not drain). In small mixer bowl beat egg whites and salt at high speed, scraping bowl often, until stiff, but not dry, peaks form (1 to 3 minutes). Fold egg whites into chocolate mixture until blended (2 to 3 minutes). Pour batter into prepared pan. Bake for 45 to 50 minutes or until torte just begins to pull away from side of pan. (Torte will be moist in center.) Let torte stand 15 minutes. Remove from pan; place on flat plate or cake cardboard round. Cool completely. Wrap tightly in plastic food wrap; refrigerate 6 hours or overnight.

In 2-quart saucepan cook <u>1 cup</u> chocolate chips and <u>1 cup</u> whipping cream over low heat, stirring constantly, until melted and mixture just comes to a boil (5 to 7 minutes). Cover; refrigerate 6 hours or overnight until chocolate is firm enough to pipe through pastry bag.

TO DECORATE TORTE
Prepare chocolate for glaze. In 2-quart saucepan cook remaining 1 cup chocolate chips and 1 cup whipping cream over low heat, stirring constantly, until melted and mixture just comes to a boil (5 to 7 minutes). Refrigerate, stirring occasionally, 1 hour or until chocolate is just beginning to thicken.

Meanwhile, in food processor bowl or 5-cup blender container place all sugar plum ingredients <u>except</u> 1 tablespoon brandy, sugar and large crystal sugar. Cover; process for 1 to 2 minutes or until mixture is finely chopped. Place chopped fruit in medium bowl; stir in 1 tablespoon brandy. Shape into 20 (1-inch) balls. Roll in sugar. Place <u>one-third</u> of firm piping chocolate mixture into pastry bag fitted with star decorating tip. Pipe small star garnish on each ball; set aside.

Pour thin layer of glaze over cake, spreading sides with glaze that has drizzled from top of torte; refrigerate 30 minutes.

With knife, design chocolate by making lines through chocolate 1 inch apart, horizontally and vertically, to form diamond shapes. With remaining chilled piping chocolate mixture, pipe rosettes around edge of torte. Sprinkle with large crystal sugar. Refrigerate at least 1 hour before serving. Place on serving plate; arrange sugar plums on torte. Decorate with pine boughs. **YIELD:** 16 servings.

*Nutrition Facts (1 serving): Calories 700; Protein 8g; Carbohydrate 65g;*
*Fat 49g; Cholesterol 150mg; Sodium 170mg*

*Chocolate Sugar Plum Torte*

# Holiday Dinner Menu

Pear & Walnut Salad
With Blue Cheese

Garlic Prime Rib

Vegetable Yorkshire Pudding

Winter Vegetables With
Mustard Sauce

Marmalade Mincemeat Tart

*Garlic Prime Rib, Winter Vegetables With Mustard Sauce*

# Garlic Prime Rib

*Garlic studded prime rib is made festive when served with Yorkshire pudding.*

*Preparation time: 15 minutes • Baking time: 1 hour 30 minutes*

1 (4 to 5-pound) rolled beef prime rib roast

6 cloves garlic, each cut lengthwise into thirds

4 medium carrots, cut into 1-inch pieces

2 medium onions, each cut into 8 wedges

$^1/_2$ cup chopped fresh parsley

2 bay leaves

1 cup water

2 teaspoons chopped fresh thyme leaves*

1 teaspoon coarsely ground pepper

$^1/_2$ teaspoon salt

Heat oven to 450°. In 13x9-inch baking pan place roast; with tip of sharp knife, cut 18 slits through fat and into meat just large enough for garlic thirds. Insert garlic third into each slit. Place carrots, onions, parsley and bay leaves around roast; pour water over vegetables. In small bowl stir together thyme, pepper and salt; sprinkle mixture over roast. Bake 30 minutes to brown outside of roast. Reduce temperature to 325°. Bake for 1 hour to 1 hour 15 minutes or until meat thermometer reaches 130°F. Let stand 10 minutes or until meat thermometer reaches 140°F. **YIELD:** 10 servings.

*1 teaspoon dried thyme leaves can be substituted for 2 teaspoons chopped fresh thyme leaves.

*Nutrition Facts (1 serving): Calories 250; Protein 26g; Carbohydrate 5g; Fat 13g; Cholesterol 80mg; Sodium 190mg*

# Winter Vegetables With Mustard Sauce

*A country-style mustard sauce flavors this hearty vegetable dish.*

*Preparation time: 25 minutes • Cooking time: 18 minutes*

2 cups water

6 medium (2 cups) new red potatoes, cubed 1-inch

1 medium (1 cup) carrot, sliced $^1/_4$-inch

1 pound Brussels sprouts, trimmed*

$^1/_3$ cup LAND O LAKES® Butter, melted

$^1/_2$ teaspoon salt

$^1/_4$ teaspoon pepper

4 teaspoons country-style Dijon mustard

4 teaspoons vinegar

2 to 3 drops hot pepper sauce

In 3-quart saucepan combine water, potatoes and carrot; bring to a full boil. Cover; cook over medium heat 8 minutes. Add Brussels sprouts. Continue cooking, stirring occasionally, until vegetables are crisply tender (10 to 12 minutes). Drain.

Meanwhile, in small bowl stir together all remaining ingredients; pour over vegetables. Toss to coat. **YIELD:** 6 servings.

*2 (10-ounce) packages frozen Brussels sprouts can be substituted for 1 pound Brussels sprouts.

Microwave Directions: Reduce 2 cups water to $^1/_4$ cup. In $2^1/_2$-quart casserole combine potatoes, carrot and $^1/_4$ cup water. Cover; microwave on HIGH 4 minutes. Stir in Brussels sprouts. Cover; microwave on HIGH, stirring after half the time, until vegetables are crisply tender (10 to 14 minutes). Meanwhile, in small bowl stir together all remaining ingredients; pour over vegetables. Toss to coat.

*Nutrition Facts (1 serving): Calories 250; Protein 6g; Carbohydrate 36g; Fat 11g; Cholesterol 30mg; Sodium 420mg*

# Pear & Walnut Salad With Blue Cheese

*Select ripe pears to make this salad tossed with walnuts and blue cheese.*

*Preparation time: 15 minutes*

2 tablespoons olive <u>or</u> vegetable oil

1 tablespoon red wine vinegar

1 teaspoon Dijon-style mustard

1/4 teaspoon coarsely ground pepper

2 medium ripe pears, sliced 1/4-inch

2 tablespoons crumbled blue cheese

2 tablespoons coarsely chopped walnuts

2 tablespoons chopped fresh parsley

In medium bowl stir together oil, vinegar, mustard and pepper. Add all remaining ingredients; toss to coat. **YIELD:** 4 servings.

*Nutrition Facts (1 serving): Calories 150; Protein 2g; Carbohydrate 14g; Fat 11g; Cholesterol 3mg; Sodium 100mg*

# Vegetable Yorkshire Pudding

*Serve this updated version of an English favorite with roasted prime rib.*

*Preparation time: 20 minutes • Baking time: 35 minutes*

1/2 cup water

2 cups broccoli flowerets

1 3/4 cups all-purpose flour

1 cup milk

1 cup cold water

4 eggs

1 1/2 teaspoons seasoned salt

1/4 teaspoon pepper

1/3 cup LAND O LAKES® Butter <u>or</u> beef drippings

1/2 cup thin carrot peel

Heat oven to 400°. In 2-quart saucepan bring 1/2 cup water to a full boil. Add broccoli. Cover; cook over medium heat until crisply tender (2 to 3 minutes). Rinse with cold water. Drain; set aside.

In large mixer bowl combine flour, milk, 1 cup water, eggs, salt and pepper. Beat at low speed, scraping bowl often, just until smooth (1 to 2 minutes).

Meanwhile, in 13x9-inch baking pan melt butter in oven (3 to 5 minutes). Pour batter into hot baking pan. Sprinkle with broccoli and carrot. Bake for 35 to 45 minutes or until edges are dark golden brown and center is set. Serve immediately. **YIELD:** 8 servings.

TIP: Make thin carrot peel by pulling vegetable peeler across length of carrot.

TIP: Batter can be made 1 hour ahead. Cover; refrigerate. Stir well before pouring into hot pan.

TIP: For a traditional Yorkshire pudding, omit broccoli and carrot.

*Nutrition Facts (1 serving): Calories 230; Protein 8g; Carbohydrate 25g; Fat 11g; Cholesterol 160mg; Sodium 430mg*

# Marmalade Mincemeat Tart

*Candied orange peel glistens on top of a twisted lattice mincemeat tart.*

*Preparation time: 1 hour • Baking time: 40 minutes*

## Pastry

2 cups all-purpose flour
3 tablespoons sugar
1 tablespoon grated orange peel
3/4 cup LAND O LAKES® Butter, cut into 6 pieces
2 egg yolks, slightly beaten
4 to 5 tablespoons ice water

## Filling

1 (3-ounce) package cream cheese, softened
2 tablespoons orange juice
1 (27-ounce) jar mincemeat
2 medium (2 cups) tart cooking apples, cored, peeled, sliced 1/4-inch

## Candied Orange

1 medium orange
1/2 cup water
1/4 cup sugar

Heat oven to 375°. In large bowl stir together flour, 3 tablespoons sugar and 1 tablespoon orange peel. Cut in butter until crumbly. With fork mix in egg yolks and 4 to 5 tablespoons ice water just until moistened. Divide dough into 2 balls making 1 ball one-fourth larger than the other ball. Wrap smaller ball in plastic food wrap; refrigerate. On lightly floured surface roll out larger ball into 14-inch circle. Place in 10-inch tart pan, pressing firmly against bottom and side of pan. Cut away excess pastry.

In small bowl, with wire whisk, stir together cream cheese and orange juice. Spread over bottom of unbaked tart. In large bowl stir together mincemeat and apples. Pour into tart. Roll remaining pastry ball into 12-inch circle. With sharp knife or pastry wheel, cut circle into 10 (1/2-inch) strips. Twist each strip 5 times; place 5 twisted strips, 1 inch apart, across filling in tart pan. Place remaining 5 twisted strips, 1 inch apart, at right angles to strips already in place. With thumb seal ends of strips and cut away excess dough. Bake for 40 to 50 minutes or until golden brown.

Meanwhile, with vegetable peeler, peel large strips of orange peel (colored part only); cut into thin julienne strips. In 1-quart saucepan bring 1/4 cup water to a full boil; add orange strips. Cook over medium high heat until orange strips are blanched (1 to 2 minutes); drain. In same saucepan stir together remaining 1/4 cup water, 1/4 cup sugar and blanched orange strips. Cook over medium heat, stirring occasionally, until orange strips are glazed and candied (12 to 15 minutes). Remove orange strips; separate on waxed paper. Arrange on baked mincemeat tart. **YIELD:** 10 servings.

*Nutrition Facts (1 serving): Calories 460; Protein 5g; Carbohydrate 70g;*
*Fat 19g; Cholesterol 100mg; Sodium 370mg*

## Southwestern Holiday Menu

Cranberry Daiquiris

Strawberry Margaritas

Yellow Squash Soup With
Cilntro Sour Cream

Pork Loin Roast With
Dried Apricots

Four Pepper Blast
With Sesame Seed

Maple Pecan Corn Bread
With Maple Butter

Fresh Fruit Flan Tart

*Pork Loin Roast With Dried Apricots, see page 228; Four Pepper Blast With Sesame Seed, see page 228; Fresh Fruit Flan Tart, see page 233*

# Pork Loin Roast With Dried Apricots

*A savory pork loin roast is garnished with dried apricots and toasted pecans,*
*then served with a rich demi-glace sauce.*

*Preparation time: 15 minutes • Baking time: 1 hour 40 minutes • Standing time: 15 minutes • Cooking time: 10 minutes*

### Roast

- 1 (3-pound) boneless center cut pork loin roast (2 loins tied)
- 2 teaspoons dried thyme leaves
- 1 teaspoon dried rosemary, crushed
- 1/4 teaspoon salt
- 1/4 teaspoon coarsely ground pepper
- 2 tablespoons olive or vegetable oil

### Sauce

- 1/2 cup pecan halves
- Water
- 1 (6-ounce) package dried apricots
- 1/4 teaspoon dried thyme leaves
- 1/4 cup brandy or apple juice
- 1/4 cup chopped fresh parsley

Heat oven to 325°. Place roast in 9-inch square baking pan. In small bowl stir together all remaining roast ingredients. Spoon oil mixture over roast. Bake for 1 hour 30 minutes to 1 hour 40 minutes or until meat thermometer reaches 160°F (Medium). Remove roast to carving board; reserve pan juices. Let roast stand 15 minutes (temperature of roast will rise to serving temperature of 170°F).

Meanwhile, pour pan juices into 1-cup measure; skim off fat. Set aside.

Place pecans in same pan. Bake for 10 to 15 minutes or until toasted. Add enough water to reserved pan juices to equal 1 cup. Place pan juice mixture in 10-inch skillet. Cook over medium heat, stirring occasionally, until mixture comes to a full boil (3 to 5 minutes). Add all remaining sauce ingredients except 2 tablespoons parsley. Continue cooking, stirring occasionally, until apricots are plump (4 to 5 minutes).

To serve, place carved roast on serving platter. Place apricots from sauce around roast; garnish with toasted pecans and remaining 2 tablespoons parsley. Serve with sauce.
**YIELD:** 8 servings.

*Nutrition Facts (1 serving): Calories 370; Protein 38g; Carbohydrate 16g;*
*Fat 18g; Cholesterol 100mg; Sodium 160mg*

---

# Four Pepper Blast With Sesame Seed

*Southwestern cooking at its best — bold, colorful and spicy.*

*Preparation time: 20 minutes • Cooking time: 7 minutes*

- 1 tablespoon sesame oil or vegetable oil
- 1 tablespoon LAND O LAKES® Butter
- 1 tablespoon finely chopped fresh garlic
- 1 large green pepper, cut into 1/4-inch strips
- 1 large orange pepper, cut into 1/4-inch strips
- 1 large red pepper, cut into 1/4-inch strips
- 1 large yellow pepper, cut into 1/4-inch strips
- 1 onion, cut into 1/4-inch strips
- 1 tablespoon chopped fresh rosemary*
- 2 teaspoons chopped fresh oregano leaves**
- 1 teaspoon salt
- 1/4 teaspoon pepper
- 1/4 teaspoon crushed red pepper
- 1 tablespoon toasted sesame seed

In Dutch oven heat sesame oil and butter; add garlic. Cook over medium heat, stirring occasionally, 2 minutes. Stir in all remaining ingredients except sesame seed. Reduce heat to low; continue cooking until peppers are crisply tender (5 to 7 minutes). Stir in 2 teaspoons sesame seed. Sprinkle with remaining 1 teaspoon sesame seed.
**YIELD:** 8 servings.

\* 1 teaspoon dried rosemary, crushed, can be substituted for 1 tablespoon chopped fresh rosemary.

\*\* 1/2 teaspoon dried oregano leaves can be substituted for 2 teaspoons chopped fresh oregano leaves.

*Nutrition Facts (1 serving): Calories 50; Protein 1g; Carbohydrate 5g;*
*Fat 4g; Cholesterol 5mg; Sodium 280mg*

# Maple Pecan Corn Bread With Maple Butter

*Serve this corn bread warm with maple butter and enjoy.*

*Preparation time: 20 minutes • Baking time: 25 minutes*

## Corn Bread

- 1 cup cornmeal
- 1 cup all-purpose flour
- $1/2$ teaspoon salt
- 1 teaspoon baking powder
- 1 teaspoon baking soda
- 3 tablespoons LAND O LAKES® Butter, softened
- 2 tablespoons firmly packed brown sugar
- 3 eggs
- $3/4$ cup buttermilk*
- $1/3$ cup real maple syrup <u>or</u> maple-flavored syrup
- 1 teaspoon maple flavoring
- $3/4$ cup chopped pecans, toasted

## Maple Butter

- $1/2$ cup LAND O LAKES® Butter
- 1 tablespoon real maple syrup <u>or</u> maple-flavored syrup
- 1 teaspoon maple flavoring

Heat oven to 350°. In small mixer bowl combine cornmeal, flour, salt, baking powder and baking soda. In large mixer bowl combine 3 tablespoons butter, brown sugar and eggs. Beat at medium speed until well mixed (1 to 2 minutes). Add buttermilk, $1/3$ cup maple syrup and 1 teaspoon maple flavoring. Continue beating until well mixed (2 to 3 minutes). Reduce speed to low; add flour mixture. Continue beating, scraping bowl often, until well mixed (1 to 2 minutes). By hand, stir in pecans. Spoon into greased 8-inch square baking pan. Bake for 25 to 30 minutes or until toothpick inserted in center comes out clean. (Corn bread may dip slightly in center.)

Meanwhile, in small mixer bowl combine all maple butter ingredients. Beat at medium speed until fluffy (2 to 3 minutes). Serve with warm corn bread.
**YIELD:** 9 servings ($1/2$ cup maple butter).

* 2 teaspoons vinegar plus enough milk to equal $3/4$ cup can be substituted for $3/4$ cup buttermilk.

*Nutrition Facts (1 serving plus about 1 tablespoon Maple Butter): Calories 380; Protein 6g; Carbohydrate 37g; Fat 23g; Cholesterol 100mg; Sodium 450mg*

# Yellow Squash Soup With Cilantro Sour Cream

*The fresh flavors of cilantro, basil and oregano season this southwestern soup.*

*Preparation time: 25 minutes • Cooking time: 1 hour 9 minutes*

## Soup

3 to 4 pounds butternut <u>and/or</u> acorn squash, each cut in half, baked

$^1/_2$ cup LAND O LAKES® Butter

1 medium ($^1/_2$ cup) onion, finely chopped

2 teaspoons finely chopped fresh garlic

$^1/_4$ cup all-purpose flour

2 cups milk

1 ($14^1/_2$-ounce) can chicken broth

$^1/_3$ cup real maple syrup <u>or</u> maple-flavored syrup

$^3/_4$ teaspoon salt

$^1/_8$ teaspoon ground red pepper

$^3/_4$ cup whipping cream

1 tablespoon chopped fresh cilantro

$1^1/_2$ teaspoons chopped fresh basil leaves*

$1^1/_2$ teaspoons chopped fresh oregano leaves**

## Cilantro Cream

3 tablespoons chopped fresh cilantro

$^1/_2$ cup LAND O LAKES® Sour Cream (Regular, Light <u>or</u> No•Fat)

Scoop baked squash from skins; place <u>half</u> of squash in 5-cup blender container or food processor bowl. Cover; blend at high speed until pureed (2 to 3 minutes). Spoon into medium bowl; set aside. Repeat with remaining squash. (You should have $3^1/_2$ to 4 cups pureed squash.)

In Dutch oven melt butter until sizzling; add onion and garlic. Cook over medium heat, stirring occasionally, until onion is soft (5 to 7 minutes). Stir in flour; continue cooking, stirring constantly, 4 minutes. With wire whisk stir in milk and chicken broth. Stir in pureed squash, maple syrup, salt and pepper. Gradually whisk in whipping cream, 1 tablespoon cilantro, basil and oregano. Reduce heat to low; continue cooking, stirring occasionally, 1 hour.

Meanwhile, in small bowl stir together 3 tablespoons cilantro and sour cream. Dollop sour cream mixture onto each serving of soup. **YIELD:** 10 servings.

\* $^1/_2$ teaspoon dried basil leaves can be substituted for $1^1/_2$ teaspoons chopped fresh basil leaves.

\*\* $^1/_2$ teaspoon dried oregano leaves can be substituted for $1^1/_2$ teaspoons chopped fresh oregano leaves.

*Nutrition Facts (1 serving): Calories 320; Protein 5g; Carbohydrate 34g; Fat 19g; Cholesterol 60mg; Sodium 350mg*

*Yellow Squash Soup With Cilantro Sour Cream*

# Strawberry Margaritas

*Serve this strawberry sensation in glasses rimmed with salt.*

*Preparation time: 10 minutes*

¼ cup powdered sugar
1 cup tequila <u>or</u> water
½ cup orange-flavored liqueur
  <u>or</u> orange juice
2 (10-ounce) packages frozen
  strawberries in syrup*
1 (6-ounce) can frozen
  limeade concentrate
4 cups ice cubes

In 5-cup blender container place <u>2 tablespoons</u> powdered sugar, <u>½ cup</u> tequila, <u>¼ cup</u> orange liqueur, <u>1 (10-ounce) package</u> frozen strawberries and <u>half</u> of limeade concentrate. Cover; blend at high speed 1 minute. Continue blending, adding <u>2 cups</u> ice cubes, until thick and slushy (1 to 2 minutes). Serve in glasses rimmed with salt. Repeat with remaining ingredients. **YIELD:** 8 servings.

\* About 20 ounces your favorite fruit in syrup (peaches, raspberries, blackberries, etc.) can be substituted for 2 (10-ounce) packages frozen strawberries in syrup.

TIP: To rim glasses with salt, dip top edge of glasses into lime juice and then salt.

*Nutrition Facts (1 serving): Calories 250; Protein 0g; Carbohydrate 40g;*
*Fat 0g; Cholesterol 0mg; Sodium 5mg*


# Cranberry Daiquiris

*Cranberry adds a new twist to daiquiris.*

*Preparation time: 10 minutes*

2 cups rum*
1 cup cranberry juice
  cocktail*
1 cup cranberry-flavored
  liqueur*
1 cup orange-flavored
  liqueur**
¼ cup frozen lemonade
  concentrate
1 (6-ounce) can frozen
  limeade concentrate
4 cups ice cubes

In 5-cup blender container place all ingredients <u>except</u> ice cubes. Cover; blend at high speed 1 minute. Continue blending, adding <u>2 cups</u> ice cubes at a time, until thick and slushy (1 to 2 minutes). Serve in glasses rimmed with sugar. **YIELD:** 8 servings.

\*1 (12-ounce) can frozen cranberry juice cocktail concentrate and ½ cup water can be substituted for 2 cups rum, 1 cup cranberry juice cocktail and 1 cup cranberry-flavored liqueur.

\*\*1 cup orange juice can be substituted for 1 cup orange-flavored liqueur.

TIP: To rim glasses with sugar, dip top edge of glasses into water and then sugar.

*Nutrition Facts (1 serving): Calories 450; Protein 0g; Carbohydrate 47g;*
*Fat 0g; Cholesterol 0mg; Sodium 5mg*

# Fresh Fruit Flan Tart

*A velvety custard is baked in a flaky pastry and topped with fresh fruit.*

*Preparation time: 1 hour • Baking time: 39 minutes • Cooling time: 1 hour*

## Pastry

1²/3 cups all-purpose flour
  2 tablespoons sugar
 3/4 cup LAND O LAKES® Butter
  1 egg, slightly beaten
  1 tablespoon milk

## Filling

 3/4 cup sugar
  2 tablespoons cornstarch
  2 cups milk
  5 egg yolks, slightly beaten
  2 tablespoons
    LAND O LAKES® Butter
  2 teaspoons vanilla

## Fruit

  1 pint strawberries, hulled,
    cut in half lengthwise
  2 kiwi fruit, peeled,
    sliced 1/4-inch
  1 mango, peeled, cut into
    1-inch cubes

Heat oven to 400°. In large bowl stir together flour and 2 tablespoons sugar; cut in 3/4 cup butter until crumbly. With fork mix in egg and 1 tablespoon milk just until moistened. Shape into ball. On lightly floured surface roll into 14-inch circle. Place in 11-inch tart pan; press on bottom and up side of pan. Trim dough, leaving 1/2-inch overhang. Fold in overhang, forming double-thick side. With fork prick bottom and side of pastry. Bake for 9 to 11 minutes or until lightly browned. <u>Reduce oven to 350°</u>.

Meanwhile, in 2-quart saucepan combine 3/4 cup sugar and cornstarch. Gradually stir in 2 cups milk. Cook over medium heat, stirring constantly, until mixture thickens and comes to a full boil (10 to 15 minutes). Boil, stirring constantly, 1 minute. In small bowl, with wire whisk, gradually stir <u>two-thirds</u> of hot milk mixture into beaten egg yolks. Gradually stir egg mixture into remaining hot milk mixture. Continue cooking, stirring constantly, until mixture comes to a full boil (2 to 4 minutes). Boil, stirring constantly, 1 minute. Remove from heat; stir in 2 tablespoons butter and vanilla until butter is melted. Pour custard into baked pastry. Bake for 30 to 40 minutes or until custard is set. Cool 1 hour. Cover; refrigerate. Just before serving, arrange fruit on top of custard. Store refrigerated. **YIELD:** 12 servings.

*Nutrition Facts (1 serving): Calories 320; Protein 5g; Carbohydrate 38g;*
*Fat 17g; Cholesterol 150mg; Sodium 170mg*

## Southwestern Hospitality Appetizer Buffet Menu

Apricot Turkey Salad
In Mini Cream Puffs

Gingered Peach Fruit Dip

Spicy Skewered Chicken
With Peanut Dip

Four Cheese & Walnut
Cheese Ball

Peach Glazed Riblets

*Apricot Turkey Salad In Mini Cream Puffs, see page 236; Peach Glazed Riblets, see page 238*

# Apricot Turkey Salad In Mini Cream Puffs

*The crunchy texture of nuts and vegetables combines with apricots and turkey in this appetizer served in miniature cream puffs.*

*Preparation time: 1 hour • Baking time: 28 minutes • Chilling time: 1 hour*

### Cream Puffs
1¼ cups water
¾ cup LAND O LAKES® Butter
¼ teaspoon salt
1¼ cups all-purpose flour
5 eggs

### Dressing
3 tablespoons mayonnaise
2 tablespoons olive <u>or</u> vegetable oil
1 tablespoon garlic wine vinegar <u>or</u> vinegar
1 teaspoon finely chopped fresh gingerroot*
½ teaspoon finely chopped fresh garlic
¼ teaspoon grated lime peel
⅛ teaspoon crushed red pepper

### Salad
1 chunk (1½ pounds) deli turkey, finely chopped
⅓ cup finely chopped dried apricots
3 tablespoons finely chopped celery
3 tablespoons finely chopped onion
3 tablespoons finely chopped red <u>and/or</u> green pepper

1 tablespoon finely chopped pecans, toasted

Heat oven to 400°. In 2-quart saucepan bring water, butter and salt to a full boil over medium heat. Continue cooking, vigorously stirring in flour, until mixture leaves side of pan and forms ball. Remove from heat; cool 10 minutes. Stir in eggs, one at a time, beating well after each addition. Continue beating until mixture is shiny. Shape tablespoonfuls of dough into 1-inch balls. Place 2 inches apart on greased cookie sheets. Bake for 28 to 33 minutes or until puffed and golden brown. Pierce puffs with sharp knife allowing steam to escape and centers to dry. Cool completely on wire cooling rack.

Meanwhile, in large bowl, with wire whisk, stir together all dressing ingredients. Add all salad ingredients <u>except</u> pecans; toss to coat. Cover; refrigerate 1 hour. Stir pecans into turkey mixture. Cut tops off cream puffs; fill each with about <u>2 tablespoons</u> salad mixture. **YIELD:** 18 servings (36 cream puffs).

\* ⅛ teaspoon ground ginger can be substituted for 1 teaspoon finely chopped fresh gingerroot.

*Nutrition Facts (1 serving): Calories 200; Protein 9g; Carbohydrate 12g; Fat 13g; Cholesterol 100mg; Sodium 410mg*

# Gingered Peach Fruit Dip

*Fresh fruit never tasted so good! You'll love the blend of ginger and peach.*

*Preparation time: 10 minutes*

1 (12-ounce) jar (1 cup) peach preserves
¼ teaspoon ground nutmeg
¼ teaspoon finely chopped fresh gingerroot*
1 (16-ounce) carton (2 cups) LAND O LAKES® Sour Cream (Regular, Light <u>or</u> No•Fat)

Fresh and dried fruit pieces (apples, bananas, pears, etc.)

In medium bowl stir together all ingredients <u>except</u> fruit. Serve with fruit. **YIELD:** 3 cups dip.

\* Dash ground ginger can be substituted for ¼ teaspoon finely chopped fresh gingerroot.

*Nutrition Facts (1 tablespoon dip only): Calories 35; Protein 0g; Carbohydrate 5g; Fat 2g; Cholesterol 5mg; Sodium 10mg*

# Spicy Skewered Chicken With Peanut Dip

*These skewered chicken strips are a take-off of Thai "satay." You'll love the fragrant and spicy flavor combination.*

*Preparation time: 30 minutes • Broiling time: 4 minutes*

### Peanut Sauce

$1/4$ cup peanut butter
$1/2$ to $3/4$ teaspoon crushed red pepper
$1/8$ teaspoon ground ginger
1 teaspoon finely chopped lemon grass*
1 tablespoon chili sauce
1 tablespoon peanut oil <u>or</u> vegetable oil

### Dip

$3/4$ cup LAND O LAKES® Sour Cream (Regular, Light <u>or</u> No•Fat)
2 to 3 tablespoons coconut milk <u>or</u> milk

### Chicken

1 pound boneless skinless chicken breasts, cut into 16 (6x$1/2$-inch strips)
1 tablespoon firmly packed brown sugar
2 teaspoons finely chopped lemon grass*
2 teaspoons peanut oil <u>or</u> vegetable oil
1 teaspoon soy sauce
16 (6 to 8-inch) wooden skewers
1 small cucumber, seeded, cut into 16 chunks, if desired

In small bowl, with wire whisk, stir together all peanut sauce ingredients. Set aside to use in dip and chicken.

In small bowl stir together <u>2 to 3 tablespoons</u> peanut sauce and all dip ingredients. Cover; refrigerate until ready to use.

<u>Heat broiler</u>. In medium bowl combine 2 tablespoons peanut sauce, chicken, brown sugar, lemon grass, oil and soy sauce; toss to coat chicken. Thread 1 strip chicken on each wooden skewer. Place on broiler pan. Broil 4 to 5 inches from heat, turning once, until chicken is fork tender and golden brown (4 to 5 minutes). To serve, thread 1 chunk cucumber on each skewer. Serve warm with peanut dip. **YIELD:** 16 appetizers.

*1 teaspoon finely chopped chives and $1/4$ teaspoon grated lemon peel can be substituted for 1 teaspoon finely chopped lemon grass.

*Nutrition Facts (1 appetizer): Calories 100; Protein 8g; Carbohydrate 2g; Fat 6g; Cholesterol 20mg; Sodium 80mg*

# Four Cheese & Walnut Cheese Ball

*This tangy cheese ball has its origins in the south of France.*

*Preparation time: 30 minutes • Chilling time: 3 hours • Baking time: 10 minutes*

## Cheese Ball

- 1 (8-ounce) tub sharp Cheddar cold pack cheese
- 1 (8-ounce) package cream cheese, softened
- 1 (5 to 5.2-ounce) package herb cheese spread*
- 1 (4-ounce) package Blue cheese, crumbled
- ³/₄ teaspoon dried dill weed
- ¹/₂ teaspoon dried basil leaves
- ¹/₂ teaspoon celery salt
- ¹/₂ teaspoon Italian herb seasoning**
- 1 tablespoon chopped garlic
- 1 tablespoon soy sauce
- ¹/₂ cup chopped walnuts, toasted
- ¹/₄ cup chopped fresh parsley

## Pita Crisps

- ²/₃ cup LAND O LAKES® Butter
- 2 teaspoons chopped garlic
- 1 (9-ounce) package (4) pita bread, each cut into 8 wedges, each wedge split

  Apple slices

In large mixer bowl combine all cheese ball ingredients <u>except</u> walnuts and parsley. Beat at low speed, scraping bowl often, until well mixed (3 to 4 minutes). Shape into large ball. Cover; refrigerate until firm (at least 3 hours).

Reshape ball if necessary. In small bowl combine walnuts and parsley. Roll cheese ball in walnut mixture to coat.

Meanwhile, <u>heat oven to 400°</u>. In large bowl melt butter in microwave; stir in 2 teaspoons garlic. Add split pita wedges; toss to coat. Place on cookie sheets. Bake for 10 to 12 minutes or until golden brown around edges. Cool completely. Serve cheese ball with pita crisps and apple slices. **YIELD:** 32 servings.

*1 (3-ounce) package cream cheese with chives, softened, can be substituted for 1 (5 to 5.2-ounce) package herb cheese spread.

** ¹/₈ teaspoon <u>each</u> dried oregano leaves, dried marjoram leaves and dried basil leaves, and ¹/₁₆ teaspoon rubbed sage can be substituted for ¹/₂ teaspoon Italian herb seasoning.

*Nutrition Facts (1 serving): Calories 150; Protein 4g; Carbohydrate 6g; Fat 11g; Cholesterol 35mg; Sodium 290mg*

# Peach Glazed Riblets

*A southern favorite, peaches, add interest to this finger-lickin' good appetizer.*

*Preparation time: 1 hour 30 minutes • Baking time: 50 minutes*

## Sauce

- 1 tablespoon vegetable oil
- ³/₄ cup chopped onion
- 2 teaspoons chopped garlic
- ¹/₃ cup soy sauce
- ¹/₄ cup firmly packed brown sugar
- ¹/₄ cup dark molasses
- ¹/₄ cup honey
- 1 (14-ounce) bottle (1¹/₃ cups) ketchup
- ¹/₄ teaspoon crushed red pepper
- 1 tablespoon chopped crystallized ginger*
- ¹/₂ teaspoon Worcestershire sauce
- 2 to 3 drops hot pepper sauce
- 2 cups unsweetened frozen peach slices, thawed

## Riblets

- 3 pounds pork riblets

Heat oven to 425°. In Dutch oven heat oil; add onion and garlic. Cook over medium high heat, stirring often, until onion is soft (2 to 4 minutes). Stir in all remaining sauce ingredients <u>except</u> peaches. Continue cooking until sauce just comes to a boil (3 to 6 minutes). Reduce heat to low. Continue cooking, stirring occasionally, 1 hour. Cool 10 minutes.

Meanwhile, place peaches in 5-cup blender container or food processor bowl. Cover; blend at high speed until pureed (1 to 2 minutes). Stir puree into cooled sauce.

Meanwhile, place riblets in lightly greased 13x9-inch baking pan. Bake 15 minutes. Drain off fat. <u>Reduce heat to 400°</u>. Pour sauce over riblets; stir to coat. Bake, basting occasionally, for 35 to 40 minutes or until riblets are tender and sauce has thickened. **YIELD:** About 4 dozen riblets.

* ¹/₂ teaspoon ground ginger can be substituted for 1 tablespoon chopped crystallized ginger.

TIP: Pork riblets are pork back ribs, cut into single rib (1¹/₂-inch) pieces. Ask the meat cutter to cut through the rib bones to form the riblets; then separate each riblet.

*Nutrition Facts (1 riblet): Calories 130; Protein 7g; Carbohydrate 7g; Fat 8g; Cholesterol 30mg; Sodium 240mg*

*Four Cheese & Walnut Cheese Ball, see page 238; Spicy Skewered Chicken With Peanut Dip, see page 237*

## Dessert Buffet Menu

Irish Cream Truffles

Raspberry Cream Angel Food

Key Lime Tart In
Sugar Cookie Crust

Chocolate Brownie Almond
Bundt Cake

Maple-Nut Cream Cheese Cups

*Irish Cream Truffles, see page 242; Raspberry Cream Angel Food, see page 242; Key Lime Tart In Sugar Cookie Crust, see page 243*

# Irish Cream Truffles

*These rich, dense, creamy candies freeze well.*

Preparation time: 25 minutes • Cooking time: 12 minutes • Chilling time: 1 hour

1 cup whipping cream
2 teaspoons vanilla
  Pinch of salt
1 pound high quality real
    bittersweet chocolate,
    broken into 1-inch pieces
4 ounces high quality real
    milk chocolate, broken
    into 1-inch pieces
4 egg yolks, beaten
3 tablespoons Irish cream
    liqueur*
⅔ cup unsweetened cocoa

In 2-quart saucepan heat whipping cream over medium heat until heated through (2 to 3 minutes). Stir in vanilla and salt. With wire whisk, stir in <u>half</u> of bittersweet chocolate and <u>half</u> of milk chocolate until melted. Stir in egg yolks. Cook over low heat, stirring often, until slightly thickened (10 to 12 minutes). Remove from heat; stir in all remaining chocolate and liqueur until chocolate is melted. Cover; refrigerate until chocolate mixture starts to firm and set (about 30 minutes).

Sift cocoa into medium shallow bowl. Drop rounded tablespoonfuls of chocolate mixture into cocoa; roll to coat. Shape into balls; roll in cocoa again. Place gently on tray; refrigerate until firm (30 minutes). Store refrigerated. **YIELD:** 3 dozen truffles.

\* 1 teaspoon your favorite flavor extract can be substituted for 3 tablespoons Irish cream liqueur.

*Nutrition Facts (1 truffle): Calories 110; Protein 2g; Carbohydrate 9g;*
*Fat 9g; Cholesterol 35mg; Sodium 10mg*

# Raspberry Cream Angel Food

*This trifle-like dessert is served scooped into balls.*

Preparation time: 30 minutes • Cooling time: 45 minutes • Chilling time: 8 hours

⅔ cup whipping cream
6 egg yolks, beaten
1 teaspoon almond extract
1 teaspoon vanilla
1 (10-inch) angel food cake,
    cut into ¾-inch slices
1 pint (2 cups) whipping
    cream
3 cups powdered sugar
¾ cup LAND O LAKES®
    Butter, softened
1 (12-ounce) bag individually
    frozen raspberries
    (not in syrup)

In 1-quart saucepan cook ⅔ cup whipping cream and egg yolks over low heat, stirring constantly, until mixture thickens (10 to 12 minutes). Stir in almond extract and vanilla. Cover loosely with waxed paper; cool completely (45 minutes).

Meanwhile, line 13x9-inch pan with <u>half</u> of angel food cake slices. In chilled small mixer bowl beat chilled 1 pint whipping cream at high speed until soft peaks form (1 to 2 minutes). In large mixer bowl beat powdered sugar and butter at medium speed until creamy (2 to 3 minutes). Add cooled egg mixture; continue beating until well mixed (1 to 2 minutes). Gently stir in whipped cream. Spread <u>half</u> of mixture over cake slices in pan. Cover with <u>three-fourths</u> of raspberries. Layer remaining cake slices over raspberries. Spread remaining cream mixture over cake. Top with remaining raspberries. Cover tightly with plastic food wrap; refrigerate at least 8 hours. With ice cream scoop, spoon into individual dessert dishes. **YIELD:** 12 servings.

*Nutrition Facts (1 serving): Calories 600; Protein 6g; Carbohydrate 69g;*
*Fat 34g; Cholesterol 210mg; Sodium 530mg*

# Key Lime Tart In Sugar Cookie Crust

*Use Key limes for traditional flavor in this refreshing dessert.*

*Preparation time: 45 minutes • Baking time: 18 minutes • Cooling time: 15 minutes • Chilling time: 2 hours*

## Crust

- $1/3$ cup sugar
- $1/2$ cup LAND O LAKES® Butter, softened
- $1^1/4$ cups all-purpose flour
- 1 tablespoon grated Key lime peel
- 2 tablespoons milk
- 1 teaspoon vanilla

## Filling

- 1 cup sugar
- $2/3$ cup Key lime juice
- 1 tablespoon grated Key lime peel
- 2 eggs
- 4 egg yolks
- 6 tablespoons LAND O LAKES® Butter

## Garnish

- 1 cup whipping cream
- 2 teaspoons grated Key lime peel

Heat oven to 400°. In large mixer bowl beat $1/3$ cup sugar and $1/2$ cup butter at medium speed until creamy (1 to 2 minutes). Reduce speed to low; add flour, 1 tablespoon lime peel, milk and vanilla. Continue beating, scraping bowl often, until well mixed (2 to 3 minutes). Press crust on bottom and up side of greased 10-inch tart or quiche pan. Bake for 18 to 23 minutes or until light golden brown. Cool completely.

Meanwhile, in 2-quart saucepan combine 1 cup sugar, lime juice and 1 tablespoon lime peel. Cook over medium heat until sugar is dissolved (1 to 2 minutes). Reduce heat to low. In small bowl, with wire whisk, stir small amount of hot mixture into beaten eggs and egg yolks. Gradually stir egg mixture into hot sugar mixture. Continue cooking, stirring constantly, until mixture thickens (6 to 8 minutes). Remove from heat. Whisk in 6 tablespoons butter, 1 tablespoon at a time. Cool 15 minutes. Pour cooled filling into crust; smooth top. Cover; refrigerate at least 2 hours.

Just before serving, in chilled small mixer bowl beat chilled whipping cream at high speed until stiff peaks form (2 to 3 minutes). Place whipped cream in pastry bag fitted with large star tip. Pipe border of whipped cream around edge of tart. Sprinkle with 2 teaspoons lime peel. **YIELD:** 12 servings.

TIP: To get the most juice from limes, grate limes first. Then microwave limes on HIGH for 30 to 45 seconds to warm slightly before juicing. If additional Key lime juice is needed, add bottled Key lime juice.

*Nutrition Facts (1 serving): Calories 360; Protein 4g; Carbohydrate 35g; Fat 23g; Cholesterol 170mg; Sodium 160mg*

# Chocolate Brownie Almond Bundt Cake

*Serve this rich chocolate cake a la mode.*

*Preparation time: 15 minutes • Baking time: 55 minutes • Cooling time: 1 hour • Cooking time: 2 minutes*

### Cake
1/4 cup unsweetened cocoa

1 (7.25-ounce) box chocolate fudge flavor dry icing mix

1/2 (18.25-ounce) box devil's food cake mix

1/2 (19.8 to 21.5-ounce) box brownie mix

1 cup LAND O LAKES® Sour Cream (Regular, Light or No•Fat)

2/3 cup half-and-half

1/2 cup chocolate-flavored syrup

3 eggs

2 teaspoons vanilla

2 teaspoons almond extract

2/3 cup chopped almonds, toasted

### Chocolate Ganache
1 (6-ounce) package (1 cup) semi-sweet real chocolate chips

3 tablespoons LAND O LAKES® Butter

2 tablespoons half-and-half

1 tablespoon vegetable oil

1 teaspoon almond extract

Heat oven to 350°. Generously spray 12-cup Bundt pan with no stick cooking spray; dust with 1/4 cup unsweetened cocoa. Spray with no stick cooking spray again; set aside.

In large mixer bowl combine all remaining cake ingredients except almonds. Beat at low speed, scraping bowl often, until well mixed (1 to 2 minutes). By hand, stir in almonds. Pour into prepared pan. Bake for 55 to 70 minutes or until cake begins to pull away from side of pan. DO NOT OVERBAKE. Cool 10 minutes; invert onto serving platter. Cool completely.

Meanwhile, in 1-quart saucepan combine all chocolate ganache ingredients except almond extract. Cook over low heat, stirring constantly, until chips are melted and consistency is pourable (2 to 3 minutes). Stir in 1 teaspoon almond extract. Drizzle over cooled cake. **YIELD:** 16 servings.

TIP: Use remaining half of boxes to make second cake. Wrap unfrosted cake in plastic food wrap; freeze. When ready to serve, let thaw. Prepare chocolate ganache and drizzle over cake.

TIP: To wrap for gift giving, cut 36-inch square of holiday fabric. Place cake on plate; cover with plastic food wrap. Place in center of fabric; gather fabric around cake securing top with rubber band. Tie with brightly colored ribbon.

*Nutrition Facts (1 serving): Calories 390; Protein 6g; Carbohydrate 52g; Fat 20g; Cholesterol 50mg; Sodium 280mg*

# Maple-Nut Cream Cheese Cups

*A creamy, rich dessert with the flavor of cheesecake.*

*Preparation time: 30 minutes • Freezing time: 5 hours • Standing time: 10 minutes*

1/3 cup sugar

1/4 cup milk

1 (8-ounce) package cream cheese, softened

1 egg

1/2 teaspoon vanilla

1/4 cup pure maple syrup or maple-flavored syrup

2 tablespoons graham cracker crumbs

1/4 cup chopped pecans

Line 6 muffin cups with paper liners; set aside.

In large mixer bowl combine sugar, milk, cream cheese, egg and vanilla. Beat at medium speed, scraping bowl often, until smooth (2 to 3 minutes). Divide cream cheese mixture evenly among prepared muffin cups. Freeze until firm (at least 4 hours).

Meanwhile, in small bowl stir together maple syrup and graham cracker crumbs. Cover; refrigerate at least 2 hours.

To serve, invert each dessert on individual dessert plate. Let stand 10 to 15 minutes; remove paper. Spoon 1 tablespoon maple syrup mixture over each dessert; sprinkle with pecans. **YIELD:** 6 servings.

*Nutrition Facts (1 serving): Calories 270; Protein 5g; Carbohydrate 24g; Fat 18g; Cholesterol 80mg; Sodium 140mg*

*Chocolate Brownie Almond Bundt Cake*

*Sweet & Sour Meatballs, see page 248; Festive Stuffed Pea Pods, see page 248; Pepper Swiss Cheese Ball, see page 249*

# New Year's Eve Appetizer Buffet Menu

Old-Fashioned
Hot Buttered Rum

Sweet & Sour Meatballs

Festive Stuffed Pea Pods

Pepper Swiss Cheese Ball

Wreath-Shaped Taco
Layered Dip

Country Chicken Nuggets

# Sweet & Sour Meatballs

*These spicy meatballs are served in a sweet and sour ginger sauce.*

*Preparation time: 45 minutes • Baking time: 25 minutes*

## Meatballs
- ½ cup dried bread crumbs
- 1 pound lean ground beef
- 1 (12-ounce) package spicy bulk pork sausage
- 1 egg
- ½ teaspoon dry mustard
- 1 tablespoon soy sauce

## Sauce
- 1 (20-ounce) can pineapple chunks in unsweetened juice, drained, <u>reserve juice</u>
- 2 tablespoons firmly packed brown sugar
- 1 tablespoon cornstarch
- ½ teaspoon ground ginger
- 2 tablespoons cider vinegar
- 1 tablespoon soy sauce
- 2 medium green peppers, cut into 1-inch pieces

Heat oven to 350°. In large bowl stir together all meatball ingredients. Shape into 1-inch balls. Place meatballs on 15x10x1-inch jelly roll pan. Bake for 15 to 20 minutes or until meatballs are browned.

Meanwhile, in 1-quart saucepan combine reserved pineapple juice, brown sugar, cornstarch, ginger, vinegar and 1 tablespoon soy sauce. Cook over medium heat, stirring occasionally, until mixture is thickened and bubbly (4 to 6 minutes). Boil, stirring constantly, 1 minute. In 2-quart casserole place meatballs, pineapple chunks, green peppers and sauce; stir gently to coat. Cover; bake for 10 to 15 minutes or until green peppers are crisply tender. Serve in chafing dish with toothpicks. **YIELD:** 5 dozen.

<u>Microwave Directions:</u> In large bowl stir together all meatball ingredients. Shape into 1-inch balls. Place <u>half</u> of meatballs in 13x9-inch baking dish. Cover with waxed paper. Microwave on HIGH, rearranging after half the time, until meatballs are no longer pink (7 to 10 minutes). Repeat with remaining meatballs. In 2-cup measure stir together reserved pineapple juice, brown sugar, cornstarch, ginger, vinegar and 1 tablespoon soy sauce. Microwave on HIGH, stirring after half the time, until mixture is thickened and bubbly (1½ to 3 minutes). In 2-quart casserole place meatballs, pineapple chunks, green peppers and sauce; stir gently to coat. Cover; microwave on HIGH until green peppers are crisply tender (6 to 9 minutes). Serve in chafing dish with toothpicks.

*Nutrition Facts (1 meatball); Calories 40; Protein 2g; Carbohydrate 3g; Fat 2g; Cholesterol 10mg; Sodium 80mg*

# Festive Stuffed Pea Pods

*Cheese and coarsely ground pepper add flavor and color to the cream cheese filling in these extra special appetizers.*

*Preparation time: 45 minutes • Cooking time: 1 minute*

- 8 ounces (approximately 50) fresh pea pods
- 1 (8-ounce) package cream cheese, softened
- ½ cup (2 ounces) LAND O LAKES® Shredded Cheddar Cheese
- ½ teaspoon coarsely ground pepper

In 2-quart saucepan bring 2 cups water to a full boil. Add pea pods; cook 1 minute. Drain well; plunge into ice water. Drain well. Cut stems off pea pods. Cut seam on side of each pea pod forming pocket; set aside.

In small mixer bowl combine cream cheese, Cheddar cheese and pepper. Beat at medium speed, scraping bowl often, until well mixed (1 to 2 minutes). Spoon or pipe cheese mixture into pocket of each pea pod. Refrigerate until ready to serve. **YIELD:** 50 appetizers.

*Nutrition Facts (1 appetizer): Calories 20; Protein 1g; Carbohydrate 0g; Fat 2g; Cholesterol 5mg; Sodium 20mg*

# Pepper Swiss Cheese Ball

*Pepper complements the nutty flavor of Swiss cheese.*

*Preparation time: 15 minutes • Chilling time: 2 hours*

2 (3-ounce) packages cream cheese, softened

$\frac{1}{2}$ cup LAND O LAKES® Sour Cream (Regular, Light <u>or</u> No•Fat)

$\frac{1}{4}$ teaspoon garlic salt

6 ounces ($1\frac{1}{2}$ cups) LAND O LAKES® Swiss Cheese, shredded

2 tablespoons chopped fresh parsley

2 to 3 tablespoons coarsely ground pepper

In small mixer bowl beat cream cheese on medium speed, scraping bowl often, until smooth (1 to 2 minutes). Add sour cream and garlic salt; continue beating until well mixed. By hand, stir in cheese and parsley. Refrigerate at least 2 hours.

Shape into flattened cheese ball or log. Roll in pepper to coat. Store refrigerated. **YIELD:** 1 cheese ball (24 servings).

*Nutrition Facts (1 serving): Calories 60; Protein 3g; Carbohydrate 1g; Fat 5g; Cholesterol 15mg; Sodium 70mg*

# Wreath-Shaped Taco Layered Dip

*A favorite party dip—layers of lettuce, tomato and cheese are shaped into a wreath and served with tortilla chips.*

*Preparation time: 30 minutes*

1 (16-ounce) carton (2 cups) LAND O LAKES® Sour Cream (Regular, Light <u>or</u> No•Fat)

1 (4-ounce) can chopped green chilies, drained

1 ($1\frac{1}{4}$-ounce) package taco seasoning mix

$1\frac{1}{2}$ cups shredded lettuce

1 cup (4 ounces) LAND O LAKES® Shredded Cheddar Cheese

1 large ripe tomato, chopped, drained

1 medium avocado, peeled, pitted, chopped

2 tablespoons sliced green onions

2 tablespoons sliced ripe olives

Tortilla chips

In medium bowl stir together sour cream, chilies and taco seasoning mix. On large serving platter, sprinkle lettuce in a wreath shape (10-inch ring). Spoon taco mixture over lettuce; mound slightly and smooth top and sides of wreath. Sprinkle top and sides with Cheddar cheese, tomato, avocado, green onions and ripe olives. Serve with tortilla chips. **YIELD:** 12 servings.

*Nutrition Facts (1 serving): Calories 130; Protein 5g; Carbohydrate 9g; Fat 8g; Cholesterol 20mg; Sodium 290mg*

# Country Chicken Nuggets

*Buttery crumb-coated chicken bites dipped in
a sour cream-mustard sauce.*

*Preparation time: 20 minutes • Baking time: 10 minutes*

## Nuggets
- 1 cup corn flake crumbs
- 1½ teaspoons dried oregano leaves
- 1½ teaspoons dried thyme leaves
- 2 (12 ounces each) whole boneless chicken breasts, skinned, cut into 1-inch pieces
- ½ cup LAND O LAKES® Butter, melted

## Sauce
- 1 cup LAND O LAKES® Sour Cream (Regular, Light or No•Fat)
- 2 tablespoons country-style Dijon mustard
- 1 tablespoon milk

Heat oven to 425°. In small bowl stir together corn flake crumbs, oregano and thyme. Dip chicken pieces in melted butter, then coat with crumb mixture. Place chicken ½ inch apart on 15x10x1-inch jelly roll pan. Bake for 10 to 15 minutes or until fork tender and crisp.

Meanwhile, in small bowl stir together all sauce ingredients. Serve nuggets with sauce. **YIELD:** About 40 nuggets.

<u>Microwave Directions</u>: In 1-quart casserole place chicken pieces. Cover; microwave on HIGH, stirring twice, until fork tender (3 to 4 minutes). In small bowl stir together corn flake crumbs, oregano and thyme. In small bowl melt butter on HIGH (70 to 80 seconds). Dip <u>half</u> of chicken pieces in melted butter, then coat with crumb mixture. On 9-inch serving plate place chicken pieces ½ inch apart around outside edge. Cover with paper towel; microwave on HIGH, turning plate ¼ turn after 1 minute, until heated through (1½ to 2 minutes). Repeat with remaining chicken pieces.

TIP: Nuggets can be baked ahead of time and reheated at 350° for 10 minutes.

*Nutrition Facts (1 nugget): Calories 50; Protein 3g; Carbohydrate 3g;
Fat 3g; Cholesterol 15mg; Sodium 70mg*

# Old-Fashioned Hot Buttered Rum

*Chase away those winter chills with this traditional hot beverage.*

*Preparation time: 10 minutes • Cooking time: 6 minutes*

- 1 cup sugar
- 1 cup firmly packed brown sugar
- 1 cup LAND O LAKES® Butter
- 2 cups vanilla ice cream, softened

- Rum or rum extract
- Boiling water
- Ground nutmeg

In 2-quart saucepan combine sugar, brown sugar and butter. Cook over low heat, stirring occasionally, until butter is melted (6 to 8 minutes). In large mixer bowl combine cooked mixture with ice cream; beat at medium speed, scraping bowl often, until smooth (1 to 2 minutes). Store refrigerated up to 2 weeks or frozen up to 1 month.

For each serving, fill mug with ¼ cup mixture, <u>1 ounce</u> rum or ¼ teaspoon rum extract and ¾ cup boiling water; sprinkle with nutmeg. **YIELD:** 16 servings.

*Nutrition Facts (1 serving): Calories 300; Protein 1g; Carbohydrate 30g;
Fat 13g; Cholesterol 40mg; Sodium 140mg*

# Success Pointers for Holiday Entertaining

Part of the fun of the holidays is the planning and anticipation. Here are a few ideas on how to get organized so you can enjoy entertaining and eliminate the party-giving jitters.

◆ Plan ahead, make lists for the grocery store and inventory the food you have on hand.

◆ Check dishes and serving pieces: Do you have enough; are they the right size? Ask friends and neighbors if you can borrow the extra pieces you need. If your group is going to be large, also check rental stores for large or unusual pieces to rent.

◆ Review recipes and plan refrigeration and storage needs. Do you need to use space at a neighbor's, or will a cooler with ice work? What foods can be made ahead, frozen, refrigerated or stored in airtight containers at room temperature?

◆ Make a time plan for the entire week, right up to the hour before. This helps eliminate last-minute surprises. Plan to shop the day before you cook, allowing enough time to accomplish all that needs to be done.

◆ Set the table a day or two ahead; then cover it with a clean sheet to keep off the dust. This also ensures having all the dishes and serving pieces on hand and helps eliminate last-minute problems.

◆ If relatives or friends are helping to prepare food, give them the recipe well in advance so they can do their planning. Coordinate who will provide the serving dishes.

◆ Take time for yourself. Plan what you are going to wear well in advance. Schedule time in the day to unwind, review your arrangements and be relaxed when your guests arrive.

◆ Remember, holiday entertaining is FUN! Do not worry if things don't go as planned. You will probably be the only one who will know. Relax. You've planned and organized well; now you can enjoy too!

# Index